The
Assertive
Manager

The
Assertive
Manager

Positive Skills at Work for You

Elaina Zuker

amacom

American Management Association

This book is available at a special
discount when ordered in bulk quantities.
For information, contact Special Sales Department,
AMACOM, a division of American Management Association,
135 West 50th Street, New York, NY 10020.

Library of Congress Cataloging-in-Publication Data

Zuker, Elaina
    The assertive manager: positive skills at work for you.

    Includes index.
    1. Organizational behavior.   2. Assertiveness
training.   I. Title.
HD58.7.Z84 1989   158'.1'024658   82-73519
ISBN 0-8144-5769-X
ISBN 0-8144-7727-5 (pbk.)

This book was originally published under the title Mastering Assertiveness Skills: Power and Positive Influence at Work.

First AMACOM paperback edition 1989.

Printing number

10 9 8 7 6 5 4 3 2 1

To Oscar and Sarah Zuker,
who always gave me permission,
and
to Aleksandra Sedillo Madsen,
who taught me about living and loving assertively.

Preface

When I was asked to write this book for the American Management Association, I had been teaching communications skills and assertiveness to hundreds of managers in corporations, government agencies, and organizations all over this country and abroad. Many participants in my workshops and seminars asked me, "Is there a book that summarizes the ideas and skills we're learning here?" After researching what was available, I was surprised to learn that there were no books that I could wholeheartedly recommend. There were quite a few general self-help books about assertiveness training, but each presented only one technique (that author's favorite) instead of suggesting several and letting readers compare them. Also, I found no books that dealt specifically with the problems of managers and employees in the workplace. To meet this need, I decided to write this book. Geared specifically to situations in the work environment, its ideas, theories, and techniques are even more vital now, as we enter the rapidly changing workplace of the 1990s.

Many events and trends have changed forever the way business works. In 1984, the giant corporation (and comforting "work home" to one million people) AT&T divested its 22 operating companies and formed seven "regionals," causing confusion among its employees, customers, stockholders, and the business community. In the two years following, almost 30,000 people in the Bell System were laid off—or given "early retirement." Other giants followed suit, displacing thousands of long-time employees from their jobs. Merger mania, leveraged buyouts, mega-acquisitions, "downsizing," streamlining—these new forms of business phenomena are happening with alarming pace and frequency. In this new and competitive environment, it is vital to have the assertive and interpersonal skills to stay afloat, advance in your career, and not get lost in the shuffle.

The techniques in this book come from the best thinking and results in the fields of psychology, management training, and business. And rather than provide you with only one technique for being assertive, I am presenting a wide variety of skills and ideas so that you can experiment and find the ones that work best for you.

The scope of this book is broad. It covers many diverse areas where assertiveness is useful; for example, delegation, body language, and written communication. For this reason, the book is meant to be digested slowly, not read through quickly and put away on a shelf. I've tried to introduce one idea at a time in a simple, straightforward way so that you can easily grasp each new technique and then try it, even before you've finished reading the whole book.

You'll find a number of exercises and self-assessment quizzes. These are meant to help you see how you are already doing in different areas, and then focus on whatever issues you need to work on most. Since each reader has a unique set of concerns and problems, I have not tried to put together one rigid system that is supposed to work for everyone.

Above all, I've done my best to make this book *practical*. The ultimate test of any self-help book is simply whether it helps. I hope this book will serve as a useful tool that will help you discover your new, assertive self. I also hope and believe that assertiveness training will help you become more effective, more productive, and more satisfied—both as a person and as a manager.

Acknowledgments

Through the many months of researching and writing this book, there were many whose expertise, support, and encouragement helped me immeasurably. My sincere thanks to all of them.

First, to Kathy Mullins, whose research and editorial contributions to the chapters on body language, writing, stress, and support systems deserve special thanks.

To Tom Gannon, my acquisitions editor at AMACOM, who saw the value of and the need for this book from the beginning and encouraged me throughout the process.

To Kathryn Cason, Nancy Lee, and Alice Sargent, who shared with me their experiences as authors.

To my dear friend Carole Hyatt, for her loving support and her personal and professional wisdom.

To Tom Quick, a dear friend and a true professional, who was an astute sounding board early in the process and a supporter throughout it.

To Alexandria Hatcher, whose negotiation skills and advice were extremely useful at the inception of the project.

To my friend and colleague Larry Schwimmer, who helped me with subject matter and structural issues, and provided loving support and encouragement as well.

To Peter Krohn, whose love and friendship gave me confidence in the value of the project.

To Louise Marinis, without whose artful editing this book would not be as clear an expression of my ideas as it now is. Her deft hands sculpted my work and took it far beyond its original form. Thanks also to Natalie Meadow and Janet Frick for their editorial help and expertise.

To my friends Dorothy Hertle, Karen Gray, Lori Samet, Nancy Miller, Minna Hilton, Mary Williams, Janet Gifford, Joanne Rogovin, and Barbara Maher, all of whom patiently listened to my fits and starts and my complaints about writer's block.

To Joan Alevras Stampfel, who has contributed many ideas to my work on this and other subjects.

To my dear friend Alec Fiorentino, who early in the game taught me about effective management.

Finally, to the hundreds of workshop participants who always contribute more to me than I do to them; who help me fine-tune my craft; and who supplied me with many examples, problems, cases, and ideas for this book.

Contents

1   The Manager in the 1990s   *1*
2   Assertiveness Defined   *12*
3   Beliefs and Attitudes Underlying Behavior   *27*
4   Attitudes That Work Against You   *40*
5   Assertive Skills and Techniques—A Tool Kit
    for Positive Power and Influence   *52*
6   The Assertive Manager: Delegation, Counseling,
    Performance Appraisal   *73*
7   Interpersonal Communication   *92*
8   Refined Listening   *105*
9   The Assertive Body   *118*
10 Criticism, Feedback, Acknowledgments, Bouquets   *130*
11 Meetings   *140*
12 Assertive Writing   *148*
13 Managing Stress   *162*
14 Building Support Systems   *183*
    Epilogue   *198*
    "How Assertive Are You?" Exercise Scorecard   *199*
    Index   *201*

The
Assertive
Manager

1

The Manager in the 1990s

"I want to be more in charge."

"I want to establish my authority."

"I want to be more firm with people."

"I want my employees to see things my way."

"I want to have greater control over things, especially my people."

These are some of the goals described by managers attending seminars on assertiveness training. When asked what they hoped to learn in the seminars, many of them said that they wanted to establish themselves as authority figures, to let their people know who was boss, and to project themselves as being more decisive, more on top of things.

Yet there is a curious irony here. First of all, as we will see in this and later chapters, take-charge authority and firm control are not what assertiveness training is all about, nor are these the best ways to gain positive influence. Second, and more important in view of the changing nature of the workforce, the changing values in American society, and the new structures emerging in organizations, these are no longer the types of skills the successful manager needs.

In the 1990s a whole new set of values, a different posture, will distinguish the excellent manager from the mediocre or average one. The new manager will *not* be controlling, but will manage others through influence and collaboration. The new manager will not be seen as the "boss," or as a remote authority figure. Nor will the manager be a rugged individualist who makes decisions unilaterally and then tells the troops about them. Rather, the manager will work with and through peers, subordinates, and superiors to reach negotiated solutions that are satisfactory to all.

Let's take a closer look at some of the factors that call for new, assertive leadership styles in the 1990s.

THE CHANGING NATURE OF THE WORKFORCE

In the 1970s a number of significant changes took place in the nature of the American labor force.*

- ○ A shift from blue collar to white collar jobs, particularly professional, technical, and clerical jobs.
- ○ A near doubling of the government's share of the labor force.
- ○ Geographic shifts, with dramatic movements toward the Sunbelt and away from the larger and older Eastern and Midwestern industrial centers.
- ○ Decline in private sector unionism.
- ○ The massive movement of women into the workforce, especially younger women.
- ○ The growth in the number of younger workers.
- ○ Decline in the participation of older men in the workforce. In 1947, 91 percent of men aged 54 to 65 were working; in 1977 only 78 percent had jobs—a drop of 15 percent. The principal factor has been the changes in the Social Security laws, especially as they affect those over 62. Other forces, such as voluntary and involuntary early retirement, the business cycle and layoffs, the problem of age discrimination on re-employment, the growing financial ability of older men to retire early, and the increased domestic income as a result of working women and two-paycheck families, have contributed to the diminishing participation of older men.

Forecasts indicate there will be several additional changes in the labor market in the next decades.

1. *The coming youth shortage.* Because of the low birth rate in the 1960s, the absolute number of young workers is expected to fall sharply in the 1980s.

2. *The midcareer bulge.* The number of workers in the 25 to 44 age bracket will increase dramatically. In 1975, there were 39 million workers in this age group; by 1990, there will be 60.5 million—an extraordinary increase of 55 percent. Typically, this is the group that vies most strongly for promotions, professional recognition, and supervisory responsibilities. In their midcareers, workers in this group could well bottleneck in the competition for higher-level jobs.

Considerable pressure will be placed on management development, human resources, and compensation programs to meet this challenge.

3. *The expanding role of women.* Women will continue to participate in

*These data are drawn in large measure from Richard Freeman, "The Work Force of the Future, an Overview," in Clark Kerr and Jerome Rosow, eds., *Work in America: The Decade Ahead* (New York: Van Nostrand Reinhold, 1979).

the workforce in greater numbers, in every type of activity, and in all kinds of businesses and institutions. It is predicted that by 1990, 61 percent of American women will be working; this is equivalent to the present level of female participation in the Swedish workforce.

4. *Competition for desirable jobs.* The competition for desirable jobs will intensify as women continue to enter occupations traditionally held by men.

5. *Increased employment of older workers.* By 1990 it is likely that employers will be motivated more strongly than ever to attract and retain older workers. This may necessitate further loosening Social Security laws and retirement policies, redesigning jobs to accommodate the physical and psychological requirements of older workers, and establishing new personnel policies that are responsive to the needs of this segment of the workforce.

CHANGING VALUES AND EXPECTATIONS

Studies conducted for the U.S. Department of Labor over the past 10 to 15 years indicate that although workers' expressions of overall job satisfaction have not changed significantly, workers have indicated growing dissatisfaction with specific aspects of their jobs. For example, more than half of American workers reported concern over improved fringe benefits, exposure to health and safety hazards, work schedules, difficulties in getting job duties changed, and inadequate time for leisure activities. More than one third of American workers reported problems related to pay inequities, inconvenient or excessive hours, ennui (the feeling that time drags at work), unpleasant physical conditions on the job, and interference between work and family life.

A number of factors have contributed to these new concerns on the part of the American workforce.

1. *Challenge to authority.* As a by-product of the youth counterculture movement of the 1960s and the focus on job autonomy in the 1970s, many workers are no longer willing to accept orders from supervisors at face value, especially if they do not agree with the orders. At the same time, a subtle shift is occurring among younger, more educated workers. Although they resent tyranny and authoritarianism, these workers do accept authority when it is exercised intelligently and appropriately. The challenge to large hierarchical organizations will be to rationalize their work policies and procedures and learn the art of conflict mediation and consensus.

2. *Decline of confidence in institutions.* There is a growing mistrust of business, government, the church, and the military. Americans are particularly skeptical about the President and Big Business. In fact, a study in 1975 showed that nine out of ten Americans expressed a general mistrust of ''those in power'' (covering business, government, and most national institutions).

3. *Decline of the work ethic.* The work/success ethic received a serious challenge in the 1960s and 1970s. The scarcity of natural resources, the struggling American economy, and the focus on ecology have dispelled the myth of two cars in every garage and abundance for all. As a result, the future-reward mentality is succumbing to a "do it now, enjoy the present" hedonism. The rugged American individualist has softened into a cooperative team player.

People are increasingly concerned about personal growth—psychological as well as physical. The current interest in the human potential movement, as well as the physical fitness crazes of the past several years, attests to this growing "me-ism."

4. *The leisure society.* Hard work is also being challenged by the leisure society. Although the workweek has remained relatively stable for the past 40 years, people are becoming more and more interested in leisure pursuits. In one study comparing work and leisure as sources of satisfaction, only one out of five Americans said that work meant more to them than leisure. Four out of five said that although they enjoyed their work, it was not their major source of satisfaction.

More and more people are stating, in different ways, that they want their work to be a balanced part of their lives. Work schedules, career pressures, and overtime should be balanced against family needs and responsibilities and should allow for recreation and self-renewal.

5. *Demand for participation in decision making.* Over the past ten years there has been a remarkable increase in employee expectations for participating in decisions at the workplace. In 1977, 54 percent of American workers expressed a desire to take part in decisions affecting their immediate jobs and work-related issues. Though the demand for participation is limited to a relatively narrow arena, many managers are reluctant to share decision-making power. Authority and responsibility should rise to the top, not drift to the bottom. Managers cherish authority; they worry about having too much responsibility. Often managers are so preoccupied with their responsibilities that they hesitate to delegate or to share authority.

Demands for participation in decision making have spawned many new forms of participative management. The Japanese version of the quality circle movement, which has recently been adopted successfully by a number of American firms, is one creative solution to workers' growing desire to have more say over issues that affect their working lives.

6. *Job content.* Double-digit inflation and rising costs reduce the incentive to work, and employees are no longer lured simply by the promise of a good salary. As the workforce becomes better and better educated, people want something more from their jobs than a paycheck and a clean lunchroom. They are not willing to settle for dull, meaningless, monotonous work. More and more workers are speaking out about the content of their jobs.

They want work that's more challenging and more creative, work that gives them greater opportunity to improve their skills so that they can advance.

CHANGES IN THE ORGANIZATION

These changes in values in the American workforce are being reflected in changing attitudes in business organizations. Power is becoming an increasingly elusive phenomenon. More and more emphasis is being placed on building a collaborative work environment in which authority and decision making are shared and differences between people are valued and utilized rather than perceived as threats. Individual achievement is giving way to group performance and group reward. Table 1 summarizes the trends.

At the same time, rapid growth and development in many companies have changed the very structure of the corporation. Fewer and fewer contemporary organizations fit the old hierarchical mold, with "bosses" at the top of the pyramid making all the decisions and "workers" at the lower levels carrying out all the orders.

The strong influence of Japanese management styles and structures on U.S. organizations bears evidence to this fact. Companies all over the coun-

Table 1. Shifts in organizational philosophy in the 1990s.

Away From	*Toward*
Viewing employees as inherently bad and lazy.	Viewing workers as basically conscientious and good.
Either/or thinking (dichotomies/ polarities).	Thinking along a continuum; allowing possibilities.
Individual performance and reward.	Group achievement.
Competition.	Collaboration and synergy.
Seeing people as static, fixed, unchangeable.	Seeing people as in constant process of learning, developing, and growing.
Fearing and resisting individual differences.	Accepting, utilizing, and valuing diversity.
Linear, rational, cognitive modes of problem solving.	Creative, intuitive forms of problem solving.
Valuing "hard," bottom-line (quantitative) information.	Balancing "hard" (quantitative) and "soft" (qualitative) information.
Distrusting people.	Trusting people.
Avoiding conflict; seeing disagreement as "bad."	Seeing conflict as healthy, productive, and creative.
Avoiding risk; playing it safe.	Valuing risk taking and "entrepreneurial" management.

try are instituting teams and task forces, quality-of-worklife programs, systems of consensus management, quality circles, and other forms of group problem solving and worker participation in management.

NEW LEADERSHIP STYLES

The older hierarchical forms of organization, and the value systems on which they are based, called for the traditional management skills of planning, organizing, controlling, implementing, and evaluating. The newer forms of organization, along with the changing values in the workforce, call for a new mode of managing—and a new breed of manager.

Peter Schwartz of Stanford Research Institute has described two styles of leadership: Alpha and Beta. The Alpha style reflects the traditional management approach. It is based on analytical, rational, quantitative thinking. It relies on hierarchical relationships of authority and looks for preset, engineered solutions to specific problems. The Alpha power style is direct and aggressive. It is based on abstracting one particular task or demand from its surroundings at a given time. Alpha managers strive competitively for an all-or-nothing outcome, expecting a clear win/lose, or "zero sum," solution. They focus on the short range, perceiving change as chaotic and disruptive and relying on "order" to control it.

The Beta style is based on synthesizing, intuitive, qualitative thinking. Beta managers exercise power flexibly according to context, with consideration for the various relationships involved. They are tuned to more complex, subtle, and less defined aspects of the work environment. They are concerned with the whole picture rather than a specific task, with growth and the quality of life rather than fixed quantities and the status quo. The Beta style focuses on sharing internal resources and establishing interdependent relationships of support. It is more attuned to the subtleties of human interaction than the Alpha style. Thus the Beta style is better equipped to deal with the overwhelming changes now occurring in society and in organizations.

Another new view of management has been put forth by Donald Michael, who suggests that planning should be viewed as a learning process and that managers should be capable of "embracing errors" as part of the learning experience. Michael notes that the competent manager

> is one who designs his or her activities to provide the maximum amount of feedback about what is happening in order to detect and respond to errors. Competence, then, is measured not by skill in avoiding errors but by skill in detecting them, and in acting on that information openly so that all can continue to learn about where they are and where they might go—about what kind of world we have created for ourselves and what we might do toward re-creating it.*

*Donald Michael, *On Learning and Planning to Learn: The Social Psychology of Changing Toward Future-Responsive Societal Learning* (San Francisco: Jossey-Bass, 1973).

As these analyses suggest, the nature of leadership in the future will involve three major shifts: from control to influence; from planning as prediction to planning as learning; and from scientific management to entrepreneurship. Influence entails the delicate orchestration of a variety of forces to produce action. Planning as learning requires a tolerance for error and multiple interpretations. Entrepreneurship requires responding to changes in the business environment with openness, flexibility, and intuition rather than relying on rigid or abstract principles of control. The entrepreneurial manager exercises control much like a skilled captain on the open sea. When the waters are calm, the captain can run the ship "by the book." But when the waters become turbulent, the leader must be prepared to develop new strategies for each unexpected twist and turn.

In short, the basic managerial skills that were adequate in a more clearly defined, hierarchical setting are giving way to a new set of skills that are responsive to current changes in the workplace. (See Table 2.) The manager who is successful in the coming decades will be sensitive to these emerging

Table 2. Traditional versus new management skills.

Situations Calling for Traditional Management Skills	*Situations Calling for New "Influence" Skills*
Decisions are unilateral.	Decisions require participation and support.
You are in control—over people, resources, projects.	Others have expertise, information, contacts, and resources that you need to get results.
Issues are simple, predictable, linear.	Issues are complex, unpredictable, nonlinear.
Impact is on single units or departments.	Impact is on several units ("ripple effect").
Narrow, contained impact and concerns.	Broad organizational impact and concerns.
Results must be produced through controlling, directing, and evaluating.	Results must be produced through spontaneity and responsiveness to organizational needs.
Structures are preset.	Structures emerge from assessing issues and setting goals.
You have official recognition.	You need informal support.
You have extrinsic power.	You need intrinsic power.
You work with autonomy.	Success is achieved via interdependence.
Your "territory" is defined and contained.	There is territorial overlap.
You are directing.	You are negotiating, persuading.

changes and will be able to adjust his or her behavior to be *appropriate* in all situations. Technical skill alone will not ensure the manager's rise up the organizational ladder. Equally important will be human relations and communications skills, along with the ability to adapt to change, to see the whole picture, to value differences, to be flexible, and to create and work in teams.

Commanding and controlling people, the old style of management, may get you *compliance:* people do what you say because you're the boss, but they may also resent you and rebel. Attentiveness to others and a more flexible style will get you *positive influence* with people. This brings you a more effective kind of power. As we'll see later, the first style is aggressive, but the second style is truly assertive.

So, although you may have picked up this book with the idea that it would help you learn more about control, authority, and power, you should now realize that the key to your success as a manager lies in the newer forms of assertive management: influence, collaboration, and communication. There are no magic formulas, no rule books. The best guide to change will be yourself—your own training, judgment, ingenuity, and flexibility. The following exercise will help you take stock.

Exercise: Examining Your Work Goals and Values*

Each of us has our own set of values which are affected by the people, activities, and events around us. These values both are influenced by and influence our participation in the workplace. This exercise is designed to help you examine your own goals and work values, those of your department, and those of your organization.

Rate Yourself

Imagine looking at yourself at work now. How do you feel as you see yourself in that setting? As you look at that picture, what needs of yours do you believe are very important for you to meet on that job? To help clarify those needs, rate the degree of importance you would assign each of the following work values. Use this scale as a measuring guide:

  1 = not important at all in my work/career
  2 = not very important in my work/career
  3 = somewhat important in my work/career
  4 = very important in my work/career
  5 = essential in my work/career

_____ *Help society.* I want my work to contribute to the betterment of the world I live in.

*This exercise was designed by Joan Alevras Stampfel and Elaina Zuker. Joan Alevras Stampfel is Executive Director of Resource Center Inc., a management development corporation located at 273 Hillside Ave., Nutley, NJ 07110 (201) 661-2195. Exercise reprinted with permission from THE EXECUTIVE FEMALE, a bimonthly magazine published by and distributed exclusively to members of the National Association for Female Executives, 120 East 56th Street, Suite 1440, New York, NY 10022 (212) 371-0740.

_____ *Affiliation/friendship/teamwork.* I want to have strong, close relationships with people and co-workers on the job.

_____ *Make decisions.* I want to have power to decide courses of action, policies, and so on.

_____ *Influence people and institutions.* I want to be in a position to influence attitudes or opinions of others.

_____ *Power and authority.* I want to be in a position to control the work activities or destiny of others.

_____ *Status.* I want to be regarded as someone with expertise, power, skills, or knowledge.

_____ *Recognition.* I want to be acknowledged in some visible or public way.

_____ *Creativity.* I want to create new ideas, programs, structures.

_____ *Opportunity.* I want to learn and grow professionally.

_____ *Change and variety.* I want work responsibilities that change over time in content and setting.

_____ *Stability.* I want a work routine and job duties that are largely predictable, that do not change much over time.

_____ *Security.* I want to be assured that I will be able to keep my position over time.

_____ *Fast pace/pressure.* I want to work where there is a fast pace of activity.

_____ *Excitement/adventure.* I want work duties which involve frequent risk taking on my part.

_____ *Independence.* I want to be able to determine the nature of my own work.

_____ *Time/freedom.* I want to be able to determine my own time schedule.

_____ *Profit/gain.* I want to earn a lot of money, have significant material gain.

_____ *Moral fulfillment.* I want to see that my work contributes significantly to a set of moral standards I believe are important.

Work Values and Goals

Now look back over your ratings. Choose three of the work values which you rated as *the* most important to you now. Fill them in on the lines below:

1. _____

2. _____

3. _____

Department's Values and Goals

Write down the three values which you see either as getting the most attention from your supervisor or as most likely to be satisfied by your work within that department:

1. _____

2. _____

3. _____

Organization's Values and Goals

List the top three values which you see being emphasized through company policies, reports, actions, messages from the CEO, and so forth:

1. _____

2. _____

3. _____

Areas of Harmony

As you look at these three lists, record below the areas of "harmony"—areas where your values and goals are *in alignment* with those of your department *and* your organization.

1. _____

2. _____

3. _____

If you were able to fill in all three spaces for areas of alignment you are likely to be experiencing a great deal of personal satisfaction on the job. Our values and goals are at the core of what keeps us "happy" at work.

Filling in two of the spaces supports the assumption that you are experiencing a satisfactory amount of personal harmony on the job. Although all of your needs are not being met, some very important ones are. This balance is probably going to keep you in your current job unless something really appealing comes along to lure you away.

If you filled in only one space, it is likely that you are not feeling much personal satisfaction in your work. This situation is a ripe atmosphere for "burn-out" to occur. You are experiencing burn-out if you are no longer able to renew your enthusiasm for tackling the problems of your job.

If there are no spaces filled in here you will want to take a hard look at the results of the next section.

Areas of Dissonance

Look at the three lists again. In this section record the areas of personal values and goals which are *out of alignment* with those of your department or organization.

1. _____

2. _____

3. _____

If you filled in all three spaces for areas of dissonance you are probably experiencing a lot of internal conflict on the job. Your most important values are not being satisfied in your work life. Often, a situation like this produces many physical symptoms, such as colds, headaches, and fatigue, owing to the stress of continually working in an unsupportive setting.

Two spaces filled in suggests that you find your values and goals only minimally supported. Although you probably have some very good reasons for staying where you are, this might be a good time for you to rethink your values and goals and how satisfied you are working there.

If only one area of disharmony is filled in you are likely to be feeling satisfied with your work. Perhaps you can put aside this one area of disharmony for now or have the values satisfied by other activities in your life. It may also be a value you do eventually want, and you may choose now to set aside time and energy for working toward that goal.

If you had no areas of disharmony, you are likely to be feeling very satisfied. This may be a good time to reassess your long-range goals and look at your growing and changing needs for the future.

Options

There are many strategies you may choose to bridge the gap between your values and goals and those of your workplace. Use your creative processes to map out how to get from the present state to where you ideally would like to be. You *may* not ever reach the ideal, but there will be no chance of reaching it if you do not work toward it. Here are some options.

1. You could work with your supervisor or someone else who has the power to help you realize your values and goals. The more clear, directed effort you put into getting your needs met, the greater the degree of satisfaction you will experience.

2. You could look for a more desirable job somewhere else. Perhaps now is a time to reevaluate whether the factors that led you to this job are important enough to keep you there.

3. You could rethink your values and see if it is realistic to maintain them in this particular work setting. Look back over the list of values and goals to see if there are other values available in this job which could be very satisfying for you. If there are, you might adjust your sights and renew your commitment to working there.

Only you can decide the benefits and costs of using any particular strategy. Talk over your options with someone whose opinions you value to get another perspective. Now, make a plan!

2

Assertiveness Defined

Assert yourself! These very words may trigger some instant negative reaction in you. "I'd better not." "They'll think I'm too pushy." "It's just not like me." These and other limiting internal messages are often what get in our way, preventing us from expressing ourselves directly and clearly—in other words, assertively.

What is assertiveness? Well, it's not a mysterious, mystical gift that some have and others don't. Rather, it's a series of skills that anyone can master with a little practice. The exciting thing about acquiring these skills is that you will suddenly find yourself being able to say no without guilt, to ask for what you want directly, and in general to communicate more clearly and openly in all your relationships. Most important, your self-confidence will improve dramatically.

In simplest terms, when you assert yourself, you communicate your *positive and negative* feelings honestly and directly. You are aware of your rights as a human being and speak and act to protect those rights. Assertive behavior demonstrates self-respect and self-confidence, along with an awareness of and respect for the rights of others.

Perhaps the best way to describe assertive behavior is to distinguish it from two other behavioral styles: nonassertive and aggressive behavior.

NONASSERTIVE BEHAVIOR

Nonassertive behavior usually arises from the belief that "I don't matter—my feelings, rights, opinions, and ideas aren't important. They aren't worth expressing." Nonassertive people sound apologetic, rambling, hesitant, hedging. They don't come to the point. They beat around the bush and are afraid to say no. Usually, when we engage in nonassertive behavior we feel hurt or resentful, sometimes anxious, often fearful. We may be angry

12

or annoyed with ourselves for not having the confidence to express our needs directly. Other people may feel irritated, impatient, or pitying toward us.

Usually, we act nonassertively out of fear—the fear that saying what we want will be considered pushy or aggressive. It's not polite. Often we feel like the victim or underdog and are pessimistic. We don't think we'll win anyway, so why try? Sometimes, especially among managers, the fear is that we *will* succeed and will be unable to handle the responsibility or other people's envy of us. Other beliefs that lead to unassertive responses are "I must be loved and approved of by everyone I meet. If I'm not, then I'm an awful person." "If I say no, I will hurt the other person." Sometimes we imagine that saying no to people's unreasonable requests or demands will utterly shatter them when in truth for the most part they will not be nearly as upset as we think.

Nonassertive people often qualify their statements with phrases like "I mean" and "you know." Worse, they preface their remarks with "This is only my opinion," "I don't know if anyone will agree with this," "I don't really have much research data to back this up." Unassertive comments like these convey a lack of self-confidence and a low level of confidence in others. How can we expect people to believe us, or to value what we are saying, if we don't believe in ourselves? This is the most common way that people destroy their credibility in the business environment.

Nonverbally, lack of assertiveness is communicated by a weak or wavering voice, excessive throat clearing or other nervous gestures, failure to make direct eye contact, and fidgety posture or stance. (The nonverbal components of behavior—all the ways in which people communicate without using words—are examined in detail in Chapter 9.)

AGGRESSIVE BEHAVIOR

Aggressive behavior is self-enhancing at the expense of others. It is dominating and controlling. Aggressive people often sound accusing or superior. They blame and label the behaviors and attitudes of others.

Aggressive people state their feelings and desires clearly and directly, but they do so in a way that violates other people's rights. Or they behave as if others' rights were not as important as theirs. Aggressive people are usually unconcerned with the feelings, ideas, opinions, or attitudes of people around them.

How does aggressiveness look? Most of us know the signs. Even if aggressive people are outwardly civil, we can tell when they are feeling angry or hostile. A great deal of the message lies in their nonverbal communication. Generally, aggressive people convey an air of superiority and distance. Often their voices are loud, demanding, authoritarian. But they can also be quiet—deadly quiet. Aggressive people rarely make direct eye contact.

Sometimes they point fingers accusingly, or make broad gestures with their hands that intrude on other people's space.

Aggressive people are usually unaware of their effect on others. Their antennae are not very sensitive, so they don't respond to feedback about when they're being offensive or annoying. They just keep on doing whatever they're doing, like children, usually ignorant of or unconcerned about the damage they are causing to their relationships.

Why do people act aggressively? Often out of fear. They may believe that others are out to get them or take away what they have, so they try to protect themselves. Sometimes people act aggressively in an attempt to appear tough, decisive, or grown up. Aggressive behavior may also be an overreaction to a past experience of having been too passive. The person vows never to let it happen again, even though current situations do not warrant protective or aggressive behavior.

ASSERTIVE BEHAVIOR

Now let's compare assertive behavior with these two styles. Assertive behavior is the expression of our wants, needs, and opinions clearly and directly, *without* violating the rights of others. We are assertive when we are open and honest, when we don't beat around the bush or try to force other people to agree with us or give in to our requests. An assertive person says no to others' requests without feeling guilty.

People are usually assertive out of a desire to be fair to themselves and to others, and a desire to *share* control and responsibility. An assertive person has a well-developed repertoire of assertiveness skills. Further in this book, we will examine these skills in detail.

Verbally, an assertive person makes an open, honest statement of desires and feelings. The messages are clear and direct. Nonverbally, an assertive person communicates both caring and strength by listening attentively and displaying a generally assured, confident manner. An assertive person's voice is firm, warm, well modulated, and relaxed. The eyes make direct contact. Posture is well balanced—not leaning, slumped, or thrusting.

Table 3 summarizes the verbal and nonverbal components of nonassertive, assertive, and aggressive behavior.

Another way to compare these three behavioral styles is to examine the varying levels of "openness of self" and "respect for others" that assertive, nonassertive, and aggressive people display. (See Figure 1.) Aggressive people are open about their feelings, whatever those feelings may be, but often show a low respect for others. Nonassertive people have a lot of respect for others—in fact, sometimes too much—but very little openness of self. Assertive people mix high openness about their needs and feelings with a high degree of respect for the needs and feelings of others.

Table 3. Verbal and nonverbal components of behavior.

	Nonassertive (No Influence)	*Assertive (Positive Influence)*	*Aggressive (Negative Influence)*
VERBAL	Apologetic words. Veiled meanings. Hedging; failure to come to the point. Rambling; disconnected. At a loss for words. Failure to say what you really mean. Qualifying statements with "I mean," "you know."	Statement of wants. Honest statement of feelings. Objective words. Direct statements, which say what you mean. "I" messages.	"Loaded" words. Accusations. Descriptive, subjective terms. Imperious, superior words. "You" messages that blame or label.
NONVERBAL General demeanor	Actions instead of words, hoping someone will guess what you want. Looking as if you don't mean what you say.	Attentive listening behavior. Generally assured manner, communicating caring and strength.	Exaggerated show of strength. Flippant, sarcastic style. Air of superiority.
Voice	Weak, hesitant, soft, sometimes wavering.	Firm, warm, well modulated, relaxed.	Tense, shrill, loud, shaky; cold, "deadly quiet," demanding; superior, authoritarian.
Eyes	Averted, downcast, teary, pleading	Open, frank, direct. Eye contact, but not staring.	Expressionless, narrowed, cold, staring; not really "seeing" others.
Stance and posture	Leaning for support, stooped, excessive head nodding.	Well balanced, straight on, erect, relaxed.	Hands on hips, feet apart. Stiff and rigid. Rude, imperious.
Hands	Fidgety, fluttery, clammy.	Relaxed motions.	Clenched. Abrupt gestures, fingerpointing, fist pounding.

AN ASSERTIVE PHILOSOPHY

Assertiveness begins with a positive, humanistic philosophy. Assertive people approach the world from the position that they are worthwhile and

Figure 1. Behavior matrix.

	Low Respect	High Respect
High Openness	Aggressive Telling co-workers they must not smoke in the office.	Assertive Telling co-workers you do not like smoke and requesting they not smoke in the office.
Low Openness	Passive Aggressive Acting grumpy and coughing loudly when someone is smoking near you.	Nonassertive Not mentioning your discomfort or wish that people would not smoke in the office.

have certain rights while acknowledging that other people are worthwhile and have rights too. The Assertive Bill of Rights on the opposite page lists the ten fundamental rights that all assertive people believe in.

Assertive people try to govern their personal and professional lives so they do not hurt others or allow others to hurt them. They stand up for legitimate personal rights in such a way that *the rights of others are not violated.* This is important. Assertiveness is not license to tread on the feelings of others, to blame people, or to make unreasonable demands.

Sacrificing our rights—by allowing others to make unreasonable demands on us—creates unhealthy emotional imbalances and ultimately corrodes relationships. Also, when we do not let other people know how we feel, what we think, and what we want, we are in essence being selfish. By concealing these parts of ourselves, we are not giving others the chance to know us and to relate to us openly and honestly. Finally, when we sacrifice our rights, we train other people to treat us without respect. If we don't tell others how they are affecting us, we deny them the opportunity to change their behavior if they want to have a more successful relationship with us.

As adults, we can decide what's important to us, based on our own personal and professional priorities. Of course, we are all constrained by a set of "shoulds" imposed on our lives—the dos and don'ts of company policy, social mores, and public law. But many of us also have an internal set of shoulds—beliefs about ourselves and others—that do not always reflect reality and that can lead us to behave in unproductive ways. It is these shoulds that we need to examine to see whether they are appropriate for us.

ASSERTIVE BILL OF RIGHTS

I have the right to be treated with respect.
I have the right to have and express my own feelings and opinions.
I have the right to be listened to and taken seriously.
I have the right to set my own priorities.
I have the right to say no without feeling guilty.
I have the right to ask for what I want.
I have the right to get what I pay for.
I have the right to make mistakes.
I have the right to assert myself even though I may inconvenience others.
I have the right to choose not to assert myself.

Having an assertive philosophy implies a specific set of attitudes toward ourselves and others. When we are assertive, we accept and act on statements such as:

1. I'm under no obligation to say yes to people simply because they ask a favor of me.
2. The fact that I say no to someone does not make me a selfish person.
3. If I do say no to people and they get angry, that doesn't mean I should have said yes.
4. The fact that other people might not be assertive doesn't mean I shouldn't be.
5. Even though someone else may be annoyed with me at times, I can still feel good about myself.

BEHAVIOR CHANGE: THE FIRST STEPS

Now that you understand the distinctions between assertive, nonassertive, and aggressive behavior you can begin to work on becoming a more assertive you. Effective behavior change usually takes place in six steps.

1. Identify your current behavior and its results. What situations in your life would you like to change? What is your current behavior in those situations, and what outcomes is that behavior creating?

2. Set goals for new behavior that will lead to better results. What new results would you like to achieve? Often it is helpful to visualize your goal. Try to imagine each situation or relationship exactly the way you want it to be. What about it impresses you—what do you see, hear, or feel in the situation that can help you? Visualizing the change can give you the motivation to try new behaviors.

3. Identify the beliefs, attitudes, and feelings that are keeping your existing behavior in place. In Chapter 4, we will look at beliefs that lead to

unassertive behavior and how you can "redesign" your beliefs in order to change.

4. Develop new skills. You can have a really clear idea of why your present behavior isn't working, you can envision the new goal, and you can be very motivated, but you still need practical skills that will reinforce your new behavior and keep you from reverting to old patterns when you encounter the situations that have been giving you problems. Chapter 5 examines a "tool kit" of assertive skills that will help you achieve your goals.

5. Practice, practice, practice. This can't be stressed enough. When you try out any new skill, you will feel awkward and clumsy. Try to build new skills in relatively low-risk situations at first, until you feel comfortable.

6. Get some positive experiences. Nothing succeeds like success. And don't forget to reward yourself after you've had a success, no matter how small.

As you begin to work on changing your behavior, you may find it helpful to seek out a role model. Is there someone in your life—personal or professional—who is assertive, clear, direct, human, someone who gets respect? You might try to emulate this person's behavior, adapting it to your own personality and style so it feels like you. Or you could talk with your model and ask for advice. Chances are your model has tried some things that didn't work, learned some lessons, and then found the things that did work.

It's also a good idea to get some feedback. Ask a colleague or friend to observe you the next time you're trying out a new behavior. Have your observer document specifically what you said, what the other person said, what you could have said differently. Also ask for feedback on your nonverbal communication—what did your body say that was assertive, nonassertive, or aggressive?

Once armed with a few simple tools and techniques, you can begin to identify and overcome your own "failure devices" and become more aware of the impact that your behavior and communications have on others. All of us can learn to be more assertive. It's usually just a question of tuning in to the fears and beliefs that hold us back.

SELF-IMAGE AND SELF-ESTEEM

Whether or not we are assertive is largely determined by our self-concept—how we view our strengths and weaknesses and how we believe other people respond and react to us. This image, in turn, forms the basis for our self-esteem—the degree to which we appreciate our own value.

Our self-image is formed by the experiences we gather as we go through life and get feedback (negative or positive) from people around us. Our parents, siblings, teachers, friends, classmates, lovers, spouses, and business associates all give us direct or indirect feedback on which behaviors

GOAL-SETTING CHECKLIST

○ What is my goal? What exactly do I want to accomplish?

○ How will assertive behavior on my part help me accomplish my goal?

○ What do I usually do to avoid asserting myself in this situation? What is my usual modus operandi?

○ Why would I want to give up the comfort and security of usual behavior and assert myself instead? What incentive or motivation can I give my-self to change?

○ What is stopping me from asserting myself? Have I been taught or con-ditioned to behave in ways that make it difficult for me to act assertively in this situation? What are these ways?

○ What are my rights in the situation? Do these rights justify changing the old "tapes" of my conditioning? What can I do to change?

○ Can I let the other person know I hear and understand him or her? Let the other person know how I feel? Tell the person what I want?

are desirable and appropriate. As we grow up, we internalize the labels and opinions of other people and incorporate them into our picture of our-selves—our self-image.

Our self-image is also built on the successes and failures that we have experienced in the past. Nonassertive people have a selective memory and remember only the failures. As a result, they have a large inventory of negative self-messages. These statements, through repetition, become im-printed on their consciousness, and they act as if the statements were true. If they have been doing this long enough, their negative self-image will be evident in how they carry themselves, how they dress, and what they say.

A strong indicator of self-image is the way a person accepts a compli-ment. People with a low self-image often discount anything positive said about them: "This old thing? I've had it for years." "I didn't think the report was quite as complete as it should have been." Or they will make self-deprecatory remarks or cracks about themselves. Many people with a poor self-image are low achievers. They know that learning brings about change and success, but they are not willing to tolerate the mistakes and setbacks that inevitably occur in the learning process. So they play it safe, forgoing the bigger challenges in order to keep their shaky self-image intact.

It is also interesting to note that people who, at first glance, appear to have high self-esteem—the blowhards and braggarts—often suffer from an extremely low self-image. They are calling out for attention. "Look at me," they are shouting. "I *am* worthwhile." But they don't really believe it. If they did, they wouldn't have such a compulsive need for the spotlight. Peo-ple with a healthy self-image do not feel hostile or resentful toward others, do not feel that other people's good fortune threatens their own, and aren't out to prove anything.

To build our self-esteem, we must take pride in ourselves as we are *right now*, not brood over the past or daydream about the future. Self-esteem is a habit, and like any other habit it can be developed with practice. The following exercises will help you assess your self-image and work on your self-esteem.

Exercise: Feeling Good About Yourself

1. Write down five statements describing your good qualities—attributes that you like in yourself or that others have commented on or noticed. Be as concrete and specific as possible. For example, you might describe positive aspects of your appearance, your intelligence, your interests, your achievements, and your loving or spiritual qualities.

_____

_____

_____

_____

_____

Add to this list whenever you can. And every time you think of another positive statement, give yourself a reward. Make positive self-statements as often as possible. You might also try telling others who are close to you what you like about yourself. This may seem like "fishing for compliments," but it will give you practice in allowing yourself to feel good about you.

2. Every time you find yourself saying something negative or derogatory about yourself, turn the statement around. Make a statement that is the direct opposite, even if you don't believe it! For example, one negative self-message might be, "I always procrastinate on important tasks." You can turn the statement around by saying, "I find big jobs challenging and turn to them right away." Write out five such statements below.

Negative _____

Positive _____

Negative _____

Positive _____

Negative _____

Positive _____

Negative _____

Positive _____

Negative ————————————————————————————

Positive ————————————————————————————

Practice this technique aloud every day. Reward yourself each time you turn a negative message around and punish yourself (for example, by doing an unpleasant task) every time you choose to hold on to a negative belief. Pretty soon, you'll be coming out with more and more positive statements.

Exercise: Choosing a Model

As noted earlier in this chapter, having a role model—someone who looks, feels, and acts the way you would like to—is an important part of behavior change. You can choose someone you know as a model, or you can create an ideal in your mind.

1. Describe your model, being very specific about how the person looks, talks, interacts with others, and so on.

————————————————————————————

————————————————————————————

————————————————————————————

2. Visualize the model doing something that you don't think you do well. Describe how she or he does it.

————————————————————————————

————————————————————————————

————————————————————————————

3. Think of a situation in which you have been having difficulty acting assertively. Imagine yourself in that situation using some of the techniques, attitudes, and behaviors of your model. Imagine that you have a strong self-image and high self-esteem, just like the model. Describe how you are handling the situation.

————————————————————————————

————————————————————————————

————————————————————————————

TIPS ON BUILDING SELF-ESTEEM

Liking yourself and feeling that you are a worthwhile, valuable person in your own way is not egotistical or bragging. Like everyone else, you have unique gifts, and you have the right to be proud of them. To continue building your self-esteem:

1. Dress and look your best. Even if you don't feel good on a particular day, force yourself to look your best. Often, this can go a long way toward helping you take pride in yourself.

2. Take stock. Make a list of all the qualities you have to be proud of. Write down all the positive self-statements you can think of.
3. Give yourself a gold star. You are the most intelligent judge or appraiser of you. Don't let yourself be run by other people's opinions or standards.
4. Use positive language when you talk to yourself and others.
5. Turn negative self-statements around.
6. Record your successes every day.
7. Acknowledge other people. You'll feel good about yourself whenever you can add value to other people's lives and strengthen their self-esteem.
8. Smile at yourself as often as you can. You'll find a friendly face who is there to support you, cheer you on, and tell you how special you are.

Exercise: Self-Image/Career Inventory*

This exercise is designed to help you explore some of the below-the-surface visions you hold about yourself and your career. Since it is an inventory, there are no right or wrong answers. It is simply a personal evaluation of your qualities. Fill in your responses to the items described below.

1. *Background.* List the ethical and cultural building blocks on which you base your life and work (spiritual values, cultural roots, and so on).

_____

_____

_____

2. *Personal principles.* List the personal beliefs that determine the pace of your life and work (for example, financial gain is of no great value; honesty is always worth its price).

_____

_____

_____

3. *Strengths.* List those qualities about your working self which you value most (assertive about getting ahead, endurance).

_____

*This exercise was designed by Joan Alevras Stampfel and Elaina Zuker. Joan Alevras Stampfel is Executive Director of Resource Center Inc., a management development corporation located at 273 Hillside Ave., Nutley, NJ 07110 (201) 661-2195. Exercise reprinted with permission from THE EXECUTIVE FEMALE, a bimonthly magazine published by and distributed exclusively to members of the National Association for Female Executives, 120 East 56th Street, Suite 1440, New York, NY 10022 (212) 371-0740.

4. *Weaknesses*. List those work habits that you value least in yourself (impatience, lack of planning, and so on).

_____

_____

_____

5. *Heart space*. What about your work life excites you and keeps you active (stimulating relationships with others, status rewards, and so on)?

_____

_____

_____

6. *Verbal communication*. How do you express yourself to others about your work? (For example, I love/hate my job, my boss, commuting.)

_____

_____

_____

7. *Internal communication*. What do you tell yourself about your job and life? (For example, I'm so bored/scared; they don't appreciate me here.)

_____

_____

_____

8. *Sensing*. What do your senses or intuition tell you about your work life before the facts have been stated? (For example, I knew that project would be canceled.)

_____

_____

_____

9. *Visions*. What do you see when you picture yourself at work now ("making it," struggling)? What do you see in the future (working full time, part time, on your own)?

_____

_____

_____

10. *Reflections.* How do you imagine others see you now (creative, shrewd, lazy)? How would you like to be seen in the future (executive material, director)?

_____

_____

_____

11. *Sound impressions.* What do you hear others tell you about yourself and your work? (You're so confident and enthusiastic. You're competitive.)

_____

_____

_____

12. *Self-impressions.* How do you hear yourself sound at work (impatient, "know-it-all," defiant)?

_____

_____

_____

13. *Brain power.* How smart do you think you are? How high up in your organization do you see yourself going (vice president, CEO, director)?

_____

_____

_____

Scoring

Rank each category with a number which represents the level of satisfaction you feel about your responses. Use the following scale:

3 = completely satisfied   2 = somewhat satisfied   1 = not satisfied

Category	Rank
1. Background	_____
2. Personal principles	_____
3. Strengths	_____
4. Weaknesses	_____
5. Heart space	_____
6. Verbal communication	_____

7.	Internal communication	_____
8.	Sensing	_____
9.	Visions	_____
10.	Reflections	_____
11.	Sound impressions	_____
12.	Self-impressions	_____
13.	Brain power	_____
	Total	_____

If your total score is 30 to 39, your self-image is in good shape. If you scored between 22 and 29, there are areas you need to pay attention to. A score below 21 indicates room for satisfaction to grow.

On the basis of your self-assessment, what three areas are you most satisfied with?

1. _____

2. _____

3. _____

What three areas are you least satisfied with?

1. _____

2. _____

3. _____

Which *one* area that you are least satisfied with are you willing to work at changing over the next six months? Write out a full description of your present behavior in that area.

_____

_____

_____

_____

_____

_____

_____

Now imagine yourself with the change *already* in place. How would you look, dress, work differently? Write out a full description of the desired behavior.

_____

_____

_____

_____

_____

_____

_____

Finally, use these action steps to begin the change process right now:

1. Observe your present behavior.
2. Keep track of your responses.
3. Concentrate on one particular situation.
4. Review your responses.
5. Observe an effective model.
6. Consider yourself using alternative responses.
7. Imagine yourself handling the situation the way you would like to.
8. Try several approaches until you find ones that work best for you.
9. Get feedback.
10. Repeat steps 7, 8, and 9 as often as necessary to reach your goal—and stay flexible. (Always consider alternatives as the situation demands.)
11. Do it!
12. Reward yourself. Think of a reward that would make it worth your while to change. This is the most important step—be good to yourself and recognize your efforts in your own behalf.
13. Save this inventory. Check your responses in six months. Satisfied? Great! Not satisfied? Go over the steps again and concentrate on one situation at a time.

3

Beliefs and Attitudes Underlying Behavior

A hundred times a day, in our work and personal lives, we make decisions about how to behave with other people. Most of these decisions do not seem like choices at all. Rather, we make them as if we were on automatic pilot. We come up against a situation, do a quick computation of the possible outcomes, decide which one is most familiar or least risky, and then immediately make our response.

The internal messages we send ourselves have a powerful influence on whether our behavior is assertive or nonassertive. For example: "If I tell my assistant his performance isn't up to standards, he'll resent me." Anticipating that a subordinate will be resentful is really a belief we have about his reaction to criticism. It may or may not be true. As long as we continue to hold this belief, we will have great difficulty acting assertively and telling the subordinate anything negative about his performance.

Another example: "If I tell my boss my new ideas, she won't be interested. She'll reject them." Here we know that we have ideas and in fact have been hired to contribute them to the organization. At the same time, we believe that if we express these ideas, the boss will think they are foolish, trivial, or not worthwhile. This belief keeps us from expressing ourselves assertively.

A third example: "If I don't do what my customers want, they'll go to the competition and I'll lose business." Doing the customer's bidding without establishing boundaries or limits can put us in a one-down situation every time. True, we may lose business if we don't meet a customer's requirements. But always acquiescing to customer demands is no guarantee of business success.

In business situations, we often act as if we had no rights, or as if other people had more rights than we do, and our behavior is motivated by a desire not to make waves. We focus our attention more on the other person's rights and authority than on our own. Certainly, it's important to be sensitive to and considerate of other people. But we rarely check out our beliefs about others to see if they are true.

Sometimes we imagine that saying no to other people's unreasonable requests or demands will utterly shatter them. Again, this is a belief we have, and one that rarely holds up against the facts. A typical situation: A stranger sits down next to you on a train or plane and starts to chat, but you don't feel like it. What do you do? You could be direct (if you're assertive) and say you're not in the mood to talk. Or you could be indirect (if you're not assertive) and stick your nose in your book or pretend to be sleeping. After a while, your would-be companion will get the message and leave you alone. Within minutes, he or she will probably strike up a conversation with a more willing passenger. It's not *your* job to entertain your seatmates—and people who want to chat will usually find someone who wants that too. Probably the other person's feelings won't be hurt at all.

Finally, it's important to be aware that you *choose* your beliefs. You are in charge of what to believe and what not to believe. And it's this choice that determines most strongly whether you act assertively or nonassertively—that is, whether you value and respect yourself or give away your rights and powers to others.

TRYING OUT NEW BELIEFS

Before you can change your behavior, you will need to try out several new beliefs to see which ones will encourage you to be more assertive and reinforce your efforts to change. The process involves four steps:

1. Identifying a situation in which you are not as assertive as you'd like to be.
2. Identifying the belief underlying your nonassertive behavior.
3. Visualizing yourself behaving more confidently and assertively in that situation.
4. Making up—creating—one or more new beliefs that you would have to accept in order to practice the desired assertive behavior.

Let's look at an example to see how the process works. Barry J. has a subordinate who complains to him chronically about how heavy the workload is. Barry rarely responds to Julie's complaints, and when he does, he usually makes apologies for the busy season or puts himself down by saying that maybe he should be doing some of the work himself.

What is the belief underlying this unassertive behavior? According to Barry, it's fear of rejection: "If I tell Julie I don't want to hear the complaining, and in fact give her suggestions on how to complete the work efficiently, she might reject my ideas and be angry with me for criticizing her attitude."

What's the new, desired, more assertive behavior? Barry would like "to be able to set limits, to tell her that this is the way I as her manager must delegate the work, and to give her some suggestions about how to complete it on time. I would like to stop apologizing and putting myself down for being a bad manager." This is the new assertive posture Barry wants to achieve.

What new beliefs will Barry have to try out in order to motivate himself to practice the new behavior? What could he imagine as a potential outcome of assertive behavior that is different from the outcome he's now imagining—the employee's further discontent and unwillingness to complete the work? Barry came up with this new belief: "If I told her what the situation was, and that it was part of her responsibility to do the work, and mine as a manager to delegate it, she might have a clearer idea of our roles and tasks, and know more clearly what to expect of me in the future. If I gave her suggestions about how to finish the work, she might welcome them, not be so confused, and quit complaining. She might actually be grateful for my suggestions and not view them as criticism at all." Once Barry has created a new scenario for the outcome that his behavior is likely to produce, he can begin to change. But first he must recognize—and dare to challenge—the old belief underlying his current behavior.

You too can develop the confidence and courage to try out different behaviors—by altering your beliefs. Remember, the original belief—the one leading to nonassertive behavior—isn't necessarily true. It's just what you *think* might happen. Or it may have happened once or twice as a result of a certain action you took, so now you think it is the only possible result. In shifting your beliefs, you're really changing your ideas about the possible consequences of your behavior. It is often simply a matter of acting *as if* you really believed the new or made-up belief, even if you don't. After all, the old belief, the one you're used to, is no less fabricated than the new one. It's just one you've grown accustomed to. You've had it longer—it's like an old, familiar friend. Often we allow ourselves to be run by old beliefs without being aware of it. Many of the beliefs we carry around assume that we don't have the same rights that others have. We give over our power to other people's needs and demands.

Table 4 lists some typical problems that managers encounter on the job and the outcomes produced by nonassertive versus assertive behavior. As the examples demonstrate, trying out new beliefs is a powerful motivator in helping managers act more assertively.

Table 4. Unassertive versus assertive responses to typical work situations.

Current Unassertive Behavior	Current Belief About Results	Desired Assertive Behavior	New Assertive Belief About Results
I have an employee who isn't performing up to standards. I'm reluctant to tell her.	If I tell her she'll get upset and resent me.	I'll tell her clearly and specifically what my expectations are, and how she is meeting them, as well as how she's not.	She will welcome the feedback—she wants to know how she's doing, and how she can improve.
I give my subordinates a great deal of detail and instructions about how to do the work.	They'll become confused and do it wrong or inadequately. They'll take it personally.	I'll give them only as much information and detail as they need.	They will feel more trusted and have a chance to use their talent and creativity. They will see that I am criticizing the work, *not* criticizing them personally.
When I'm in a meeting with my peers, I don't speak up or express my opinions.	I'm afraid my ideas will be seen as stupid or unrealistic. !	I will challenge others' ideas if I think they lack merit, and also present my own.	My ideas are solid and interesting. I have many worthwhile contributions to make. Even if people don't agree with me, they will still respect me for participating.
One of my peers is much more knowledgeable than I am. I hesitate to call on her for advice or information.	She will find out how ignorant I am and use it against me.	When I need information, I will ask her for it.	She will be flattered that I value her input; she'll use me as a resource when she needs to.
I never disagree with my male colleagues in meetings.	They will say I'm a pushy, aggressive female.	I will disagree when I see things another way.	They will respect my honesty. They will trust me to say what I feel and not to mask it with politeness.

30

When my boss gives me a project that I know I can't complete on time, I'm reluctant to say so. I go away and worry about it—or do it and neglect other important work.	He will think I'm a poor manager, lazy or inefficient. He will be angry, and never again consider me for important work.	When I get a new project and cannot deliver it realistically by the deadline my boss tells me, I will speak up right away, let the boss know my situation, and try to negotiate a satisfactory solution.	He will appreciate knowing the situation now, rather than finding the project not done at the last moment. He will respect my assertiveness and realistic assessment of the situation.
In a meeting with my boss and other members of our department, I am afraid to let on that I don't know something. Usually, I just nod; then I am unclear about what I'm expected to do.	She (and they) will think I'm stupid—and inexperienced.	When I don't understand or don't hear something, I will question until I do.	She will welcome the fact that I'm paying attention and will want to understand exactly what's expected of me. She will respect me for taking the time to get clear on my duties.
When colleagues ask me for a favor, I hardly ever say no.	If I say no, they'll be upset and angry, and they won't want to be my friend.	I will say no when I feel I don't want to comply with the demand or request.	They will have a clearer understanding of my limits—and respect me. They will find it easier to say no to me. Our relationship will become more honest.
I don't ask for what I want—with my boss and colleagues.	They will think I'm greedy or pushy. They will say no.	I will ask for what I want. Even though I may not get it, I will have stated clearly what I want.	They may say yes to me. Whether or not they do, they will see me as a person who has self-respect, and they will respect me.
I hesitate and "sit on the fence." I ask everybody else's opinion. I hardly ever make a decision.	1. Someone will prove me wrong. 2. I'll have to change my mind. 3. I'll look silly or, worse, incompetent.	I will make a decision when I have a reasonable amount of information, even though I may be wrong.	1. I may turn out to be wrong, but it's okay to make mistakes. 2. If I change my mind, that will be a sign of my flexibility as a good manager. 3. I'll look even sillier and more incompetent by sitting on the fence and not taking a stand.

Exercise: Building New Beliefs

A major goal of assertiveness training is to build a personal belief system that will help you support and justify your new assertive behaviors. This is important so that you can:

1. Continue to believe in your right to act assertively.
2. Deal with any guilt feelings you may have when you begin practicing assertiveness skills.
3. Be proud of your assertiveness, even if others don't acknowledge you.
4. Be motivated to continue asserting yourself.

Take a look now at your own life—both personal and professional. In each case, think of a situation in which you're not as assertive as you'd like to be. In the first column of the Behavior Chart on the opposite page, write down the unassertive current behavior you'd like to change. In the second column, write down the current belief that is keeping you in the unassertive behavior pattern. Now try to visualize yourself being more assertive in that situation. Imagine yourself in a conversation with the other person. How do you see yourself and hear yourself? How do you feel? Walk yourself through a scene or conversation with the person. In the third column, write down, in one sentence, what your desired assertive behavior is. In the last column, write down one or more new beliefs about the outcomes your assertive behavior is likely to produce. (It's helpful to brainstorm this part of the exercises to come up with as many new beliefs as you can. You can use some or all of them.)

BELIEF-CHANGERS

A favorite belief-changer of mine is "nothing personal." I try to remember it when I feel under attack by other people, or when I have to say no to someone's request. It means that everyone in the world is doing his or her own thing, behaving in the way that has some personal meaning or payoff. So if your pal Jim is critical and you happen to be in his path, you'll get some of that criticism—and it's probably *nothing personal.* Chances are that most people in Jim's life get some of that criticism. Jim is a critical person, and he is just doing what he does. Similarly, if your friend Sarah is sweet and loving and gives you a lot of positive feedback, it may be nothing personal. Sarah probably gives positive strokes to everyone! If you say no to someone, you are simply taking care of your own needs. Remember, you are not necessarily saying no to the *person;* you are simply stating your limits—saying no to the request. If you can stress to someone else that it is nothing personal, that can help soften your refusal.

Another good belief-changer is "rewriting the rules." Whenever you notice that you're operating under some unstated assumption, ask yourself what it is. You'll probably find that you have unrealistic expectations about yourself or others (such as, "If Larry is my friend, he *should* always be available to talk to me on the phone.") Rewrite your shoulds—you may be quite surprised at the ways they are limiting your relationships.

BEHAVIOR CHART

Current Unassertive Behavior	Current Belief About Results	Desired Assertive Behavior	New Belief About Results
Personal Life	*Personal Life*	*Personal Life*	*Personal Life*
_____	_____	_____	_____
_____	_____	_____	_____
_____	_____	_____	_____
_____	_____	_____	_____
Professional Life	*Professional Life*	*Professional Life*	*Professional Life*
_____	_____	_____	_____
_____	_____	_____	_____
_____	_____	_____	_____
_____	_____	_____	_____

A related belief-changer is "renegotiating a bargain." Most of us make unwritten bargains or agreements with people in our lives that keep us stuck in a certain behavior pattern. For example, Joanne was never able to refuse Bob when he asked her to stay late at work, even though he always asked her at the last minute and she had to rearrange her personal plans. She became aware that her bargain went something like this: "I won't refuse you when you ask me to stay late, in return for your thinking I'm a loyal, conscientious person who never disagrees." Most of us are unaware of the unspoken bargains in our lives. We may never discuss the terms of the agreement or even enter into negotiations with the other person, but both parties act as though the bargain is in place.

Generally, we maintain these bargains because we get some positive benefit or payoff or because we don't know (or are afraid of) what the payoff would be if we were to change the bargain. Suppose Joanne suddenly decided to change her bargain and act assertively. Suppose she said to Bob, "No, I can't do this report. It's unrealistic to think I can do a good job in such a short time." What might she get from Bob that's better than what she's getting now? Maybe she'd get him to respect her. Maybe she'd get him to see that she has a realistic view of what she can accomplish in a certain time period. Joanne's new bargain might go like this: "I will assert myself by saying no to your unreasonable requests for me to stay late, in return for your respecting me."

Exercise: Changing a Bargain

Here is a chance to practice changing a bargain you have made in your life, one that you're not completely satisfied with. Think of a situation in which you're not as assertive as you'd like to be. Think about the other person in the situation, and what your bargain is. How does the person act toward you in the situation? What are you getting in return? The person's approval or acceptance? Whatever it is, write the bargain down.

I will not assert my self when you ——————————————————————,
in return for your ————————————————————————.

Now think about the negative consequences of the situation. What are you *not* getting? Self-respect? Do you feel dishonest, as if you're letting yourself down? Or perhaps you do not like the feelings the other person has toward you when you behave nonassertively. What would happen if you were more assertive? What could you get that would be better than what you're getting now? Could you get a changed attitude from the other person that would make you feel better about yourself, better about the relationship? Rewrite your bargain in the space below.

I will assert myself by saying ——————————————————————,
if you will ——————————————————————————.

Identifying your beliefs and bargains, and working toward turning them around, can be a powerful first step toward becoming more assertive. When you begin to see that the beliefs you hold are merely ideas you have been telling yourself, and that they can be changed, you'll be well on your way to a more powerful, more assertive you.

Exercise: How Assertive Are You? Assessing Your Business Relationships

Many of us are familiar with measuring business skills through profit and loss statements. More difficult to measure are the results produced through interacting with others. This exercise is designed to help you assess your *beliefs* and *actions* (both negative and positive) in several arenas of your business relationships.

The four categories you will be looking at will be: a) your beliefs and actions as they relate to yourSELF, b) your beliefs and actions with your PEERS at work, c) your beliefs and actions with your BOSS and finally, d) your beliefs and actions with your SUBORDINATES—if you are a manager or supervisor.

There are 64 questions in all. As you go through each one, work as quickly as possible. Be honest with yourself, so you can get the most accurate picture when you score the answers.

For each question indicate, with an "x" in the appropriate place, whether the sentence is:

1 = never true
2 = seldom true
3 = sometimes true
4 = usually true
5 = always true

Complete all 64 questions this way, and then follow the scoring instructions at the end of the questionnaire.

	1	2	3	4	5
1. I set specific goals and time frames for my work.	—	—	—	—	—
2. I do things that will make me liked by others.	—	—	—	—	—
3. I am an ambitious person.	—	—	—	—	—
4. It is selfish to ask for what you want.	—	—	—	—	—
5. I express my positive feelings to others easily.	—	—	—	—	—
6. I rarely tell people if I'm angry with them.	—	—	—	—	—
7. I am able to control or change my feelings.	—	—	—	—	—
8. It's not a good idea to take too many risks at work.	—	—	—	—	—
9. I reward myself for good performance even when others do not.	—	—	—	—	—
10. I usually work alone, rather than with others.	—	—	—	—	—
11. I have the right to say "no" to other people's requests.	—	—	—	—	—

	1	2	3	4	5
12. It is important to get the approval of others.	—	—	—	—	—
13. I take on challenging tasks even when I don't know how they will turn out.	—	—	—	—	—
14. I challenge people and try to prove them wrong.	—	—	—	—	—
15. I am responsible for my own happiness.	—	—	—	—	—
16. It's not a good idea to state your ideas directly.	—	—	—	—	—
17. When meeting with my peers, I speak up easily.	—	—	—	—	—
18. I usually compete with my peers when the boss is around.	—	—	—	—	—
19. Many of my peers are as competent as I am.	—	—	—	—	—
20. I would be uncomfortable if I were promoted and had to supervise my current colleagues.	—	—	—	—	—
21. I make an effort to make my peers look good in the boss's or management's eyes.	—	—	—	—	—
22. I don't acknowledge my peers when they have demonstrated competence.	—	—	—	—	—
23. If I support my peers in their careers, it will benefit me.	—	—	—	—	—
24. When a peer is acknowledged by management I feel envious and threatened.	—	—	—	—	—
25. When one of my peers is more knowledgeable than I am, I call on him/ her for advice and information.	—	—	—	—	—
26. If I have inside information, I don't share it with my peers.	—	—	—	—	—
27. My peers have rich resources and expertise to offer me.	—	—	—	—	—
28. I often feel my peers know more than I do.	—	—	—	—	—
29. I help my colleague when he/she is having trouble meeting a deadline.	—	—	—	—	—
30. If one of my peers is not doing his/her job, I tell the boss.	—	—	—	—	—
31. If a peer were in trouble, I would put my own work aside to help out.	—	—	—	—	—
32. My peers would blow the whistle on me if I wasn't doing my job well.	—	—	—	—	—

	1	**2**	**3**	**4**	**5**

33. I let my boss know when I disagree with him/her. ___ ___ ___ ___ ___

34. I only ask the boss for the information I need to do a specific task. ___ ___ ___ ___ ___

35. My boss is an example of a person I would like to become. ___ ___ ___ ___ ___

36. I assume my boss always knows what he/she is doing. ___ ___ ___ ___ ___

37. I ask my boss for help when I need it. ___ ___ ___ ___ ___

38. When people say negative things about the boss, I agree with them. ___ ___ ___ ___ ___

39. I could step into my boss's job without too much difficulty. ___ ___ ___ ___ ___

40. When I don't know or understand something I try to hide it from my boss. ___ ___ ___ ___ ___

41. When my boss asks me to go "an extra mile" I never hesitate to say "yes." ___ ___ ___ ___ ___

42. I let the boss figure out what's wrong when things get delayed or become disorganized. ___ ___ ___ ___ ___

43. If I needed my boss to go to bat for me with higher management, he/she would. ___ ___ ___ ___ ___

44. I'm never certain where I stand with my boss. ___ ___ ___ ___ ___

45. I tell my boss when I appreciate something he/she has done. ___ ___ ___ ___ ___

46. I talk to others about it when I'm angry with my boss. ___ ___ ___ ___ ___

47. My boss makes as many mistakes as I do. ___ ___ ___ ___ ___

48. Supervisors rarely understand or appreciate me. ___ ___ ___ ___ ___

49. I give career advice to my subordinates. ___ ___ ___ ___ ___

50. I take complicated projects rather than spending time explaining them to subordinates. ___ ___ ___ ___ ___

51. Subordinates should be coached to take over my job. ___ ___ ___ ___ ___

52. I believe it's important to give subordinates detailed instructions for every job they do. ___ ___ ___ ___ ___

53. I help my subordinates get the results they need to do their jobs better. ___ ___ ___ ___ ___

54. When subordinates don't do their jobs well, I hesitate to tell them I am displeased. ___ ___ ___ ___ ___

	1	**2**	**3**	**4**	**5**
55. Most subordinates welcome and can handle responsibility.	___	___	___	___	___
56. Good managers don't give a subordinate too much responsibility.	___	___	___	___	___
57. I let my subordinates know that I respect their competence.	___	___	___	___	___
58. I put off confronting an incompetent subordinate.	___	___	___	___	___
59. I can count on my subordinates to support me.	___	___	___	___	___
60. Subordinates who demonstrate outstanding ability make me uncomfortable.	___	___	___	___	___
61. I will set limits on a subordinate if I consider it necessary.	___	___	___	___	___
62. It's not my task to teach subordinates.	___	___	___	___	___
63. My subordinates take pride in their work.	___	___	___	___	___
64. You must closely supervise subordinates or they will shirk their duties.	___	___	___	___	___

How to Score

Using the scorecard on page 199, *write* the score you gave yourself for each question in the blank space provided next to that question number.

For example: on the upper left-hand portion of the chart, under "BE-LIEFS," Positive, question numbers 3, 7, 11, and 15 are listed. In the space next to 3, write the score (1 through 5) you gave yourself for that item. Then do the same for the lines beside 7, 11, and 15.

Follow the same procedure for each section, until you've completed the chart, then add up each sub-section. For example, for BELIEFS, Positive, add up the four scores (for 3, 7, 11, and 15), and you will get a total of your Positive Beliefs regarding "SELF." Put that number in the blank box.

Going across, add up your four scores under "SELF AND PEERS," "SELF AND BOSS," and "SELF AND SUBORDINATES."

Moving across, add up the four sub-totals (following the arrows across), and you will get your "TOTAL BELIEFS" in the right column. This is your Total Positive Beliefs, for all your relationships. Now move to the question numbers under "BELIEFS," Negative. Again, total your scores for questions 4, 8, 12, and 16, for your Negative Beliefs about SELF. Then total your scores for questions 20, 24, 28, and 32 for your Negative Beliefs about SELF AND PEERS. Then complete the next two columns, for SELF AND BOSS and SELF AND SUBORDINATES. If you add those four sub-totals across, you will get your total "Negative Beliefs" score, in the far right column.

Follow the same procedure for "ACTIONS," Positive and Negative.

When you have filled in all the spaces next to the questions, and the sub-totals in the extreme right-hand column, go back to each vertical column. Here, add up your scores for "Positive Beliefs" and "Positive Actions" (the totals of questions 3, 7, 11, 15, 1, 5, 9, and 13), and you will have a total for Positive Beliefs and Actions about SELF.

Do the same for each vertical column: SELF AND PEERS, SELF AND BOSS, and SELF AND SUBORDINATES.

Now go to the vertical columns for "Negative Beliefs" under SELF (questions 4, 8, 12, and 16) and "Negative Actions" under SELF (questions 2, 6, 10, and 14). Here you will have a total of "Negative Actions" for SELF.

Do the same for each vertical column: SELF AND PEERS, SELF AND BOSS, and SELF AND SUBORDINATES.

How to Interpret Your Scores

Look at each sub-section. A high score is a score over 15 (out of a possible 20) for each sub-section of 4 items. A low score in a sub-section is one under 10. If you have a high score in *any* "positive" column, your Beliefs or Actions are Assertive in your interactions with Self, Peers, Bosses, or Subordinates. Of course, you can always improve, but you are well on your way to a Strong Self-Image and Relationships.

If you have a low score in the "positive" column, go back to the specific questions and see which situations had a low response. These will be areas for further work.

If your "Positive Beliefs" in any of the columns were low, you will find some practical and powerful techniques for turning Negative Beliefs into Positive ones on pages 28–34.

If you have a high score in the "Positive Actions" columns, then your behavior is already quite assertive. You may have higher scores in some interactions than in others—for example, higher Positive Actions with Subordinates than with Bosses. Again, look back over the specific questions to find where the trouble spots are. The theory, ideas, and practice exercises in this book will help you in your actions with *any* of these relationships.

If you have a high negative score in the ACTIONS columns, go back to the questions and pinpoint where you have scored low.

After you've worked with the ideas and techniques in this book, you will have improved your Assertive Beliefs and Actions, and strengthened your Assertiveness Quotient and your Success Potential. If you take the test again a few months from now, you will be surprised at the change in your results! You will be a more Positive and more Assertive You!

4

Attitudes That Work Against You

Many of our basic emotional responses have their origins in our primitive survival instincts. Our earliest ancestors had two basic ways of coping with danger and promoting their survival: (1) fight, or aggressively combatting the predator or antagonist, and (2) flight, or running away.

Many of us still act as though we had only those two choices. Of course, sometimes we do our fighting or fleeing in subtle ways. When we are in the "fight" mode, we may feel aggressive and angry and walk around the office slamming drawers and barking at people. Or we may clam up and drag our feet. We think that other people will pick up the message that we are in fact angry. This is called "passive aggression," because on the surface we do not appear to be hostile. But people who are the least bit sensitive will certainly pick up the emotions underlying our behavior.

When we are in the "flight" mode, we are usually afraid, and our fear makes us want to leave the scene. Sometimes we actually do leave it; at other times, we leave in spirit, even though our bodies are still there. Another common flight response is depression—or complete withdrawal. This is like not playing the game at all. We all experience depression from time to time, whether it is the mild "down in the dumps" feeling of a winter afternoon or the more severe depression that results from a serious life upset or loss.

Anger, fear, and depression are not "sick" responses. But they are inefficient ways of coping with life's real, hard problems. When we become angry, afraid, or depressed, our emotional brain centers shut down many of the operations of our more efficient rational centers. We are less capable of seriously tackling the problems of everyday life. Many of these feelings are simply conditioned responses, variations of our basic survival instincts. The important point is that they do not help us get what we want.

What we sometimes forget is that we are born assertive. The infant in her crib has a very direct way of making her needs and desires known to whoever is within earshot. The growing child, not yet taught or conditioned about what is polite, naturally and constantly asks for what he wants. He isn't always sure he'll get it, but he asks anyway.

Many of our feelings of anxiousness, fear, or guilt are instilled by our parents, who use negative reinforcement and the fear of punishment to manipulate our behavior. Our parents do this emotional training in simple and subtle ways. We learn from them beliefs and ideas about ourselves and other people that often produce feelings of anxiety, ignorance, and guilt.

Let's take Mom as an example. Instead of asking you not to do X simply because she doesn't want you to, Mom will tell you that X is bad. Or that little Susie next door is a good child and never does X. Now, Mom has taken the responsibility off herself as the bad guy and no longer has to say, "I don't want you to do what you're doing"—playing, watching TV, whatever. She has now imposed a good/bad external standard, so that you can be your own bad guy.

Dad gets into the game too. He asks you, "Why do you always leave your Y lying around?" You don't know why; you just do it—maybe because you like to have Y lying around where you can see it, or you were having more fun doing other things, or you just plain forgot. But at the moment you're asked why, you feel terribly ignorant, as if there should be a perfectly good reason but you just didn't know it. Ironically, all the asking why or saying should is less effective than if Mom and Dad simply told you what they wanted you to do. This would be direct, clear assertion.

Now let's translate some of these basic emotions into adulthood and how they affect you and your performance as a manager.

MIND OVER MATTER

All your feelings come from your thoughts. You have a thought, and your emotional system, because it doesn't know any better, believes it entirely. This then triggers your behavior—assertive, aggressive, or nonassertive.

Some thought processes involve a kind of twisted logic, called "cognitive distortion." This is like a house of mirrors of the mind where people twist the evidence before them and create distorted and usually negative thoughts. Dr. David Burns has identified ten cognitive distortions that form the basis of most depressions.* Let's look at them in the light of how they affect your ability to act assertively as a manager.

* David Burns, *Feeling Good* (New York: Morrow, 1980).

1. *All-or-nothing thinking.* If you are an all-or-nothing thinker, you evaluate yourself and others in the extreme. This is known as "dichotomous thinking"—believing that something is either wonderful or terrible—and leads to a perfectionist attitude. You begin to fear any mistake. A typical statement of an all-or-nothing thinker is, "I made a mistake last week. I'm a lousy manager." Of course, such an attitude is completely unrealistic. Life is rarely black or white.

2. *Overgeneralization.* Here you conclude that just because something happened once it will continue to occur, or always has been true. If you mess up once on a project, or fail to complete a report, you might say, "That's just like me. I always goof up on projects in midstream. I'll never be able to do one right." Of course, this kind of thinking is likely to paralyze you. You may never take on another project again or, if you do, you'll be filled with fear and trepidation.

3. *Mental filter.* Here you pick out one negative aspect of a situation and dwell on it exclusively. You then see everything as negative. For example, if one of your employees is late, you say, "These people can't be trusted. They never show up on time."

4. *Disqualifying the positive.* Another form of filtering is changing neutral or even positive experiences into negatives. You go further than just ignoring the experiences; you turn them into their opposites. A classic example is handling a compliment. When someone acknowledges your work, your style, or your qualities, you say, "She's just trying to be nice." Or, worse, "He must want something from me." If you are intent on finding evidence to support your negative hypothesis, you will never get positive results.

5. *Jumping to conclusions.* This takes two forms—mind reading and fortune telling. Both involve jumping to a conclusion that is not justified by the facts.

If you are a mind reader, you make arbitrary assumptions about other people and then react accordingly. For example, you are making a presentation at a meeting and you notice someone's eyes getting glazed over. You assume that she is bored and doesn't like you. The fact is she might not have had enough sleep, might have some personal problems, or might just be otherwise preoccupied. But you *think* you read her mind accurately.

If you are a fortune teller, you assume that something bad is going to happen, even though it is unrealistic and unlikely, and defeat yourself before you start. You say to yourself, "I'm going to forget all that I wanted to say when I get up to speak at the national meeting." For the past six years you have always had outstanding presentations and have never forgotten anything. In fact, you've often thought of things to add, while you were on your feet, to make your presentation better. Still, you insist on imagining that this time you will forget everything.

6. *Magnification and minimization.* Magnification involves looking at one error or imperfection and enlarging its significance. "I miscalculated the budget by $10,000. My credibility will be ruined!" This is sometimes called "catastrophizing," or turning ordinary setbacks into large-scale tragedies.

Minimization involves shrinking your good points into oblivion, without giving yourself credit or acknowledgment for them.

7. *Emotional reasoning.* Here you treat your emotions as if they were objective fact. "I feel incompetent; therefore I am a total dud." Of course, if you engage in this type of thinking long enough, you *will* become a total dud. The truth is, even though you may feel incompetent—as all of us do at times—you probably get the job done quite well. Instead of letting feelings rule your mind, challenge the perceptions that are creating those feelings.

8. *Shoulds.* This distortion is sometimes called the "tyranny of the shoulds." It refers to the musts that you tell yourself every day so you can feel guilty when you don't live up to them: "I should talk to my employees more." "I should get more paperwork done." When you direct "should" statements toward others ("You should work harder on your reports") you will only feel frustrated and disappointed. You are in effect scolding others because they're not doing things the way you, with your own set of values, want them done. And other people will feel resentful toward you for your self-righteousness.

9. *Labeling.* Labeling involves stereotyping yourself or others, usually in a negative way. It is an extreme form of overgeneralization. You are labeling yourself whenever you say, "I'm a _____" (procrastinator, loner, poor time manager, whatever). More than likely, this conclusion is based on a few isolated incidents. Labeling yourself is self-defeating. You create a negative self-image on the basis of your errors. Remember, you are an ever changing, growing individual. What was true last week may not be true next month. When you label others, they will become hostile and resentful. If you've ever called someone a "slow starter" or "secretive," you have probably discovered how much the person resents it.

10. *Personalizing.* Here you assumed responsibility for a problem or an error when there is no real basis for your part in it. You conclude that what happened was all your fault, even though you had very little influence over the event. For example, you discover that a subordinate is an alcoholic or drug abuser. You begin to blame yourself for not having tried to help. You have assumed responsibility for much more than your share—the employee's personal life and habits are not your concern. True, you might have been able to help had you been asked. But you weren't asked and didn't know anything about the situation. Personalizing leads only to guilt and blame.

Exercise: Clearing Up Distortions

Go back over the list of cognitive distortions described in the preceding section. Think of examples in your own life. Write down five "distortion statements" below. Then rewrite each statement, turning it around so it reflects the situation as it really is.

Distortion _____

_____

Reality _____

_____

Distortion _____

_____

Reality _____

_____

Distortion _____

_____

Reality _____

_____

Distortion _____

_____

Reality _____

_____

Distortion _____

_____

Reality _____

_____

HOW TO HANDLE ANGER

There are two common and unhealthy ways to deal with anger. You can turn it inward—on yourself. This can lead to guilt, depression, and many physical diseases. Or you can turn it outward—on other people. Usually, this generates hostility and defensiveness, and if you aren't skilled at expressing anger in a healthy way, you will alienate people. There is a third way, however, which is healthier and less stressful and leads to more productive, positive results. This will be covered later in this chapter.

We all believe that external events cause our anger. We think that other people's stupid, self-centered, inconsiderate actions upset us. The fact is that other people cannot make us angry. They may behave in ways that we don't approve of or like, but *we* choose our response. Several of the cognitive distortions mentioned earlier are the biggest contributors to angry feelings.

1. *Labeling.* By giving people labels—"inconsiderate," "mean," "lazy"—you can then resent what they did. It is a way of writing people off, ignoring their positive attributes. It does help you feel indignant and morally superior. Usually this happens when your self-esteem seems threatened—you immediately jump to the defensive and label the other person.

2. *Mind reading.* An easy way to make yourself angry is to *imagine* that other people's actions reflect on you personally. "Jack was late for the meeting because he wanted to get back at me for not giving him a promotion!"

3. *Magnification.* Here, you exaggerate the importance of an event, blowing it up out of all proportion. "This company has the worst benefits in town. I'm leaving!" You're not leaving, of course. You're just making up an excuse to feel angry.

4. *Shoulds.* When people's actions aren't up to your standards or your style, you barrage them with statements of what they *should* have done. Then you get angry because they didn't do it. Often "should" statements are accompanied by the comment, "It's not fair"—as though fairness and justice should always prevail. That is a nice idea, but life just doesn't work that way. And your sense of what's fair may be different from other people's. This is why it is so important, in both business and personal relationships, to establish the groundrules. Typically, anger develops when you get confused between your rules and society's rules or other people's rules.

Exercise: Dealing with Anger

Take a moment to reflect on your attitudes toward and ways of dealing with anger. Check one or more answers, as they apply.

Your Own Anger

1. Attitude: When you are angry with people, you usually
   ＿＿＿ are afraid to say anything directly because you don't want to hurt anyone's feelings.
   ＿＿＿ are afraid that if you do say something, it will come out very aggressive.
   ＿＿＿ are afraid that if you say anything, the other person won't like you.
   ＿＿＿ feel okay about saying whatever is on your mind.
   ＿＿＿ feel anxious and confused about what you want to or should say.

2. Behavior: When you are angry with someone, you usually
   _____ drop hints about your feelings, hoping the other person will get the message.
   _____ tell the person in a direct manner what it is that you want and feel okay about doing so.
   _____ avoid the person for a while until you calm down and the anger wears off.
   _____ blow up right there and tell the person off.
   _____ express your anger sarcastically—getting your point across with some humor or a dig.

Other People's Anger

3. Attitude: When someone gets angry with you, you usually
   _____ think he or she doesn't like you.
   _____ feel too threatened to ask why or try to work things out.
   _____ feel confused and want to cry.
   _____ think you have a right to understand why the person is angry and respond to it.
   _____ immediately feel wronged.
   _____ feel angry in return.
   _____ feel guilty.

4. Behavior: When someone gets angry with you, you usually
   _____ end up crying.
   _____ back off.
   _____ ask the person to explain his or her anger further; get at the reasons.
   _____ get angry in return.
   _____ apologize, even though you may not understand the reason for the anger.
   _____ try to smooth it over.
   _____ make a joke out of it and try to get the other person to forget the whole thing.

Go back over your responses. Ask yourself whether you are expressing your own anger in healthy forms, *without* blaming the other person. When dealing with the anger of others, are you reacting appropriately, not taking it too personally, or feeling devastated? Coping with your own and others' anger effectively is not easy, but practice in assertive techniques can help you use anger constructively as a vehicle to more open and honest relationships. Everyone gets angry at times. It's how you cope with it, express it, and react to it that makes the difference between constructive and destructive communication.

Constructive Anger

Not all anger is unhealthy. Anger can be constructive when it forces you to take action to heal an emotional injury or change a relationship. Anger is constructive when it empowers you to stand up for yourself, to break through fixed patterns, and to gain new understanding.

The most important step in developing a constructive approach to anger is to accept responsibility for your feelings. This is called "ownership," and it is exactly the opposite of making other people feel wrong, blaming them, or making them responsible for how you feel. You take ownership of your feelings by declaring them directly and openly and acknowledging yourself as their source. For example:

Ownership	*Blame*
I am very angry.	You make me so angry!
I don't like what you've said.	How dare you say that to me?
I think that's unfair of you.	You're an SOB.
Stop bothering me.	Would you mind . . .
I am extremely upset.	You always upset me.

The next time you feel angry, you may find it useful to ask yourself, "Is my anger directed toward someone who has knowingly, intentionally, and unnecessarily acted in a harmful way to me? Is my anger constructive? Does it help me achieve a desired goal, or does it defeat me and take me further from my goal?"

If your anger is generated by another person's remarks, you can deal with it constructively by seeking additional data. Be curious:

"I'd be interested in hearing how you came to that opinion."
"When did you first become aware of that?"
"That's an interesting point of view. Can you tell me more?"
"What makes you say that?"
"Why do you suppose that's true?"

You might also find it valuable to assess all the advantages and disadvantages to you of feeling and remaining angry.

Advantages	*Disadvantages*
I like it. It feels good.	I am distancing myself in this relationship.
My anger will keep me from focusing on what is really bothering me.	My anger is keeping me from performing my job effectively.

Make up your own list the next time you feel angry. Do the disadvantages of staying angry outweigh the advantages? More than likely you'll conclude that you will get more benefits if you let go of your anger.

The assertive expression of anger means knowing your rights and appropriately expressing your feelings when someone tries to interfere with those rights. Uncontrolled lashing out or blaming is *not* assertive; it is aggressive. And you are being passive-aggressive if you are covert in expressing anger—for example, by giving people the silent treatment instead of letting them know straight out how you feel. Destructive anger weakens your self-esteem and leads to a feeling of powerlessness. It creates emotional distance by forcing other people to turn away from you.

To make sure you are not blaming, dumping on, or labeling another person when expressing your anger, follow these steps:

Prepare Yourself
> This is going to upset me, but I will know what to do.
> I can work out a way to handle this.
> This may be nothing personal—the other person is having problems.
> I will take a deep breath.
> I've got to keep my sense of humor.

Keep Calm during an Angry Exchange
> I will stay calm.
> I will keep breathing.
> I don't need to prove every point.
> I will look for the positive.
> No matter what the other person says, I am still competent and valuable.
> The person must be very unhappy or frustrated to be acting like this.
> There is no point in retaliating or losing my cool.
> I will be rational and discuss this step by step and point by point.

Reflect after the Angry Experience
> What can I learn from this?
> How could I have handled it differently?
> What did I do that worked?
> How can I calm myself down, sooner, when this happens again?
> I should not take everything so personally.
> I must remember to relax. It can help me get through experiences like this.
> I overreacted—got things out of proportion. How can I have a better perspective next time?

Hot and Cool Thoughts

Another useful technique for handling anger constructively is to distinguish between "hot thoughts" and "cool thoughts." Hot thoughts are all our angry, vindictive, and resentful feelings. Cool thoughts are rational explanations for the things that made us hot. For example:

Hot Thought	*Cool Thought*
How dare he turn down my request for a new machine?	Easily. He's not obliged to do everything I ask, and I know he has budget problems.
She doesn't care about anybody but herself.	So what? She's entitled to be self-centered.

When we sort out our hot and cool thoughts, we will begin to see the difference between *intent* and *effect*. Someone's actions may have had a harmful effect on us and may have led us to feel angry; but that may not have been the other person's intent at all. Very often, we attribute motives to others that they do not have.

Exercise: Keeping an Anger Record

Keeping a daily record of your anger can help you channel it in constructive ways and help you focus on the positive results you would like to achieve instead of dwelling on negative thoughts. The first step is to define the provocative situation—the one in which you feel hostile or angry. Then describe your hot or vengeful thoughts and your cooled-down thoughts. Finally, think about the outcome that your behavior or the other person's behavior is producing. What new, more desirable outcome would you like to achieve? What steps would you have to take to change? Can you begin now to work on even the smallest step? Start your record today by filling out the Anger Record on the next page.

HOW TO HANDLE GUILT

Over and over again, managers who attend assertiveness training workshops say that guilt is the number-one inhibitor to acting more assertively: One young manager, Gil, received a promotion and had to supervise six people who were formerly his peers. He had a very difficult time delegating work to anyone, because he still felt like he was "one of the crowd" and couldn't adjust to the idea that he was now the boss. He was afraid that others wouldn't like him if he started acting like a boss and giving orders. His unassertive response to the problem was to do most of the work himself rather than risk alienating his former co-workers. As a result, he was overworked and overburdened; worse, he wasn't being effective as a manager. In his new position as supervisor, Gil would be evaluated for how well he planned, coordinated, and delegated the work—not for how well it was actually done.

Still, he had a hard time letting go. When he was asked what his worst scenario was—the worst thing that could possibly happen—he said, "These people all used to be my buddies. If I ask them to do something, they'll say that I'm using my power as a manager to get them to do the dirty work—the stuff I don't want to do and no longer have to do as a manager. They'll say that Gil isn't the nice guy he used to be, and then I'll feel guilty."

Guilt—there's that tough little word that's at the heart of most of our difficulty with assertiveness. We feel that we owe other people something, our time, our emotions. Guilt also implies, on at least a feeling level, that we have done something bad to the other person, as though it were *intentional*. And usually it isn't.

ANGER RECORD

Situation _____

Hot Thoughts	Cool Thoughts	Current Outcome	Desired Outcome	Behavior Steps

Situation _____

Hot Thoughts	Cool Thoughts	Current Outcome	Desired Outcome	Behavior Steps

We often use cognitive distortions to create feelings of guilt. For example, we jump to the conclusion that someone will feel terrible and be really upset if we have to change a lunch appointment to another day. In such a situation, we might also use magnification by overestimating how important we are—or the lunch date is—to the other person.

Another cognitive distortion that produces guilt feelings is all-or-nothing thinking—believing that just because something has happened once, it will continue to happen. For example, suppose that once, when your colleague asked you to stay late to help out, you felt guilty because you weren't able to stay. Will you thereafter feel guilty every time you have to say no to someone's request?

One way to help overcome your guilt feelings is to go back over the Assertive Bill of Rights in Chapter 2. Review each right and ask yourself whether you really accept it. For example, if you feel guilty when you make a genuine mistake, then perhaps you don't really believe you have the right. Find out which of the rights in the Bill of Rights are producing your guilt feelings. Once you have identified them, keep a note of the situation, the person, and the right involved the next time you feel guilty. Keep a running log of these feelings. Be aware of your thoughts in the situations that create the feelings. Eventually you will be able to change your feelings by changing your thoughts.

5

Assertive Skills and Techniques— A Tool Kit for Positive Power and Influence

Just as there is no one best way to manage, so there is no one best way to become more assertive. Some situations call for a certain set of skills or strategies; others call for a different set. This chapter examines a number of techniques for becoming more assertive. These techniques have been used in a variety of settings—some in individual or group therapy sessions, some in training programs in business or other organizations.

Acquiring a broad repertoire of assertive skills will give you the flexibility you need to succeed as a manager. You will be successful to the extent that you can sense the situation—the people and feelings involved—and the desired goals or outcomes. You must then *try* different approaches. Be open to experimentation. Give yourself permission to fail once in a while. But don't call it failure; call it learning. By trial and error you will be fine-tuning your assertiveness skills so that you have a wide variety of techniques at your disposal.

Many of the techniques described in this chapter begin with self-assessment. Before you put them into practice, examine your beliefs, attitudes, and feelings—about yourself, the other person, the situation, and the likely consequences.

IDENTIFYING PERSONAL RIGHTS

Often people don't know how to respond in a situation because they aren't sure what rights they have and what rights others have. Since many of your actions have to do with these rights and your perceptions of them, it is important to be aware of what rights you really believe you have. Try the following exercise:

1. Go back to the Assertive Bill of Rights listed in Chapter 2. Look through the list and choose one right that you believe in and are certain you have. Now think of a situation in the past when you acted upon that right. What did you say or do? What did the other person say or do? How did you feel about yourself?

2. Now imagine that someone told you that you no longer had that right. How would you act? How would you feel about yourself and the other person? How would your behavior change if you no longer had this right?

3. Next, go back over the list and choose another right that you sometimes have trouble accepting—one that you don't really believe you have or deserve. Picture a situation in which you find yourself acting as if you did not have that right—either because you have denied it to yourself or because someone else has violated that right. What methods have you been using to deny yourself this right? How can you help yourself to accept it instead? Now imagine that you do have that right, and that no one can take it away from you. How do you feel? How do you feel about the other person?

4. Finally, review the list and identify all the rights you have been denying yourself. Then add some that are not on the list—rights that you wish you had but aren't behaving as if you do have. For each one, begin a sentence with "I have a right to _____." List all the rights you have been denying yourself so that you can look over the list when you're in doubt. This will be a strong reality check for you.

CHANGING IRRATIONAL SELF-MESSAGES

Feelings of anxiousness, depression, or hostility are usually based on the irrational messages that we send ourselves. By changing these negative self-messages, we can free ourselves to act more assertively.

Think of a situation in which you'd like to be more assertive. Every time you're in that situation, your emotions take over and you act aggressively or nonassertively. What negative thoughts come to your mind as you think about acting assertively in the situation?

For example: "At meetings where people in my department are very competitive, I become silent and afraid to speak up, even when I have intelligent things to say." Some of the negative thoughts underlying this attitude might be:

"They will think my ideas are stupid."
"They will think I don't understand what's going on."
"They will think I'm trying to upstage them."

Try to come up with as many negative thoughts as you can. Then *challenge* these thoughts. What you're doing is challenging the clever (but irrational) thinker inside you who is making up all these negative thoughts and preventing you from acting more assertively. So for the first statement, "They will think my ideas are stupid," you might offer this challenge: "Have they ever thought my ideas were stupid before? Even if they have, has anyone said so in front of the whole meeting? Even if someone said so in front of the meeting, what would be the worst thing that could happen—would I get fired? And even if I did get fired, would it be the end of the world? Could I handle it?"

You might challenge the situation further by taking another tack: "Even if people think my ideas aren't very smart, everyone is allowed to make a mistake. It's not the end of the world. I don't have to be brilliant and clever 100 percent of the time." By continuing to challenge your irrational thoughts, you will begin to uncover some of the paralyzing emotions you may feel. These challenges are *not* the same as saying to yourself, "Don't worry, everything will turn out just wonderful." You are not being a Pollyanna. Rather, each challenge is forcing you to be more rational and more precise.

Finally, think about all the benefits you might get if you did act more assertively: What would be valuable about speaking up? How would you feel about yourself? What might you *gain* by presenting a good idea at the meeting?

USING POSITIVE EMOTIONAL ANCHORS

Another helpful assertive technique is to anchor your feelings about a person or situation in positive emotions so you will always act constructively in that situation. Think of a situation in which you are currently experiencing negative emotions and are not being as assertive as you'd like to be. Focus on the person involved, on the relationship. Think of a time when you were with this person and felt good about yourself, good about the other person, and positive about the relationship. Try to re-create the feelings that went with the experience. How did you look? How did the other person look? What did you say? What did he or she say? And how did you feel about yourself? What *specific* positive feeling did you have—safety, security, pride, love, confidence?

Now, retaining the positive feeling, run through a practice conversation with the other person in which you behave assertively. Try to imagine the other person's reactions to you. Every time you feel a negative or fearful emotion coming up, acknowledge it and try to replace it with the positive emotion that you recalled a moment ago. You might even practice this technique with a friend or partner, or with your spouse, until you can eliminate all the negative feelings that you experience.

SELF-DISCLOSURE

Fundamental to the philosophy of assertiveness is the belief that people should be open and honest with each other. Most of us have been socialized into presenting a public face to our workmates, bosses, and subordinates, and to revealing our private face only to ourselves and to a few of our intimates. As a result of this dichotomy, we often believe we are fake, phony, or inauthentic. When we have one personality for the office and another for the rest of our lives, we inevitably feel conflict.

Self-disclosure involves revealing parts of your intimate, private self in public in a way that lets others really see and hear who you are. When you practice self-disclosure, you will feel more honest and more open in communicating with others and will encourage others to be more open and assertive in their dealings with you.

Think of a time when you were having a casual conversation over lunch or drinks with someone you didn't know well. Suddenly the flavor of the conversation began to change and you started to feel as if you had known the person for years. The relationship became a lot deeper than a passing encounter. What caused the shift? Chances are one of you revealed some hidden part of yourself. This created a bond of *trust* that allowed the other person to make some personal disclosure. As the bond of trust grew, both of you opened up further.

Of course, self-disclosure involves risks as well as rewards. In revealing intimate and often vulnerable parts of yourself to someone, you are putting aside attempts to manage and control the situation—and the other person. You may even feel that you're giving up an advantage, that you are revealing more about yourself than you want the other person to know about you.

Also, there are degrees of risk. One factor involves the topic at issue. If you are offering your opinion about a new piece of equipment or the latest company ad, this is not as risky as disclosing your feelings about another person—unless, of course, you're discussing the new piece of equipment with the purchasing agent who bought it or the ad campaign with the advertising manager who created it. In these cases, the other person is closely identified with the topic and has invested a lot of ego in it. Only you can decide what degree of risk you're willing to take in dealing with others.

Another factor influencing the degree of risk is your self-esteem. People with high self-esteem do not anticipate rejection as often as people with low self-esteem. So if your self-esteem is shaky and you think every new con-

Figure 2. The five steps from awareness to assertion.

versation is a potential rejection, you probably will not engage in much self-disclosure. You are likely to play it safe and stay on neutral ground.

A third factor influencing the degree of risk is the nature of your relationship with the other person. How much trust have you created? Will the other person take advantage of your weak spots and vulnerabilities when you reveal them? Much of this will be conjecture on your part, and you won't know until you try. Ironically, although at first it may seem as though you're jeopardizing the relationship by saying what's on your mind, you're probably strengthening it by sharing your real feelings. You might consider taking a small risk initially to see how the other person reacts. If you sense that the climate is trusting and supportive, you can go on to more intimate disclosures—and probably a closer relationship.

SELF-AWARENESS

Self-awareness is essential if you are to disclose yourself to others. There are five key steps in assessing a situation and becoming aware of what you intend to do: your sensations, interpretations, feelings, desires, and intentions. These five steps are shown graphically in Figure 2.* Each step is the foundation for those after it.

Sensations

When we tune in to our senses, we become aware of the rich and valuable data around us. All the information we receive from the external environment comes in through the senses—that is, we see, hear, taste, touch, and smell the world around us. For example: "As I stand in the doorway of your office, I see you writing at your desk and frowning."

Interpretations

No sooner does a message enter our sensory channels than we begin to interpret it. Our *mind* wants to make sense out of it. Interpretations consist of impressions, beliefs, conclusions, assumptions, evaluations, ideas, opinions, expectations, and reasons. These are the sometimes conscious, some-

---

*This model is the basis of the book *Alive and Aware: Improving Communications in Relationships,* by Sherod Miller, Elam Nunnally, and Daniel B. Wackman (Minneapolis: Interpersonal Communications Programs, 1975).

times unconscious thoughts that we have as soon as we see, hear, or feel something around us. For example: "Because you are frowning and writing even though I am standing here, I think you are very busy and would rather not talk to me now."

It is important to note that our interpretations are not based on any objective reality or on anyone else's sense of the way things are. They are based on what we perceive *plus* all the beliefs, assumptions, and expectations we bring to the situation. Thus, it is not surprising that two people will interpret the same situation entirely differently. For example, if I see you writing while I'm waiting in your doorway, I may interpret it as "You don't like me; you're not interested in what I have to say." This interpretation could be due in part to bad feelings I had before I even came into your office. Your actual interest or lack of interest in me may be very different from what I've interpreted it to be. That's why it's important to treat all interpretations as tentative. Later in this chapter, we will go through a skills exercise for checking tentative interpretations to get accurate feedback from other people.

Feelings

Your feelings are your emotional responses to the interpretations you make and the expectations you have. Feelings are the barometer of what's going on inside you, and can often help you understand your reaction to a situation. Most feelings have outward signs as well. When you feel angry, your outward signs are tense muscles, flushed skin, and loud speech. When you feel sad, the outward sign may be tears. Feelings include the broad categories of emotions (happy, sad, afraid, mad) and a host of more subtle ones (anxious, hopeful, cautious, eager, excited, uneasy, surprised, disappointed, confused, bored). It is not always easy to pinpoint your feelings, because they occur in very mixed or shaded tones. You may feel vaguely insecure, mildly anxious, highly motivated and excited, and somewhat fearful when you are assigned a challenging new project.

It's important to remember that feelings are based on our *interpretation* of a situation, not the situation itself or our simple perception of it. If I think you are still writing at your desk because you simply haven't noticed me standing in your doorway, my feelings will be very different from what they would be if I thought you were deliberately ignoring me. In both cases what I actually *see* is the same.

Desires

The next step after being aware of your feelings in a situation is to be aware of what you want from that situation. In the example about waiting in the doorway, my desires might be: "I want to talk to you right now, but I also want your full attention when I talk to you."

For many people, their desires are the hardest thing to get in touch with. The two little words "I want" are the most difficult ones for people to say to themselves, let alone to others. Becoming aware of what you want is one of the first and most important building blocks to assertiveness. If you know what you want, you may not always get it, but you will at least have a reasonable chance. If you don't know what you want, you may go right by it and never know what you missed.

Intentions

Intentions are plans of action, the final step before we assert ourselves and actually do something. In forming intentions, we automatically take into account our sensations, interpretations, feelings, and desires about a given situation. We sort out the things we want, decide which of them are most important, and plan how we will try to achieve them. Often this process takes place so quickly that we are consciously aware only of the final intention.

To follow through with our example once more, I may decide that getting your undivided attention is more important than talking to you right away; therefore I might intend to come back later. Or I might decide that I must talk to you now even if you are too busy to give me your full attention; in that case I might intend to interrupt you.

Although you may not like to admit it, your actions are probably the truest indicator of your intentions. If you were willing to be honest with yourself, you would see that sometimes what you say you want is not what your actions are revealing that you want. For example, if your intention is to become a more assertive manager, how come you're hiding under your desk? From your actions, I would only guess that your intention is to stay out of sight and out of trouble.

Many people have conflicting intentions. You want to be seen as a nice, helpful person and a good boss; you also want to be powerful, to have influence. So you act helpful and supportive with your subordinates, sometimes doing their work for them. Then you are puzzled because you're not seen as very powerful! Obviously you're working at cross-purposes, and your actions seem to indicate that your concern with being nice and supportive is stronger than your intention to be seen as powerful.

Once you understand the different dimensions of awareness and can distinguish between your sensations and your interpretations, or between your feelings and your wants, you can move ahead to becoming more assertive. The action-assertive skills described here will help you in any relationship or encounter with another person.

MAKING "I" STATEMENTS

Making "I" statements is one of the most important skills of assertiveness. It is also the one most easily forgotten. When you speak for yourself, you are announcing that you are aware of your own needs, feelings, thoughts, and opinions. You are the expert on you. You are the only one who knows what your feelings are. No one else can report on your inner state as accurately as you can. Also, *your* inner state is the only one you can be sure of. You can't presume to know what another person is feeling.

Most people have been taught that it's selfish or egotistical to focus on themselves. But if you think about it, it's almost impossible to communicate your needs and wishes clearly without using the word "I."

When you make "I" statements, you are being responsible for yourself. Underresponsible statements begin with expressions like "most people," "some managers," "the average employee." It is as if the speaker were not willing to take ownership or responsibility for the statement. Overresponsible statements involve speaking for others, using the words "we" and "you." Here the speaker acts on behalf of both parties, even when he or she isn't sure of the other person's feelings. Or the speaker implies blame, as in the statement "You make me angry when you're late." The *responsible* way to state this ideal is, "When your late, I feel angry." Underresponsible communication conceals differences, while overresponsible communication coerces people to agree with you even if they don't.

When you speak for yourself as a responsible, assertive communicator, you demonstrate that you are aware and clear, that you are the source of the messages you send, that you are the *owner* of your perceptions, thoughts, feelings, wants, and actions. You show others that you have self-respect, and you add to the accuracy and quality of your communications. You also leave room for other people to see the world differently and to speak for themselves. You don't presume to know what other people are thinking, what their intentions or motives are. This cuts down on the blaming that all of us fall prey to sometimes (even inadvertently) and so generates less defensiveness in others.

Sense Statements

Sense statements are descriptions of what you see, hear, touch, taste, and smell—in other words, what your senses are receiving. Reporting on your sensory data gives other people a clearer understanding of how you view the world, of where you're coming from. When you make sense statements, it is important to be accurate and to state only what you actually perceive. For example: "I see that your desk is piled high with unprocessed orders." This is reporting on what you see with your eyes. It is different from saying, "I see that you never process the orders on time." Here you are interpreting or analyzing what your eyes are reporting to you.

It is also helpful to describe what you see or hear as specifically as possible. For example: "This morning, after the meeting, I heard your phone ringing about 15 times." This is an accurate description of what you heard and is quite different from a generalization like "Your phone *always* rings

off the wall." Such an implied accusation leaves the other person with nowhere to go, except to get defensive and deny the accusation or to retaliate
in some way later.

Interpretive Statements

Generally speaking, it is risky to offer interpretations to other people, but
it can sometimes be helpful in clarifying your assertive communication. If
you look upon an interpretative statement as a flexible hypothesis for organizing your thoughts and letting the other person know how you arrived at
them, it can be a positive contribution to the communication. Here are some
examples:

> "I think you're angry with me."
> "I imagine you don't have time to complete this report for us."
> "I guess you're bored with your job."

These are simply your interpretations or assumptions about what is going on
with the other person; they may or may not be accurate. You are saying, in
effect, "This is what I'm thinking right now. It is subject to change if I get
new information. It is my unique way of interpreting the situation, and not
necessarily the way the world is. In fact, the way you see it may be entirely
different, and that's fine. I will want to know that, and I'll want to check
out my interpretation against yours, so we can begin to hear each other."

Feeling Statements

In the workplace it is considered inappropriate and unprofessional to have
or express feelings. Yet the toughest and most powerful people in the business world are the ones who are *not* afraid to share their feelings with others. I have seen very powerful managers express their feelings and become
even more powerful, because they were not afraid to let others know who
they were and where they stood. Of course, disclosing feelings always involves some risk. You're opening the tight little door around you and are
letting someone else know a little about yourself. This can make you feel
vulnerable and frightened at first. But it is one of the most powerful—and
underrated—skills of assertive communication.

Like most people, you probably express your feelings nonverbally all the
time. These nonverbal messages can speak louder than words. When you
are angry and walk around frowning or slamming things or looking grouchy,
don't you think people know? So why not be up front about how you feel?
The most important thing to remember is that your feelings are uniquely
your own. No one else can express them in your place. Nor can anyone
deny their validity for you.

Expressions of feelings begin with the words "I feel"—followed by a
specific emotion (happy, sad, afraid, mad, and so on). The comment "I feel

that you should be more conscientious about your work'' is not a statement of feeling but a strong expression of opinion. You are blaming or proscribing how the other person should behave. This is guaranteed to make the person defensive.

A real statement of feeling would be, ''I feel disappointed when you don't complete your work on time.'' That is responsibly announcing your own inner feelings.

''I Want'' Statements

Putting it out—saying loud and clear what we want—is a critical part of being assertive. How in the world can people let us have what we want—how can they say yes to us—if we haven't asked the question? But many of us have the childish notion that if we hint, or sulk, or beat around the bush, people will ''get the picture'' and give us what we want without our having to ask for it. This assumes that other people are really sensitive to us and are finely attuned to our every gesture and pout. The truth is most people are too involved with their own lives to pay close attention to us.

An ''I want'' statement is a way of being direct about what we would like or not like. Many people are indirect and confuse others with their ambivalent or qualified statements. For example: ''I would like to help you out with the accounting project. I suppose I might be able to, if I didn't have all this other stuff to do before Friday. But maybe if we don't today, we could get started next week, if nothing else comes up.'' What does that mean? How can someone operate from this kind of muddled information? Fuzzy words like ''might,'' ''suppose,'' and ''maybe'' only fog communication. Yet this is what most of us will settle for, because we aren't assertive enough to insist that other people tell us exactly what they want. Nor are we assertive enough to announce our own desires clearly.

If you want to communicate with and respond to people, rather than control and direct them, you have to let them know where you stand. So, if you agree that stating what you want is the assertive way to go, and the surest chance you have of getting there, begin now to practice making ''I want'' statements. You will not always get what you want, of course, and you have to be ready to accept plenty of nos to your requests. But if you practice this skill long enough, you will also get many more yeses than you've ever gotten before. And you will feel more assertive, more proactive, more in charge of your life, instead of being reactive, letting life take you over, and simply accepting whatever comes along.

Intention Statements

Intention statements let other people know what action you have taken or are planning to take to see that you get what you want. For example: ''I want to get that promotion; I have been learning about data processing for

the past eight months and have enrolled for an extension course in programming." Often, intention statements involve a commitment to doing or not
doing something. "I will do everything I can to make sure that these records
are kept up to date." They let the other person know what to expect of you
in the future. Making intention statements is a very powerful assertive skill.
It tells others that you are committed to getting what you want. It establishes
a trajectory, or path, for getting you toward your goal.

I-LANGUAGE ASSERTION

Now that you have looked at the five dimensions of self-awareness and
have examined the different self-disclosure skills for each, let's put them
together as a process. Suppose that your boss has asked you to work overtime several nights this week. You feel put upon and think that your boss
has no concern for your personal life. You might approach the boss in this
way.

I SEE	*(what you objectively perceive in the situation)* that you've asked me to work overtime three times this week.
I THINK	*(what you think or imagine is true; your assumptions)* that you are not aware of or concerned about my personal life.
I FEEL	*(your feelings or reactions to the thought)* pressured, exploited, taken advantage of, upset, anxious.
I WANT	*(a positive, clear description of what you want)* to be given at least four days' notice when you need to have me work overtime.
I INTEND	*(what you are prepared to do to see that you get what you want)* to remind you every Friday to review and estimate the workload for the next week and fill me in on what your anticipated needs will be.

Practice this technique before you engage in any important communication
with someone. Use the five steps shown earlier in Figure 2 to get in touch
with your sensations, thoughts, feelings, desires, and intentions. Then communicate them assertively by making "I" statements.

Remember too that speaking for yourself means expressing your feelings
and opinions as direct, clear assertions. Often, even without realizing it,
people ask questions instead of making statements, as in the following example:

"Don't you think we ought to proceed on the Taylor job?"

This person really wants to say, "I think we ought to proceed on the Taylor
job," but cannot act assertively and instead defers to other people and their
opinions. It's all very well to be polite and include others in the decision-
making process. But when you always ask questions and never make a direct statement, take a stand, or state a preference, you are giving over all

your power and authority to other people. So try to determine when you are asking a question because you are really seeking an answer (which someone else has) and when you are asking a question because you're afraid to assert yourself.

Another method of I-language assertion, based on the work of Thomas Gordon, involves making a four-part statement in which you describe (1) the other person's behavior, (2) its effect on you, (3) your feelings, and (4) your preferences in the situation. Here's how you might use it to assert yourself when a friend or colleague is late for lunch appointments:

WHEN   (*an objective description of the other person's behavior*) you arrive late for our lunch appointment.

THE EFFECT IS   (*how the person's behavior affects your life or feelings*) that we lose our reservations and then have to rush through lunch.

I FEEL   (*your feelings; without accusation or blame*) insulted, disappointed, anxious.

I'D PREFER   (*a description of the behavior you want*) that you show up on time.

By describing the other person's behavior without judgment or blame, you are acting assertively. If you had told your lunch partner, "When you're late for lunch, you really make me mad. Who do you think you are? What's wrong with you?" you would have certainly made the person defensive with your blaming, aggressive tone.

This technique is especially effective for assertively expressing negative feelings. It will help you determine when your feelings result from some violation of your rights and when they are caused by trying to impose your own values and expectations on others. In describing feelings, remember to state only the effect of the behavior on *you*. "I feel you are being unfair" is a judgment, not a feeling.

Exercise: Speaking for Yourself

1. Think of a situation in your own life in which you would like to be more assertive in expressing your feelings or intentions. Describe the situation below, using the five dimensions of self-awareness. After you've written your statement, practice it aloud, and then with a friend to get feedback. Finally, try it out in the real situation. How did you do? You're on your way to becoming more assertive.

I SEE _____

I THINK _____

I FEEL _____

I WANT _____

I INTEND _____

2. Now think of a situation in which you feel very strongly that your rights are being violated by someone else. What effect does that person's behavior have on you? What new behavior would you prefer? Describe the situation below:

WHEN —————————————————————————————————

THE EFFECT IS ————————————————————————————

I FEEL —————————————————————————————————

I'D PREFER ————————————————————————————————

Again, rehearse the statement to yourself and get some feedback before you try it out in the real situation. Remember always to state only the effect of the person's behavior on you, without accusing or blaming. You'll have a much better chance of getting the other person to do what you want.

SCRIPTING

Another very simple strategy for being assertive involves writing an "assertiveness script." Here you are both the director and the protagonist. You are in charge of the plot, the setting, and the script—the messages between the players (you and at least one other person). Think of a time in the past when you bungled a scene, or were not as assertive as you would have liked to be. Scripting can help you think through your *next* scene, like a playwright, and give you the opportunity to create an action plan for the future. Writing a script will also:

1. Give you a small concrete task to focus on as a starting point in acting assertively in a situation.
2. Help you get clear about the situation and define your needs.
3. Make you more confident the next time you are in that situation, because you have thought about it in advance and have "plotted out" some of the likely interactions.
4. Give you a chance to use words that are more assertive than the nonassertive or passive language you might use spontaneously.

Scripting is a concrete way for you to take charge, to take responsibility for the interactions you have with others. A very simple method of scripting called DESC involves a four-step process: *d*escribe, *e*xpress, *s*pecify, *c*onsequences. This method was first used by Sharon Bower and Gordon Bower.

Describe

You begin the script by describing to the other person the exact behavior you do not like (without psychoanalyzing or interpreting that behavior). Use simple, concrete, and objective terms. Instead of saying, "Your attitude is bad,'' state the problem specifically: "The last five times I asked you for a file, you walked away." Instead of making a generalization like "You never do the reports right," say, "This report could use more backup data." You can soften the description by opening with a comment like "I would like to discuss something with you now," or "Are you aware that . . .?"

Express

Express what you feel and think about the person's specific behavior in the situation. Again, do not use accusatory language like "You make me angry" or "You're impatient and insensitive." Even if you have these negative feelings, remember that you're trying to negotiate a mutually satisfactory solution. Negative statements will only make the other person defensive. Instead, make a goal-oriented statement, such as "I think we could have more productive meetings if you didn't take phone calls while we were all together in your office."

"I" statements take the burden off the other person and suggest that the combination of the person's behavior and your reaction to it is causing the problem.

Specify

After describing the person's behavior and expressing your feelings about it, you should specify what behavior you would like. Basically you're saying, "Please stop doing X and do Y instead." The other person then has a choice of doing Y or not. It's best to limit the request to one specific behavior, because people will get overwhelmed if you ask for too much at once.

The request must be reasonable and within the power of the other person to change. You are really asking for a contract—or rather a different contract from the one you have now. Here is where you can begin to negotiate and have an open, assertive exchange of feelings, opinions, and requests. Remember, you won't always get what you ask for. This is important to realize when you begin to practice assertive behavior. Successful salespeople know this—and have learned to be resilient. They get turned down dozens of times, but just chalk it up to the law of averages and keep trying. Not getting what you want the first time does not mean you should stop asking. You are assertive when you openly and directly ask for what you want. The assertiveness lies in speaking out and feeling good about it—not only in the result you get.

Consequences

The final part of the DESC process involves specifying the consequences (payoffs or penalties) to both parties of making or not making the desired change. You can offer material rewards when you are asking someone to make a behavior change—for example, dinner at an expensive restaurant or tickets to the theater. You can also offer intangible social rewards, which are often even greater incentive to change. They can take the form of "I will feel better (or I will not be so anxious and upset) if you stop doing X."

You should also make a clear statement of the negative consequence of failure to change. At the workplace, penalties might include removing certain privileges, taking the person off a plum project, or even demotion. Such tactics should be used only in extreme cases, of course. As every good manager knows, wielding power by punishment will not usually get the desired long-term results. People will be suspicious and resentful, and the manager's creditability will suffer.

To summarize, creating a DESC script can be a powerful way to get clear on what aspect of a person's behavior you don't like, your feelings about the situation, what you would prefer, and the consequences or outcomes. Here are two examples:

Asking for Information

DESCRIBE	I have asked you about half a dozen times to teach me about the new system, but you haven't gotten back to me yet.
EXPRESS	I feel insulted—that there's a part of our business I should know about to do my job better, and that I'm not learning it.
SPECIFY	Sometime in the next month I'd like to arrange a block of four to six hours for us to get together so you can explain this system to me.
CONSEQUENCES	(Positive) When I know all about it, I won't have to ask you anymore and will do my job much more quickly. (Negative) If I don't get this expertise soon, I will fall behind and may cause the rest of the department to be inefficient.

Asking for a Raise

DESCRIBE	I have been here in this department for 18 months and have only had two cost-of-living increases totaling $100 per month.
EXPRESS	I feel unvalued around here, as if you feel I have no contribution to make to the organization.
SPECIFY	I want $300 more per month, starting in June.
CONSEQUENCES	(Positive) I want to continue working here, because I believe I am a valuable asset and also because I enjoy it. (Negative) I won't be able to remain here much longer, at my present salary.

Exercise: Writing a DESC Script

Now write your own DESC script for a situation in your life in which you are experiencing or having difficulty acting assertively. Use the guidelines listed below each step to check your scripting.

DESCRIBE _____

_____

_____

- Does your description clarify the situation, or does it just complicate matters? Replace all terms that do not objectively describe the behavior or problem that bothers you. Be specific.
- Have you described a single, specific behavior or problem or made a long list of grievances? Focus on one well-defined behavioral problem you want to deal with *now*. One grievance per script is generally the best approach.
- Have you focused on the other person's attitudes, motives, or intentions instead of objectively describing the situation? Avoid mind reading and psychoanalyzing.

Revise your DESCRIBE lines now, if necessary.

EXPRESS _____

_____

_____

- Have you acknowledged your feelings and opinions as your own, without blaming the other person? Avoid words that ridicule or shame the other person. Swearing and using insulting labels (dumb, cruel, selfish, racist, sexist, idiotic, boring) will only provoke defensiveness and arguments.
- Have you expressed your feelings and thoughts in a positive, new way? Avoid "old phonograph record" lines that the other person is tired of hearing and automatically tunes out.
- Have you kept the wording low-key? Aim for emotional restraint, not dramatic impact.

Revise your EXPRESS lines now, if necessary.

SPECIFY _____

_____

- Have you proposed only one small change in behavior at this time?
- Can you reasonably expect the other person to agree to your request?
- Are you prepared to alter your own behavior if the other person asks you to change? What are you prepared to change about your behavior?
- What counterproposals do you anticipate, and how will you answer them?

Revise your SPECIFY lines now, if necessary.

CONSEQUENCES _____

_____

_____

○ Have you stressed positive, rewarding consequences?
○ Is the reward you selected appropriate for the other person? Perhaps you should ask what you might do for the other person.
○ Can you realistically carry through with these consequences?

Revise your CONSEQUENCES lines now, if necessary.

SETTING LIMITS

Setting limits is one of the most difficult—and rewarding—aspects of being assertive. Setting limits means defining yourself to yourself: "This is who I am." It means deciding, independent of other people's demands, how you want to devote your energies or spend your time, and how you want to be treated. By setting limits you are also teaching other people how you want to be treated—in other words, you are training them in how to behave with you!

You may not want to issue an unconditional, irrevocable "no" in a given situation, but you still need to state your bounds. For example, when things are not busy at the office, you may welcome a visitor who pops in unannounced with a cup of coffee in hand. When you are very pressured and busy, you will need to set a limit on your time and attention. Often your body will tell you when your limits are being violated. If your face becomes flushed or your stomach knots up, it may well be that you are feeling invaded, intruded upon. It is important to become attuned to these inner signals so that you are more aware of when your personal boundaries are being invaded and when you should be setting limits.

Rules for Setting Limits

1. *Make your limits clear.* Let the other person know exactly and specifically what your limits are in a particular situation at a particular time. "I will be available for about 15 minutes between ten and noon on Tuesday if you want to come over and talk about the next quarter's budgets." "I don't want to talk about the bowling team now. I would like to stay with our budget conversation."

2. *Set partial limits.* Limits need not be an all-or-nothing proposition. "I am interested in the bowling team, but let's talk about it some other time, over lunch." This lets the other person know that your business time is limited and that you'd like to stick to business topics during that "prime time" between ten and noon. It also tells the person that you are not uninterested in talking about bowling and would be willing to discuss it at another time.

3. *Be firm.* Once you have articulated your limits, it is important that you remain firm in the particular situation to see that they are kept. This is important for two reasons. First, you will lose self-respect if you find your-

self allowing a limit to be violated. Also, you will lose credibility in the other person's eyes.

4. *Set meta-level limits.* "Meta" is a Greek root meaning after, beyond, or higher. A meta-level assertion develops after an interaction has begun. It is usually a comment on the situation, above and beyond the content of what is being discussed. For example: "I am uncomfortable about the way you keep persisting with a social topic when I've said several times that I want to stick to our budgets during this meeting." This establishes the context of your request.

5. *Separate intent from effect.* Sometimes we have great difficulty distinguishing between our feelings and other people's intentions. Your showing up late to a meeting with me may have the effect of making me feel rejected, but that may not have been your *intent*. Once you become clearer on your own intentions, you can set limits more easily without being overly concerned about the effect on the other person. You are not solely responsible for other people's feelings.

Pitfalls in Setting Limits

1. *Reinforcing the behavior you don't want.* This is a simple principle of behavioral psychology. By paying too much attention to behavior you don't like, you may be encouraging others to keep doing what they are doing. Suppose your colleague Marty continually comes to you with tales about people in the department. Because you haven't set any limits, you find yourself sitting and listening politely to the tattling. You are reinforcing the behavior by your positive response.

How do you get Marty to change his behavior? Stop rewarding the tattling by listening. Either assertively set a limit and let him know you don't want to hear it, or ignore the tattling when he does come to you.

2. *Being "reasonable" when people make unreasonable requests.* You may rationalize to yourself that you're being nice and reasonable by complying, but in so doing you will not be setting limits.

3. *Making excuses.* We all make excuses at various times. We think it is kinder than being direct or assertive. This carries over into the social arena, when we find ourselves having a regular lunch date with someone we have no interest in cultivating as a friend, or when we go away for a weekend with people just because they asked us. If you make an excuse, you will probably have to deal with that situation and that person again. It's better to be direct the first time, even though it may be uncomfortable. It is often kinder, too, to let other people know how you feel than to mislead them.

4. *Responding by reacting.* If your limits have been intruded upon once, and you are anticipating that it will happen again, you can respond by waiting and *reacting* to the next occurrence. Or you can *initiate* by speaking up before the situation happens again. So the next time your friend Marty drops

by with a piece of gossip, take the initiative by saying, "I only want to spend five minutes on this conversation, and I really would not like to talk about people in the office."

5. *Rescuing*. If you've been a manager for any length of time, you've probably had people come to you with a problem or conflict, expecting you to protect them or come up with a clever solution. This is a common way that a manager's boundaries are invaded. You think that you have to take care of people and "rescue" them. If you genuinely want to preserve your boundaries, you must stop thinking of yourself as a savior and let people fend for themselves. What's more, people will feel more self-respect and self-esteem if you encourage them to stand up for themselves.

THE LAST WORD: SAYING NO

One of the most frequently mentioned problems in assertiveness training is learning to say no—to the boss's requests for something, to employees' demands, to people asking for time, information, or attention. Many of us have difficulty saying no and feel that people will not like us, or will be angry with us, if we refuse them. For many of us, too, no is still a dirty word, and the one that we find most difficult to utter.

Most of the time, we say yes instead of no because we don't want to hurt people's feelings, don't want to explain, or feel obligated to people for some past situation in which they said yes to us. Sometimes we would like to oblige, but the timing or situation is inappropriate. The result is that we spend lots of time and energy feeling resentful, wishing we had been able to muster up the gumption to simply say no when we didn't want to comply.

The Value of Refusing

Learning how to say no will save you time and energy. You will no longer have to waste time simply because you lacked the assertiveness to turn down a request. Of course, being able to say no when you want to requires self-respect and self-confidence. You will have to rely on your own standards and judgments. You will have to be in touch with your own needs and wants—and the fact that your self-worth does *not* depend on other people's judgments about you. Most important, you will have to have a strong sense that you are not responsible for other people's feelings.

Here are some steps you can take to change a situation from one in which you've said yes to one in which you can assertively say no.

1. Choose the relationship or situation you want to work on.

2. Think about your reasons for saying yes. Are you trying to please? Do you think saying no will injure the relationship? Do you think you will hurt the other person's feelings?

3. Decide what *you* want in the situation. Get very clear about your preferences.

4. Think about what the other person wants, and what he or she might accept from you as a counteroffer or substitute for the request. For example, your boss has asked you to go to a meeting that you cannot attend because you'll be out of town. You might suggest that one of your subordinates fill in or that the meeting be held at another time. What can you offer that will satisfy at least *part* of what the other person is requesting? If there is no substitute for the person's request, you will have to be brave enough to say no simply and directly.

5. Practice the conversation in advance. Write down the person's request in the words that he or she might use, and then write your own response. Try to word your response in a way that will strengthen your credibility as well as soften the blow to the other person.

Skills for Saying No

Whenever you must refuse someone, try to add that it's "nothing personal." Remember, your refusal has nothing to do with the person; you're just setting limits for yourself. "Sandy, it's nothing personal, but I can't go out with the group for drinks on Wednesdays. I have stopped drinking, and being in bars is stressful for me. But thank you for thinking of me and inviting me." In this way, you are letting Sandy and the group know that you are not rejecting them as individuals but rather are turning down the activity. This can soften your refusal and make other people more understanding of your position.

Another effective technique for refusing someone is called Broken Record.* Very simply, you learn to be persistent in the face of pressure and stick to your point, trying to ignore all side issues and not be swayed into doing what you don't want to do. The technique is somewhat contrived, but it is very effective in dealing with a persistent manipulator, such as someone who is trying to sell you something that you've already indicated you don't want. For example:

SALESPERSON: I think you will really enjoy this cruiser boat for summer weekends.

YOU: Thank you for suggesting it. But we don't want a boat.

SALESPERSON: It's equipped to go up to top speed, and is fully outfitted for long trips.

YOU: It certainly looks like it can do that. Still, we don't want a boat.

SALESPERSON: And the price is a once-in-a-lifetime special.

YOU: It may be, but we don't want a boat.

You continue saying "we don't want a boat" while conceding the truth of all the things the salesperson is saying. You are acknowledging that even

---

*This technique was originally named by Dr. Zev Wanderer. It was described by Sherwin B. Cotler and Julio J. Guerra in *Assertion Training: A Humanistic-Behavioral Guide to Self-Dignity* (Englewood Cliffs, N.J.: Prentice-Hall, 1976). The skills were later made popular by Manuel J. Smith in the bestselling book *When I Say No, I Feel Guilty* (New York: Dial, 1975).

though everything may be true, you are unshakable in not wanting a boat.

You can also use Broken Record when you want something that someone is trying to refuse you. A good example is seeking a refund from where you've purchased a product you're not satisfied with.

YOU: I bought this radio and I'm not satisfied with the sound. I want the money-back guarantee you promised in the ad.

CLERK: There's nothing wrong with this radio.

YOU: It may seem that way to you, but the sound is not what I expected. I want the refund.

CLERK: It sounds okay to me, and I'm around this music department all day, so I know the difference between good sound and bad.

YOU: That could be, but I want the refund.

One of the things that makes this technique effective is that other people will usually give up after the first try; this encourages you to keep after what you want. With practice, Broken Record will come quite naturally to you and will help you feel in greater control in difficult situations.

6

The Assertive Manager: Delegation, Counseling, Performance Appraisal

As noted in the previous chapters, your beliefs, attitudes, motivations, and behavior dramatically affect your effectiveness as a manager. Many managers are unaware of how much these underlying factors influence three vital managerial functions: delegating work to subordinates, coaching and counseling employees on present and future work, and appraising performance to improve productivity.

YOUR MANAGERIAL STYLE

There are two basic sets of emotional resources that we call upon to get results:

1. Feelings and emotions that generate action, and help us fight against obstacles that stand in our way. These are the *assertive* (or sometimes aggressive) feelings we use to push, shape, and influence the environment.
2. Feelings and emotions that enable us to tune in to the environment, to flow with it, to be influenced by events and other people around us. These are our *responsive* emotions.

At certain times managers accomplish results by moving out into their environment and making things happen. They shape events, push, probe, and act upon the world around them. At other times, good managers take in *from* the environment. They react and respond to other people, and they are

73

sensitive to the cues and clues that can make them more effective in their shaping, influencing behavior.

In one research study, an assertive/responsive test instrument developed by Malcolm Shaw was administered to 1,000 high-level managers. The results indicated that:

1. Higher-level managers generally had balanced assertive/responsive scores. Very few had higher assertive scores than responsive scores.

2. First-level supervisors had higher responsive scores than assertive scores and higher responsive scores than upper-level managers did. The implication here seems to be that higher-level managers are more ready to state their views, and lower-level managers are more responsive to their environments.

3. Assertive and responsive scores vary with the organizational context. In a highly controlled situation, with constraints placed on them by their own superiors and by organizational policies, higher-level managers often show higher assertive scores. One possible explanation is that in such situations managers feel they must be even more assertive than usual to break through the constraints and get things done.

Many managers, accustomed to the decisive model of behavior, feel that they will be compromising their position by responding. They feel that by listening to and supporting others, they will be indicating agreement with them and will therefore be seen as weak. However, as we will see in this and further chapters, much rich and valuable information can be gained by listening to and supporting other people long enough to understand their viewpoints and to establish rapport. Once we are aware of the other people's needs and motivations, we can tailor our assertive communications to them so that we have a higher probability of getting the results we want. This is true whether the communication is with the boss, a subordinate, a peer, or someone outside the organization.

This chapter shows how you can use assertive/responsive skills to delegate work, coach employees, and appraise their performance more effectively.

Exercise: How Assertive a Manager Are You?*

Check the statement indicating your most likely response to each situation below.

1. When there's an unpleasant job that has to be done, I . . .
   a. do it myself.
   b. give it as punishment to someone who's been goofing off.
   c. hesitate to ask a subordinate to do it.
   d. ask someone to do it just the same.

*Reprinted, by permission of the publisher, from *Supervisory Management,* October 1978 © 1978 by AMACOM, a division of American Management Associations. All rights reserved. This is an excerpt from *Taking Charge of the Job—Techniques for Assertive Management* by Lyn Taetzsch and Eileen Benson, published by Executive Enterprises Publications Co., Inc., 33 West 60th Street, New York, N.Y. 10023.

2. When the boss criticizes me, I . . .
   a. feel bad.
   b. show her where she's wrong.
   c. try to learn from it.
   d. apologize for being stupid.
3. When an employee isn't working out, I . . .
   a. give him rope to hang himself.
   b. do everything I can to help him work out before I have to fire him.
   c. put off firing him as long as possible.
   d. get rid of him as quickly as possible if the guy is no good.
4. When my salary increase isn't as large as I think it should be, I . . .
   a. tell the boss in no uncertain terms what to do with it.
   b. keep quiet about it.
   c. say nothing, but take it out on the boss in other ways.
   d. feel bad.
5. When a subordinate continues to ignore instructions after I've explained something for the third time, I . . .
   a. try to give her something else to do.
   b. keep telling her until she does it.
   c. tell her that if she doesn't do it right this time, she's out the door.
   d. try to explain it in a different way.
6. When the boss rejects a good idea of mine, I . . .
   a. ask why.
   b. walk away and feel bad.
   c. try it again later.
   d. think about joining the competition.
7. When a co-worker criticizes me, I . . .
   a. give her back twice the dose she gave me.
   b. avoid her in the future.
   c. feel bad.
   d. worry that she doesn't like me.
8. When someone tells a joke I don't get, I . . .
   a. laugh with the rest of the group.
   b. say it was a lousy joke.
   c. say I didn't get it.
   d. feel stupid.
9. When someone points out a mistake I've made, I . . .
   a. sometimes deny it.
   b. feel guilty as hell.
   c. figure it's only human to make mistakes now and then.
   d. dislike the person.
10. When a subordinate fouls up a job, I . . .
    a. blow up.
    b. hate to tell him about it.
    c. hope that he'll do it right the next time.
    d. don't give him that job to do again.

11. When I have to talk to a top executive, I . . .
    a. can't look the person in the eye.
    b. feel uncomfortable.
    c. get a little nervous.
    d. enjoy the interchange.
12. When a subordinate asks me for a favor, I . . .
    a. sometimes grant it, sometimes not.
    b. feel uncomfortable if I don't grant it.
    c. never grant any favors if I can help it. It sets a bad precedent.
    d. always give in.

Scoring

1. Nonassertive managers hate to ask people to do unpleasant work, and they often wind up doing it themselves (answers *a* and *c*). The aggressive manager might give such odious tasks as punishments (answer *b*). The assertive manager might hesitate to ask the subordinate, but would ask just the same (answer *d*).
2. The aggressive manager argues with the boss when criticized (answer *b*). Feeling bad or guilty, though a common reaction, is a nonassertive response (answer *a*). But apologizing for being stupid is the limit (answer *d*). The assertive response, assuming the criticism is valid, is to try to learn from the remark (answer *c*).
3. The hard-nosed, authoritarian manager would get rid of a "bad" employee as quickly as possible (answer *d*). The nice-guy manager would put if off—forever, if possible (answer *c*)—and would give the poor performer rope to hang himself so the manager would feel justified in firing him (answer a). The assertive manager would try hard to help the employee work out, but would fire him in the end if necessary (answer *b*).
4. When people don't like a situation, but they say nothing about it, resentment builds up in them. This resentment often leads to forms of passive aggression; they "get back" in other, devious ways. Answers *b, c,* and *d* are compliant reactions. Choice *a* is an aggressive reaction. No assertive choice was given here.
5. Choices *b* and *d* are both assertive ones. Choice *a*—giving the employee something else to do—is evading responsibility and a compliant reaction. Threatening is the hard-guy approach (answer *c*).
6. Planning to join the competition is passive aggression: "I'll get even; they'll be sorry!" Choices *a* and *c* are assertive responses.
7. Choice *a*—"giving her back twice the dose she gave me"—is the aggressive response. Choices *b, c,* and *d* are all nonassertive. No assertive choice was given here.
8. Choices *a* and *d* are nonassertive responses. Assertive people are not afraid to say they didn't get the joke (answer *c*). The aggressive person blames the guy for telling a lousy joke (answer *b*).
9. A common reaction when someone points out a mistake we have made is to feel guilty, to dislike the person for telling us about it, and perhaps

even to deny we did it. But assertive people know they have the right to make mistakes.

10. Blowing up at an employee is a tough-guy approach, showing no respect for the employee's rights and feelings (answer *a*). Choices *b, c,* and *d* are all nonassertive responses to this problem. No assertive response was given.

11. It's normal to be a little nervous when you have to talk to an executive, but feeling so uncomfortable that you can't even look the person in the eye is extreme nonassertiveness. If you enjoy the interchange, that's assertive (answer *d*). And that's great.

12. Managers who don't feel comfortable negotiating with subordinates sometimes make a policy of not granting any favors. Nice-guy managers just about always grant favors and feel uncomfortable if they don't. The assertive manager feels free to say yes or no, depending on the circumstances (answer *a*).

ASSERTIVE DELEGATION

"I don't have time to delegate."

"I'd rather do it myself than go to all the trouble of telling someone else how to do it."

"If I delegate this job and it doesn't work out, I'm responsible."

These are some of the many reasons managers cite for failure to delegate. True, it takes time—and assertiveness—to delegate properly, and there are some risks. But what are the consequences of *not* delegating? If you do not delegate, you have less time to train and develop employees, to plan ahead, to develop new ideas, and, most important to your own career, to become more promotable by taking on new projects.

What is Delegation?

Delegation has been defined in various ways:

"Getting things done through other people."

"Giving people things to do."

"The art of passing along authority to other people."

"Achieving specific results by empowering and motivating subordinates to accomplish some of the results for which the manager has final accountability.

Why Delegate?

Delegation is an important tool for every manager. There are several reasons why managers must know how to delegate.

1. *To use time effectively.* Delegation frees you to tackle more important jobs—to plan, to set goals, to track the progress of your department or work unit. Delegation multiplies your productivity.

2. *To save money for the organization.* Figure out what an hour of your time costs your organization compared with an hour of your subordinates' time. Every task you delegate represents a substantial cost saving.

3. *To help subordinates grow.* People who are growing are more productive. People who are learning gladly accept increased responsibility. When your subordinates are capable of taking over all your work, you are available for promotion with no threat to the organization's continued smooth operation.

4. *To perform your own job better.* Your subordinates can help you do your job more effectively. Some of the most successful managers rely on their subordinates and use them productively. You can judge from your own experience. Consider the managers you admire and respect for their ability to get things done, feel good about their accomplishments, and deal with ongoing pressures assertively. These people look at their responsibilities as challenges. They see their work environment as a resource for progress, growth, and development—for themselves as well as for those they supervise and those with whom they work. They project an attitude of strength, which they develop through techniques that lead them to the bottom line of profit, productivity, and progress.

This attitude is transferred into action through delegation—getting things done through other people. The ability to delegate, in turn, strongly influences the manager's own effectiveness. When you delegate, you give your subordinates opportunities to be challenged, motivated, and involved. You give yourself more time to create more effective techniques to use within your company. While your subordinates are developing, you are making your business or department more productive.

Your Delegation Style

The extent to which you delegate and the manner in which you do so depend on many factors, including your own style of managing. For example, some managers enjoy doing things themselves; they prefer a more active role and delegate only routine work to subordinates. Other managers prefer the team approach, with everyone given generally equal responsibility within given areas of expertise. Such managers may delegate a great deal to subordinates.

If you're managing people, you need to know how to delegate effectively. Your skills in delegating must be as sharp as they are in other technical and managerial areas. You will benefit from delegation to the degree that you tailor it to your own management style, to the types of job activities you're involved in, and to your staff, time, and budget constraints.

The Assertive Delegator
○ Is secure and confident.
○ Has confidence in subordinates' abilities.

○ Is willing to accept delegated work that is less than perfect.
○ May be afraid of criticism, but delegates the work anyway.
○ Is clear and direct when explaining work to subordinates.
○ Doesn't hover.
○ Allows employees to use their own methods and creativity whenever possible.
○ Rewards and acknowledges good performance.
○ Criticizes fairly, objectively, and constructively.

The Nonassertive Delegator
○ Delays asking subordinates to do work out of fear that they will feel overburdened.
○ Is paralyzed by fear of criticism and ends up doing all the work.
○ Does not give any feedback when an employee turns in poor performance.
○ Does not acknowledge good performance.
○ Is secretly afraid of being "shown up" by employees.

The Aggressive Delegator
○ Is insensitive to employee's needs, skills, and workloads.
○ Hovers over employees after delegating the work, giving directions and making them feel childlike.
○ Snatches back the task in midstream, without explanation.
○ Criticizes employees in front of others.

There are many reasons managers fail to delegate, ranging from fear of failure to an overwhelming desire to be needed. One of the most common reasons for failing to delegate work, authority, and responsibility is lack of assertiveness. Many managers feel that employees will be annoyed or feel put upon, and consequently will resent being asked to do work. Of course, these managers are forgetting that that is their job, to get work done through others.

Guidelines for Delegation

1. *Accept delegation.* Delegation is not just desirable but necessary to a successful department. Even if employees do not do things the way you would do them, you should be prepared to accept and live with their results.

2. *Specify goals and objectives.* Employees must know not only what is to be done, but why, how well, when, with what resources, by whom, and according to what priority.

3. *Know employees' capabilities.* If you don't know what your people can do, you may ask them to perform tasks they aren't qualified or trained to do or have little liking for.

4. *Agree on performance standards.* It's important for you and your subordinates to agree on the standards against which their performance will be measured. These include such information as the quantity of work, the time of completion, and other criteria.

5. *Include training*. Delegating doesn't mean simply handing employees something they've never done before and saying, "Let me have this by next Monday." You must provide the necessary training that will enable employees to do the new task.

6. *Take an interest*. Managerial snooping will not be welcomed by employees. But the boss who really cares about the delegated assignment and takes the trouble to find out how it's going won't be resented. On the contrary, employees will be pleased that their efforts are being noticed and appreciated.

7. *Assess results*. Carefully appraise an employee's performance of a delegated task. Only then will you know what's needed to improve that performance, such as further training or motivation.

8. *Give appropriate rewards*. An employee who successfully completes a delegated assignment deserves recognition and praise. The manager should recommend pay increases and promotions for employees who effectively handle greater responsibilities.

9. *Don't snatch back the delegated task*. An employee may not be doing as well as you'd hoped with an assignment, but think twice before you take it back—unless, of course, the problem is serious. Making mistakes, finding out about them, and correcting them is a valuable learning experience. And if you take back the tasks you delegate, your employees will wonder how sincere you are in your talk about delegating.

How to Delegate Assertively

Assertive delegation requires understanding the skills, needs, attitudes, and preferences of each of your subordinates. This means you must stay attuned to the daily workings of the environment and be aware of each person who reports to you. Successful delegation occurs when there is a "fit" between the task, the person, and the situation. The effective manager uses an assertive or responsive style that is appropriate in each case. Here are some tips on delegating assertively.

Let someone else do the work you enjoy. This may be difficult, but it will give you a chance to find out what *else* you enjoy. Or you may find that someone does something better than you! Let others do work you don't enjoy; a task distasteful to you may be fun for someone else.

Let someone else participate in or make decisions you normally make. Then back the person with your dignity and authority. If you undercut people, they may be timid or reluctant the next time. Ask your people what they want to do—find out their likes and dislikes. Delegate some of each.

Accept less than perfect results. The person who demands perfection instead of the best way under given situations will not react in time. Have a tolerance for mistakes. Expect them in any learning process. Exercise restraint. Once you delegate, you must stay out. You must make clear what

DELEGATION CHECKLIST

When to Delegate

- ○ When someone else can do it as well as you or better.
- ○ When you might do it poorly because of lack of time.
- ○ When subordinates can do it well enough for the cost or time involved.
- ○ When a subordinate can't do it as well but your doing it interferes with something more important. Delegate, coach the subordinate on how to do it, and expect less satisfactory results than you would achieve. If this can't be done, subordinates may be unqualified to do this job. You need controls on this situation.
- ○ When a project will be useful for developing a subordinate, if costs or time permit, and if you can afford the risk.
- ○ When it actually costs too much for you to do it.
- ○ When you are spending too much of your time on operations.

When Not to Delegate

- ○ When no one can do it as well as you and when the time it will take you isn't out of proportion with its importance.
- ○ When it's confidential or beyond what subordinates can handle.
- ○ When it doesn't cost too much for you to do it, or when the time of passing it on would consume the savings.
- ○ When you have to set the pace and pattern, to show how to take long steps.
- ○ When you must keep close enough to see trends, keep informed, maintain controls, and so on. If delegating keeps you too far from certain matters that you must be informed on, then the question is not, "Can the employee do it?" but rather "Can I keep necessary control by delegating?"

you *give* and what you *retain*. Patience is an important virtue in delegation. If you direct, then you haven't delegated. Get feedback from subordinates willingly, not demandingly. Have frequent casual talks with each subordinate if possible.

Delegate problems rather than tasks. Give old projects to a newcomer, new ones to an oldtimer, potential ones to a thinker.

Delegate to your secretary. Teach your secretary, or assistant, how to screen telephone calls, and refer as many as possible back to him or her for follow-up. Callers will then learn in which situations they can work directly with your secretary. Orient your secretary on how to screen incoming mail selectively, keeping him or her informed about your priorities and interests. When uncertain, the secretary should direct the mail to you until more secure about how you want it handled.

Delegate with discernment. See that subordinates clearly understand what you expect. Let them know that you sincerely believe in their ability to carry out the task. Secure commitments that they will follow through. Set deadlines. Give people latitude to use their own imagination and initiative. Do not do the job for them, even if they fail. Reward them commensurately with the results they produce.

Don't sit on projects. Pass them off to people who may be able to do them faster and better. Plan schedules regularly with those who most directly influence what you do with your time. Ask others: "What can I do to help you make better use of your time?" They will reciprocate your request.

Exercise: Making Sound Delegation Decisions

Making sound delegation decisions can save you—and your company—valuable time and resources and can reduce stress. Despite time and risks, delegation *does* work; how well depends on a number of factors.

The art of delegation requires thinking through a number of key variables and how they interact. The success of your project will often depend on the appropriateness of a particular person to a task.

This exercise is designed to help you sharpen your delegating skills. It will assist you in planning for a specific project, by asking you questions about your current attitudes and information regarding the *task,* the *person* to whom you're considering delegating it, and your own *style*.

Try to answer all the questions—then go back over the information you have written. You will then be equipped to make your decision, and be ready for a clear communication with your subordinate to produce the results you want.

Task

The following questions will help you identify, specifically, the nature of the task you want to delegate.

1. What is the task? (Describe it in terms of concrete, *measurable* results.)
2. When is it due? Is it due incrementally? Is it due in total?
3. What resources (people, materials, money. time) are needed to accomplish this task?
4. What authority is needed to carry out this task effectively?
5. Is this task a high priority to the organization? To the department?
6. Is this task of a confidential nature?
7. Is this a routine task? A complex one? In what way?
8. Is my major concern that the correct result or target be accomplished, according to the objectives (and not *how* it's done)?
9. Does the task have to follow a certain procedure or methodology?
10. What are the consequences of the task being done poorly? adequately? excellently? late? What are the consequences of its not being done at all?

Person

The following questions will help you assess the appropriateness of this particular person for this specific task, and help you identify the person's skills, interests, and learning styles.

1. With respect to this task, what are the person's best skills? most relevant experience? preferences? areas of difficulty?
2. Will this task be a training or development experience for this person?
3. Will accepting and accomplishing this task give the person visibility?
4. What might the person's attitude be toward this task, when asked to do it?
   ____ pleased
   ____ displeased
   ____ overwhelmed
   ____ bored
   ____ burdened
   ____ challenged
   ____ flattered
5. In what *form* does this person prefer to receive information?
   ____ small chunks
   ____ large picture
   ____ pictures, graphs
   ____ charts
   ____ numbers
   ____ examples or analogies
6. What do you know, from past experience, about the person's work style?
   ____ ability to take on new projects (without established procedures or precedents)
   ____ reliability
   ____ trustworthiness (respecting confidentiality)
   ____ flexibility
   ____ creativity
   ____ perseverence
   ____ stress tolerance
   Which are most vital to the successful completion of *this* task?
7. What might be this person's resistances or barriers be to (a) accepting and (b) accomplishing this task?
8. What might motivate the person to accomplish the task?

Your Communication and Management Style

Now that you've considered the task and the person, think about what style or approach you can use to communicate the nature of the *task* to the specific *person* in a way that will accomplish your goals.

1. What are my positive and/or negative attitudes toward the task?
2. What are my positive and/or negative attitudes toward the person?

3. Are the objectives clear and concise? Are they stated in terms of concrete results, with dates and methods if applicable? Are they realistic and attainable?

4. Will I communicate to the person in a form and language that he or she is comfortable with and can understand?

5. Will I check to be sure that he or she understood me perfectly?

6. Am I willing to turn over appropriate authority? Sufficient resources?

7. Is accountability consistent with the competence/experience of the person? Is it concentrated unnecessarily in one individual?

8. Can I give the person enough information—the "whole picture"—and explain why the task is important?

9. Do we set up agreements, groundrules, operating methods, controls?

10. How can we establish assessment/evaluation criteria and procedures?

11. What will the rewards be for successful completion?

12. Am I willing to let go?

Now review the information in all three categories, evaluate the benefits and costs of delegating this project to this individual, and make your decision. Use the information as a guide to *plan* your communication to maximize a successful outcome.

ASSERTIVE COACHING AND COUNSELING

One of the important tasks of management is the development of people. This is a continuing process in which the manager acts as a coach/counselor for the subordinate.

Strictly speaking, coaching and counseling are separate activities. Coaching focuses on improving job skills and job knowledge, whereas counseling focuses on problems of attitude and motivation or on interpersonal problems. For example, if a salesperson doesn't know the correct way to demonstrate the benefits of a product, coaching is needed; if the person refuses to mail call reports to the district manager because he or she thinks "the call report system is a lot of baloney," counseling is needed. In practice, the two terms are often used interchangeably or used in a single phrase to suggest a combined activity.

Coaching and counseling involve a manager in helping a subordinate do some self-analysis to produce self-understanding. Often this combines with the manager's own insights and knowledge to produce commitment to mutually accepted goals and a plan of action for achieving them. As this definition makes plain, coaching and counseling should lead to optimal development for the subordinate and therefore optimal results for the organization.

Managers who are secure in their own skills and strengths assist employees in developing on the job without fear that subordinates will take over. Ideally, the goal is to groom the subordinate so that the manager can assume wider responsibilities. Specific objectives include:

1. To make certain that employees know what is expected of them.
2. To help employees understand how they are doing compared with what is expected of them.
3. To help employees outline a plan for improvement and to encourage them to improve.
4. To develop the potential of employees for transfer and promotion.
5. To enable employees to learn something new.

Coaching Pitfalls

Every manager recognizes the need to develop and train subordinates. Even so, many managers perform this task poorly. Here are a few reasons why.

Lack of time. A busy manager often feels that today's pressing needs must take priority over the longer-term return from devoting time to coaching. Perhaps managers in this position should reflect that they might have fewer pressing problems if they had abler subordinates.

Lack of confidence in others. The act of giving responsibility should imply confidence that the task will be achieved. It is unreasonable to expect people to give of their best if they know that the boss does not really expect them to succeed and is only waiting for them to fail before taking over the task.

Shyness. Many managers are reserved with their subordinates, particularly when it comes to offering criticism. Few managers today try to cover up their own inadequacies by blustering or bullying, but they still shy away from conversations with subordinates which might lead them to make direct criticisms. Like other people, managers like to be liked, and they think that criticism is a sure way not to win friends and influence people. Although destructive criticism is certainly not the best approach to developing subordinates, we'll see later that constructive feedback can be a very effective management tool.

Adherence to traditional concepts of organization. Traditional management concepts hold that superiors should plan, organize, control, and expect their subordinates to apply their decisions in a rather rigid way. This attitude, of course, limits true participation in decision making, since subordinates inevitably have less opportunity for developing and applying their own ideas and for learning from their mistakes than they would in an environment where mistakes (as opposed to ineptness or gross stupidity) are tolerated. Coaching gives more responsibility to subordinates. If done skillfully, it empowers them to use their own initiative.

Lack of skills. One of the biggest reasons managers do not engage in effective coaching with their subordinates is lack of skill. Coaching requires an intricate combination of interpersonal skills, including listening, problem analysis, reflection and rephrasing, and assertiveness. The assertive coach takes an active part in the employee's day-to-day development and performance concerns, takes the initiative in discussions, and gives constructive but direct feedback.

Principles of Good Coaching

Good coaches are good listeners. In order to be effective as a coach, the manager must be both a willing and a skilled listener. One of the most difficult tasks in coaching is getting a subordinate to open up and talk about problems. Many people have learned from bitter experience that it is better to say nothing. The ability to encourage a subordinate to talk requires (1) taking an active and sincere interest in the person and the problem, (2) conveying a sincere desire to offer assistance, and (3) understanding the general aspects of the situation well enough to ask the right questions at the right time.

The coaching session should be a discussion between equals, not a superior/subordinate conversation. It is concerned with diagnosis and solution of work problems, rather than with issuing instructions or imposed solutions. Coaches have to be particularly careful in how they present their ideas. Many a manager has put forward an idea for discussion only to find that the subordinate takes it as an instruction to be acted upon. Good coaches, therefore, conceal their own thoughts until the end of the discussion in order not to influence the thinking of their subordinates. A readiness to admit one's own responsibility for mistakes is a further means of convincing subordinates that the meeting is an open discussion of a problem, not an occasion for issuing orders. The phrase "Can you help me?"—sincerely stated—is a useful way to initiate a problem-solving coaching session.

Good coaches are interested in their people. To take an interest in subordinates is not a charitable act or mere good manners. Nor does it have anything to do with the "prying" approach that is so often recommended. ("How is your spouse?" "Where are you going for the holidays?" "Are the children doing well at school?") To some subordinates, this type of questioning is aggressive. In the work situation, taking interest in subordinates means demonstrating a desire to develop them so that they are able to think for themselves, accomplish objectives, have ambitions, develop emotional maturity, be self-reliant and self-confident, be tolerant of others, and, above all, never want to stop learning.

The manager's effectiveness as a coach may be judged by the extent to which his or her people develop such traits. These traits cannot be taught in a formal sense; they can only be nurtured by an environment that encourages self-development and self-criticism while offering constructive help. In this sense, good coaches are *people-centered,* even though coaching is ultimately a work-centered activity aimed at improved job performance.

Good coaches look for potentialities. Two characteristic management fallacies are assuming that a person is incapable of taking on a more demanding task and assuming that a person who performs well can be given new tasks without training or guidance. Most workers are capable of mastering new challenges, provided they are given adequate coaching, guidance, and encouragement.

What a manager expects of subordinates and the way he or she treats them will have a significant influence on their performance and career progress. It is the boss who sets the pattern of behavior; it is the boss who brings out the best in a person; it is the boss who in the long run makes attendance at development courses worthwhile by encouraging employees to apply what they have learned.

Managers are the people who can make or break their subordinates. It is they who know—or should know—their employees' strengths and weaknesses better than anyone else. It is they who are in a position, and who have the opportunity, to give them tasks that will help to overcome weaknesses and build on strengths.

Superior coaches create high performance expectations that subordinates fulfill. Poor coaches fail to develop such expectations; as a consequence, the productivity of their subordinates suffers. Subordinates, more often then not, do what *they believe they are expected to do.*

Assertive Counseling Skills

As mentioned earlier, counseling is distinct from coaching in that it focuses on problems of attitude and motivation, or interpersonal issues. Of all the roles that a manager may fill, the role of counselor is the most difficult for many managers to understand, since in many ways it seems to conflict with the role of disciplinarian.

It is useful to think of counseling in terms of a helper/receiver relationship. Both helper (manager) and receiver (subordinate) must understand that the helper is trying to influence, change, and develop the behavior of the receiver in a way that will be useful and productive for both of them. To do this effectively, the manager must be finely attuned to the needs, values, beliefs, and self-image of the subordinate. The helper must have a great deal of skill in assertive communication in order to counsel subordinates without injuring their self-esteem or provoking defensive behavior. *The key to effective counseling is giving subordinates the freedom to choose the course of action that they feel is best under the circumstances.* Subordinates will be much more likely to carry out a course of action when they have chosen it themselves and are responsible for the outcome.

The helper's task is to let the receiver know exactly what is expected. This may include joint goal setting to improve peer relations, increase promptness, or improve efficiency in performing the job. The helper who has done everything possible to assist the receiver in exploring alternatives and arriving at a personal decision can feel more certain that the desired change will be achieved.

Counseling Guidelines

Here are some guidelines to get the most out of the helper/receiver relationship:

1. *Don't argue*. The subordinate will try to preserve his self-concept by meeting your arguments with resistance. If you become more argumentative or continue to pound away, you will generate even more resistance and denial.

2. *Be prepared to listen*. You must understand the subordinate's point of view before you can explore alternatives. This does not mean that you must agree with or support the subordinate's position. There's a difference between empathy and sympathy. Let the subordinates do more than half the talking. Don't let your experience as a supervisor trap you into a prescribing or lecturing role. Such a know-it-all position may threaten subordinates so much that they mentally leave the scene or become defensive.

3. *Direct your comments to behavior that the subordinate can change.* Giving people unfavorable feedback about actions over which they have little or no control only increases their feelings of frustration and their need to defend themselves.

4. *Give timely feedback.* Feedback is most helpful to a subordinate when it is given at the earliest opportunity after an event has occurred.

People can take in only so much unfavorable feedback. When their tolerance level is reached, no further learning takes place. For this reason, you should give feedback often and in small quantities. A comprehensive, once-a-year performance review is not sufficient feedback. It will not help subordinates develop on the job and may even hinder their growth. Small changes effected through frequent feedback over a long period of time will be better for the subordinate and better for you.

5. *Look at subordinates as subjects—not objects that make up your personnel resource.* They are human beings with feelings, needs, and values of their own. Try to see the world from their point of view.

6. *Reflect the feelings of the worker.* If during the counseling session you can focus on reflecting back the feelings and attitudes of the worker, you will be less tempted to give advice, and the worker will be better able to find his or her own solution. Keep the conversational ball bouncing back over the net—by nodding frequently or saying, ''I see,'' and ''Is that so?''—so the subordinate has a chance to elaborate.

7. *Ask open-ended questions.* The skillful counselor avoids questions that can be answered with a simple yes or no. Questions that begin with ''How do you feel about . . .?'' or ''What do you think about . . .?'' give the

worker a chance to let feelings and attitudes emerge along with a multitude of facts, details, and excuses. Since the purpose of the session is to solve a problem, past facts are far less important than present feelings and attitudes.

8. *Be on the lookout for signals that the subordinate is willing to commit to change or ownership in the outcome of the helper/receiver relationship.* Once a subordinate assumes responsibility for overcoming his or her own shortcomings, your task as a counselor is almost complete.

The Assertive Coach/Counselor
○ Makes certain the employee knows what's expected.
○ Is interested in developing and grooming people.
○ Is prepared to listen.
○ Knows each subordinate is an individual, with unique values, interests, attitudes, and skills—and treats the subordinate that way.
○ *Makes* time for regular coaching/counseling sessions with employees.
○ Gives timely feedback.
○ Directs feedback to behavior the subordinate can do something about.

The Nonassertive Coach/Counselor
○ Waits until small problems build up before initiating discussions.
○ Is insecure about his or her own promotability, so is reluctant to help employees with their own growth.
○ May *seem* compassionate, but usually avoids confrontation and difficult issues, preferring to maintain the status quo and keep people in line.
○ Confines people to narrow jobs and responsibilities, because of fears of letting things get out of control.

The Aggressive Coach/Counselor
○ Gives only negative feedback—complains and criticizes when people do poorly.
○ Delivers criticism at will, with little sense of timing or sensitivity to the individual's other pressures.
○ Criticizes the whole *person,* rather than the specific behavior or task.
○ Treats the person as "one of the pack," not someone with unique skills and values.
○ Runs a coaching/counseling session in a directive, prescriptive, show-and-tell fashion. Doesn't give the employee much time to talk.

ASSERTIVE PERFORMANCE APPRAISAL

Performance appraisal is a management tool for evaluating employee performance against a set of predetermined criteria. The appraisal is generally discussed with the employee in a one-to-one session in which the manager reviews the evaluation with the employee. The interviews are confidential and usually take place in the manager's office. Some managers actively solicit employees' feedback by allowing them to complete a self-appraisal form and compare their evaluation with that of the manager. Other managers prefer a session where employees must assert themselves and make their comments known.

There is no set rule on how often an employee should receive a performance appraisal. Company policies vary. Informally, of course, a manager appraises employees daily. In general, enough time should be allowed between the formal performance appraisal and the salary review date to give employees adequate opportunity to know the manager's feeling about their performance and to correct substandard performance.

Performance appraisals are usually given by the person directly responsible for (1) managing and supervising the employee, (2) recommending and/or approving raises, and (3) determining hiring and firing for that position. If you manage a department of five employees and each one of these employees reports directly to you, then you should be responsible for five separate performance appraisals.

Performance appraisal has three key objectives:

1. To measure and document employee performance for employee records and wage and salary administration.
2. To prepare (usually in writing) a development plan with specific placement and training recommendations for the next year.
3. To assist in the assessment of people in relation to their promotability/mobility.

All employees like to know how they are doing. The performance appraisal provides that information. From management's standpoint, the appraisal is a formal document reflecting the employee's performance—a document that assumes even greater importance when it is signed by the employee as proof that the employee has been made aware of its contents. From the employee's standpoint, the performance appraisal provides an excellent opportunity to catalog past achievements. Unlike the job description, which is an impersonal list of the functions and duties of a given position, the performance appraisal is a statement of individual performance in that position.

The Assertive Performance Appraiser
○ Is honest but tactful.
○ Describes the performance, not the person.
○ Is caring and concerned about people's feelings.
○ Is careful not to use language that may hurt the employee.
○ Remembers to give positive feedback as well as criticism.
○ Is supportive of the employee's own goals and interests.
○ Creates a mutual problem-solving environment.

The Nonassertive Performance Appraiser
○ Is hesitant, uses unclear language, beats around the bush.
○ Doesn't give feedback when it's appropriate, but stays silent and allows problems to build up.

o Does not take the initiative, but waits until the employee brings up the subject of performance.

The Aggressive Performance Appraiser
o Evaluates the whole person, not just the specific task or performance.
o Interprets and analyzes the employee's attitudes, values, and motivations without hearing the employee out.
o Dominates the performance interview.
o Offers criticism (and calls it "feedback") in areas that are not job-related.
o Does not make clear to subordinates the criteria for effective performance.

7

Interpersonal Communication

Communication is the cornerstone of business. Every time we come in contact with another person, we are communicating—verbally or nonverbally. We speak to people at many different times and for many reasons during the average business day. A recent survey of how managers allocate their time indicated that they spend between 50 percent and 90 percent of their day in communication of one kind or another. The people with whom they interact are subordinates; peers; vendors, suppliers, customers, or other people outside the organization; and bosses. Managers also use many different channels to communicate with others. They speak with other people face to face, on the telephone, or via a memo, letter, or report.

In the early stages of career development, many managers concentrate on their technical or other job-related skills, unaware that communication is a separate set of skills vital to their success. If you're in data processing, engineering, or manufacturing, the chances are you've learned and are continuing to learn a vast amount of information about your industry, the competition, your company, its products and their applications, and how your department works with and through other departments.

But what about the very glue of business—the skills of communication? Every time you give directions to someone, or receive a memo, or send out a sales letter or a report to your boss, you are communicating. How effectively you do this often determines the quality of the work you do—and of the work you get back, when you're the one who's delegating.

Even if you're in sales, you may have an encyclopedic knowledge about your product or service and how it rates against the competition; you may even be a sophisticated marketer and know a great deal about your customer population in general and about specific market segments, or even about individual customers and their particular needs. But how much have you learned about the specific, step-by-step skills of communication?

Communication between people would seem to be the easiest and most simple thing in the world. It doesn't have anything to do with computers, management information systems, word processing, or balance sheets. It does have to do with people's attitudes, who they are, who they have been, and their impressions of themselves, as well as their notions and ideas of other people. The Latin root for "communicate" (*communicare*) means "to make common." When we are communicating, we are attempting to "make common" our separate and different experiences.

Some managers have the misguided notion that communication is a gift, and that either you have it or you don't. They are wrong. *Communication is a set of skills you can learn.* In this chapter, we'll be looking at the various parts of the communications process and how they fit together.

ELEMENTS OF SUCCESSFUL COMMUNICATION

Congruence

What are the elements in the communications process? First, there is what I like to call straight talk—that is, clear, concise communication that is *congruent*. When you communicate congruently, you are sending verbal and nonverbal messages that are very close to what you are feeling inside. This can also be described as authentic communication. It simply means that you are saying clearly what is going on for you—what you really mean. You put out direct pieces of information, without qualifiers or discounts. The opposite type of communication is sometimes described as two-faced, covert, talking out of both sides of the mouth. For example, the statement "I like your shirt, but that patterning is a little too small" gives the listener a mixed message. The "I like your shirt" part is flattering; but the "but" takes it all back.

According to Dr. Carl Rogers, congruence occurs when what we overtly express to the other person (verbally and nonverbally) is consonant with what we are actually experiencing internally, and when we are aware of what we are feeling. In a sense, it means allowing the other person to see into us. The other person then has a real concept of who we are and senses that we are not intentionally hiding anything. Being congruent requires that we get in touch with our own feelings and assumptions and recognize when they become barriers to our ability to really hear other people.

Empathy

Another important element of communication is empathy—our capacity and willingness to understand the inner experience of another person. When we empathize, we seek to understand others through their eyes and ears, from their frame of reference. Basically we're trying to understand their thoughts and feelings as if we were in their shoes; we are trying, especially, to capture the quality of the feelings they are expressing. Empathic understanding requires that we temporarily let go of our mental set and really tune into the other person's reality. We don't necessarily have to agree with other people's viewpoints—we merely have to understand and accept those viewpoints as *theirs,* without judging or evaluating.

One important by-product of empathy is helping the other person gain self-knowledge. The more empathy we display, the more the other person will be encouraged to explore his or her own feelings. In order to do this, we must not evaluate or judge someone else's perceptions, ideas, assumptions, or insights. Typically, people attempt to "understand" or empathize with others from an external, analytic, or evaluative point of view:

> "I understand you perfectly." (before the person has finished the thought)
> "Let me tell you how to do it."
> "Here's where you're being unrealistic."

When we respond to others with judgments and evaluations, they will stay away from topics about which they are uncertain, for fear that they will be misunderstood or labeled incompetent. They will be less willing to explore new ground or to try new solutions. Also, when we impose our own ideas or judgments on others, we rob them of their own insights.

Often we are reluctant to listen empathically because we are afraid that our own view will be changed if we allow ourselves to be truly open to how another person feels. So we distance ourselves from the other person's inner world by screening what he or she says through our own set of assumptions. The truth is, getting in touch with another person's world is one way to broaden our own world and to enrich our repertoire of experiences and viewpoints.

True empathy is difficult to achieve, especially for any sustained periods of time. But the very posture of empathy—of trying to understand the other person's world view—has a beneficial effect. It is in itself an indication of respect for the person.

Acceptance

Another key aspect of communication is acceptance, or what Carl Rogers has termed "unconditional positive regard." The more willing we are to accept others as people and accept the validity of their feelings and perceptions, the better they will be able to accept themselves, good or bad. Rogers has also used the word "prizing" to describe this attitude, saying that it has

ACTION CHECKLIST

If action needs to be taken or if something needs to be said:

○ Take the initiative. Pick a time and setting when you feel in control. Avoid discussions when you feel uncomfortable or distracted.

○ Decide what you want to say and how you want to say it. Consider rehearsing it with a friend. For important telephone conversations, write out the first few sentences as well as the essential points you want to communicate.

○ Get to the point simply and directly without a lot of distracting preliminaries. Be sure that you say what you intend to say. Don't drop hints and hope you'll be understood.

○ Describe your feelings without attacking the other person's behavior. Use "I" statements rather than "you" statements—for example, "I am upset that you didn't complete the assignment on schedule," rather than "You never complete assignments on time!"

○ Don't ask questions unless you want the answer.

○ Make sure your body language—your nonverbal communication—reinforces your verbal statements. Speak firmly and audibly and maintain good eye contact. Sit or stand comfortably with your shoulders back. Look confident—avoid nervous mannerisms and don't negate a serious message by smiling.

○ Tune in on the way your body feels. If you find your stomach tightening or your hands getting clammy, it should be a sign that it's time to take action, *not* to avoid it.

If you are responding to a request:

○ Answer promptly and to the point. Don't hedge because you fear the reaction to your answer.

○ Request more time or information if necessary, but don't do so just to stall. Get it over with.

○ If a request seems unreasonable, say so, and try to focus on the area of conflict. Suggest a compromise only if you're willing.

○ Don't overexplain. Learn when to stop talking.

○ Don't apologize for your decision.

"somewhat the same quality of feeling that a parent has for a child, prizing her as a person regardless of her particular behavior of the moment."

Acceptance is not mere neutrality. We are neutral in terms of not taking a position on other people's values, as we try to understand who they are. But we are not neutral or uninterested in terms of the concern we display. Acceptance is not tolerance, or simply putting up with what the other person says. Neither is it sympathy or pity, which implies condescension and superiority. Rather, it is an unconditional caring that creates trust in others and lets them feel that they are in a safe environment when they are with us.

"LAWS" OF COMMUNICATION

The communications industry today is quite sophisticated, though many of us would hesitate to call communication a science. Even so, there are certain principles of communication that seem as constant as the laws that govern our physical world.

Edgar B. Wycott, associate professor of communications at the University of Central Florida in Orlando, has pointed out certain similarities between Newton's laws and those of communication.* For example: *For every communication action, there will be some receiver reaction.* Those of us who have been managers for any length of time know that there are consequences to everything we do. Making a hasty remark or giving someone a quick putdown may have little effect in the short run, but it will certainly affect our long-term relationship and future interactions.

Every time we send out a communication or initiate contact with someone, there will be some action or assimilation on the part of the person receiving the message. Just as we wouldn't pitch a ball without some consideration of who is at bat—the batter's strengths, weaknesses, and habits— we should not send out a communication without being aware of the other person and the subtle ways he or she might receive or interpret our message.

The late Irving Lee, author of *How to Talk with People,* listened in on over 200 business meetings for nearly ten years and concluded that the number-one contributor to misunderstanding was assuming that another person uses words in the same way that we do. Further on, in the chapter on listening, we will examine in more detail the different cues and signals people send out that can help us "package" our communications so they are received accurately and favorably.

Here is another "law" by Edgar Wycott, a communications version of the law of gravity: *One person's thoughts are attracted to another person's thoughts with a force directly proportionate to the similarity of their experience.* Often, we find ourselves attracted to people who are like us, or at least those we think are like us. When we sense that someone is similar to us and has had the same experiences, we feel less alone. The problem is that people are a mixture of hundreds of different experiences and impressions—and often we make the mistake of thinking they're just like us when in many subtle and larger ways they aren't. This is why learning to listen is such an important part of the communications process. No one can truly climb inside someone else's skin and have the same experiences. But we can go a long way toward really hearing and receiving someone else if we tune up our listening skills.

A seemingly paradoxical law of communication is: *In order to have others see things your way, you must first see things their way.* Every good

* Edgar B. Wycott, "Canons of Communication," *Personnel Journal,* March 1981.

negotiator and salesperson knows this. People want what they want, first. You must tune in to their needs, motivations, concerns, and preferences before you can get them to ride with you on your journey.

Another helpful principle which successful marketers and advertisers use all the time is: *You must have the other person's attention and interest before reasoning and communication can begin.* With the confusion and time pressures of the modern work organization, and all the clatter of typewriters, telephones, and conversations, it is a wonder that anyone hears anyone. Although most people pretend to be listening when others are talking, and may even believe that they are listening, they are often thinking of other things, distracted by noises, or tuning out. So it's really important for you as a communicator to be aware of what will get the other person's attention: Will it be something visual, something dramatic, something heard, something that appeals to feelings? The best way to get someone's attention will vary from one person to another. You should be flexible enough to use whatever attention-getter works best for each specific individual.

It is also vital for you, the communicator, to be sensitive to timing. When you want to tell your boss about a great new time-saving idea, you certainly wouldn't approach her when you've just found out that there's a crisis in the department and that her own job is in jeopardy. That would only guarantee that your message, as valuable as it may be, will not get heard. At that moment, your boss is much more concerned about survival. If, however, you can find a way to link *your* ideas to the problem she is experiencing, and address yourself to *her* concerns, you may have a receptive ear. The important thing is to be aware of the other person's situation and problems.

WIN/WIN COMMUNICATION

The kind of communication we are talking about is win/win communication. This is truly assertive—it's valuing yourself and the fact that you have rights, and also valuing the other person and his or her rights. In win/win communication, both people get what they want. Win/lose communication is usually associated with aggressiveness on the part of one party, who finds it necessary to triumph over someone else. In lose/lose communication, neither person gets what he or she wants, usually because both parties are unassertive about expressing their needs directly or too stubborn or short-sighted to compromise.

For example, you ask one of your subordinates to stay late because of an extra workload. You are thinking of your own needs, the other work you must do, and the good of the company and the department. You're not thinking very much about the other person's life or concerns. Jean, your subordinate, has plans for dinner with some friends for the evening. She is thinking about her evening and how working late is likely to interfere with that. So it looks like you're headed for a win/lose situation. You're in conflict. If you win, she loses. If she wins, you don't get to have her work with you, and you lose.

If you were to take a win/win approach, you would both be asking some different questions. Instead of asking, "How can I get Jean to stay late and give up her dinner plans?" you might ask yourself, "What results do I want?" Answer: the work completed by Friday. "What results does Jean want, and what does the company need?" Jean wants to go to dinner; she also does want to pull her load, and she is interested in results for the company. "What outcome can we both aim for so that we both can win?"

Jean might ask herself, "What do I really want?" Answer: to go to dinner with my friends. "What results does my manager want, and what does the company need?" He wants the report completed by Friday, and that's what the company needs. "What results can we both try for so that we both can win?" With such questions, you both have a chance to win, because you're working *with* each other *against* the problem or situation.

According to Bill Gellermann, a communications consultant, there are three key elements in win/win thinking:

1. Aiming at a result or goal that will enable both you and the other person to get what you want.
2. Caring that the other person gets the results he or she wants.
3. Being open to changing your goal, if necessary, to avoid a win/lose trap.

Win/win results are most likely when both you and the other person adopt a win/win attitude. If either of you does not believe in the possibility of such an outcome, you may block out some creative possibilities and solutions. Of course, you can take a win/win approach even if the other person seems to be taking a win/lose position. But you will be much less likely to achieve acceptable results. So, to avoid the win/lose trap, ask yourself, "Is there anything I can do to develop the other person's trust in my taking a win/win approach?"

All successful negotiators seek win/win results—negotiated solutions in which both parties come out feeling that they gained something. Of course, they may lose something as well, but the important thing is that no one feels like a total loser.

BARRIERS TO COMMUNICATION

Why do people have such difficulty communicating with one another? One would think that face-to-face communication would come as naturally as breathing instead of being something people have to talk about, analyze, take courses in, and read about.

The truth is, few of us learned how to communicate well. As children, we started out being extremely assertive, making known loud and clear our needs and wants. Then, like Huck Finn, we got "sivilization." We were taught how to behave. We were told to control our feelings, and not to talk back. We began to hold our feelings inside and, afraid of being punished, to control our natural urge to be assertive. As we grew up and entered the business world, these shut-off ways of communicating became reinforced. Competition is the rule in business, and disclosing feelings is considered a sign of weakness. So we are on our guard, careful not to reveal ourselves.

What can we do to *unlearn* these nonassertive, self-defeating behaviors? We can begin by identifying the barriers that keep us from communicating well with others.

Fear

One important factor is fear. We are afraid that if we speak up or disagree, or let others know how we feel, they will think we are crazy, misguided, stupid, or at the very least naive. Fear keeps us locked into tried-and-true patterns of communication; even if something doesn't get us very much in the way of results, we at least can predict the outcome fairly accurately. Breaking our rigid pattern requires a little risk, and a willingness to be more trusting of other people and of ourselves.

Avoidance of Feelings

Many of us have learned to turn feelings on at home and off at work. It's as though we were two different people: warm, emotional, and sensitive with family, friends, and loved ones; but cool, rational, and almost unfeeling with co-workers. The strange thing is that everybody feels that way—so we're not fooling anyone by pretending not to have feelings at the workplace.

Being unaware of or out of touch with feelings, our own and others', is one of the biggest barriers to clear communication. For example: You're feeling resentful toward Norm, who just got the promotion you wanted, but you have pushed that feeling out of your conscious awareness. Instead, whenever you see Norm at departmental meetings, you act as if nothing's happened. Or so you think. But your resentment comes out in other ways— you interrupt him, put down his contributions to the group, avoid eye contact with him. You're not fooling Norm, but you may be fooling yourself. If you were more in touch with your feelings, you might be more direct. You might approach Norm and even acknowledge that you're feeling a little envious and resentful. How much better to be honest and direct. You would save yourself considerable stress and probably add immeasurably to your relationship.

Expressing feelings freely is important not only to your physical and psychological health but to the health of your relationships. When you deny anger, it usually comes out in other ways. It takes its toll on your body—in ulcers, heart ailments, and other stress-related diseases. The best way to become more aware of feelings is to listen. Listen to your body, and start becoming more attuned to what it's telling you. If you feel tightness in your chest, or a lump in your throat, that may be an indication that you're literally blocking your feelings. If you look at your hand, and notice that it's in a fist, you are probably feeling hostile or angry. How much less "bruising" you'd inflict on your physical and psychological self if you could first acknowledge what you're feeling inside and then announce your feelings to the other person.

Defensive Communication

Defensive behavior occurs when we perceive or anticipate threat in a group situation. Even though we may be giving attention to the task at hand, most of our energy is devoted to defending ourselves. Even while we are talking about the topic, we are busy thinking about how we might create a more favorable impression, or how we might dominate others, escape punishment, or avoid an anticipated attack.

Defensive communication is a response, not to an actual physical threat, but to a perceived psychological threat—a threat to our ego, to the characteristics we value about ourselves. A certain amount of defensiveness is healthy and constructive. It signals to us that something may be wrong in the other person's communication. But when our feelings totally control our responses, defensiveness becomes destructive.

Defensive speakers. Some people have a way of speaking that generates defensiveness in others. They are often prescriptive, parental, and evaluative. You get the impression that you're being judged, and in fact you probably are. These people have not learned to trust others, and they are full of blame, accusations, and contemptuous talk. More than likely, if they're speaking so disparagingly of others, they're doing the same about you.

If you are sensitive to other people's situation and feelings, and are reasonably tactful in how you phrase things, the chances are that you won't put out defensive messages. Sometimes timing is important. It's not a good idea to ask a colleague why he didn't show up at a meeting when you know he's been having a terrible week.

Defensive listeners. Some of us are defensive listeners. We take everything someone says as a personal attack, and become offended. For example, your boss says, "Pat, do you have the papers on the Smithtown project?'' You react with, "You gave me the project only five days ago. How do you expect me to have it so soon?'' In fact, your boss was not accusing you of being late with the papers, shirking the project, or anything of the kind. The boss was simply making a request for information.

HOW TO AVOID SENDING DEFENSIVE MESSAGES

1. *Address the problem or situation.* Don't criticize the person or his or her personality. Try not to look for ways to "nail" the other person. Focus on joint problem solving rather than on fault finding. Statements that begin with "you always" and "you never" inevitably generate defensiveness in others. How do *you* feel when someone says, "You're always late for our lunch meetings"? You can think of at least five occasions when you've been on time, and you'd like credit for those. Instead you are being told you are always late. Grrr!

2. *Try to appeal to common goals.* Be a mediator, a negotiator. Get people to share a vision or inspiration with you. It's easy for a manager to exercise control or authority, but that's not the way to get people motivated. If you exert control, you *can* force them to do your bidding; but you'll pay the price by making people defensive.

3. *Respond to the person and the message.* Don't overreact. Sometimes, one word or phrase will "push your button," causing you to have a violent emotional or judgmental response to the other person. Often this is a result of faulty listening—you jump to a conclusion before you've heard the person out.

4. *Don't blame others or pass judgment.* Many of us have a strong need to be right, and to make others wrong. We look for ways that other people aren't doing it right and then zap them with our judgments and, worse, with our advice on how to do it better or differently. One sure way to get people's defenses going is to blame them or evaluate their behavior. For example, someone complains to you about a co-worker, and you say, "I think you're being unfair to George." This is a judgment on your part. The speaker probably didn't want your opinion; he or she just wanted you to *listen*.

5. *Don't interpret or analyze other people's behavior.* Even though your insights might be brilliant and your analyses worthy of Freud, keep them to yourself. Most people don't appreciate being slotted, analyzed, or "read"; for the most part, they want to be heard and understood. And chances are that your interpretations, clever as they may seem to you, have more to do with you than with the other person. That is, you are probably projecting what might be true for *you* in a similar situation. But that is often very different from what is going on in the other person's head.

Right or wrong, analysis and interpretation usually lead to defensiveness. It's a no-win situation. If you happen to be right, others will resent you for

COMMUNICATION CHECKLIST

○ If there is one thing more important than any other to good communication, it is self-knowledge. To get better acquainted with yourself, take 15 to 20 minutes in quiet each day to reflect upon yourself, your purpose, your feelings, and your relationships to those around you.

○ What is said and done, day to day, is the most important part of communicating. Intellectual honesty, living what is said, and acting with cooperation as well as asking about it—these are essential to developing good communication.

○ No matter what you say or how you say it, no one else gets quite the meaning you intended from the words you use. By the same token, you never get quite the meaning anyone else intends.

○ One of the biggest obstacles to communication is the tendency to evaluate, to pass judgment on, to agree or disagree with statements before finding out what is meant. Another important obstacle is feeling that you have to defend your ego by defending what you have said.

○ When listening, look for what the speaker intends, not just at what he or she says. When talking, consider every indication of the listener's response, not just whether he or she understands the instructions or directions.

○ Ask questions to see whether your listeners have understood what is intended. Have your instructions repeated to see if "you've said what you meant." Check for understanding at the time of talking.

○ Misunderstandings are inevitable. Therefore you need to create the kind of atmosphere that will encourage people to ask questions when they don't fully understand.

○ When difficulties have arisen, try to keep the talk centered on the problem rather than on personalities.

○ When people disagree, get them to state each other's position to the satisfaction of the other.

○ Recognize that, in any discussion, disagreement is normal and inevitable. Expect it, prepare for it, use it to obtain greater awareness of the various aspects of the problem at hand.

○ Control your own natural, ego-building desire to get the upper hand, to uncover weaknesses in the other person's point of view. Reveal the weaknesses when they are important, but do it in a manner that leaves the other person's ego intact.

○ Take every honest opportunity to make the other person feel better or more important.

○ An important function of communication is to make known or bring to light misunderstandings and misapprehensions before they develop into serious problems.

○ After you have heard out someone's gripe, ask the person to describe the situation again so you can be sure to "get it straight." Telling it a second time often makes it seem less "charged" for the other person and clearer to you.

○ Very rarely will people change their minds by being asked to, told to, or argued with. They must come to see the situation differently, and they are not likely to do so as long as they perceive a threat in the situation or feel the need to defend themselves.

○ When talking, pause frequently to think through what you are about to say. You create strong impressions by the way you phrase your ideas—for example, by making rambling remarks or concise statements.

○ When talking, think in terms of the total impression you create, not just the words used.

○ Tone of voice is more important than you might think. Consider what impressions you are conveying with your voice.

○ A winner listens; a loser waits until it's his or her turn to talk.

seeing into a part of them that they wish to keep private. If you're off the mark, they'll resent you for misinterpreting.

6. *Don't give advice.* Telling people what is good or helpful usually makes them feel incompetent and inferior and is likely to put them on the defensive. Even when people ask for advice, usually what they really want is a sympathetic ear to support them in finding their own solutions. As one wise psychologist said, "Help is not helpful." The best "helping" technique is to allow others to help themselves, encouraging independence and self-reliance.

7. *Don't give commands or orders.* You will make people feel childlike. And in the same way that adolescents react to parental strictures, they will become rebellious, resentful, and angry.

8. *When you are criticizing someone, observe the rules of supportive, constructive feedback.* Offer feedback in a caring manner—let the person know you're interested in improving the relationship. Give feedback in private, and be sensitive to timing. Feedback should be offered when the other person is ready to receive it, and it should be limited to behaviors that the person can change. Describe the behavior that displeased you or that caused a negative emotional reaction in you. Don't analyze, judge, or evaluate the person. Don't interpret the "meaning" of the behavior. Just give the facts. Offer feedback as soon as possible after the event, so the person can remember what you are talking about. Respect the other person's right to do what he or she wishes with the feedback. You have no right to demand a change in the person's behavior.

HOW TO RESPOND TO DEFENSIVE MESSAGES

Many people will communicate with you in all the wrong ways described above. What do you do when their communication provokes you and makes you feel defensive? The key here is using simple listening skills that allow

you to get more information—other than your initial emotional reactions—
before you respond. Here are some guidelines.

1. *Paraphrase what you hear.* After you've listened to the other person,
repeat what you *thought* you heard. Or put it in your own words.

BOSS: Where is that report I asked you for?

YOU: Are you saying that I'm late getting it back to you?

This lets your boss know that you heard a veiled accusation in the question
and gives the boss an opportunity to confirm or deny it. In this way, you
can clear up a potentially defensive communication early on.

2. *Check your perceptions.* Sometimes a spoken message says one thing
while nonverbal behavior, the "music," says another. It can be very helpful
to check this out, since you are getting conflicting messages.

BOSS: There's no rush at all to complete this project. (*Nonverbals:* Not making eye
       contact, tapping pencil nervously on conference table, rocking foot back and
       forth.)

YOU: Boss, I hear you saying there's no rush, but I see you tapping the pencil and
      rocking your foot, and I'm feeling there's a bit of urgency going on. Is that
      accurate or is it just my imagination?

This gives you a chance to announce what you're feeling or surmising. *But
say it as a guess,* rather than as a pronouncement or judgment that you're
sure of. This gives the other person an opportunity to refute or confirm your
interpretation.

3. *Ask for clarification.* This simple technique can eliminate a lot of stress,
confusion, and anxiety. Many of us do not ask for clarification because
we're afraid of looking ignorant or stupid. We want people to think we are
smart, that we got it the first time. But the fact is that people often speak in
vague, fuzzy, and muddy ways, and if we don't ask for clarification we
cannot hope to understand what they mean.

BOSS: I want those reports to be more efficient and better looking next time.

YOU: What specifically do you mean by "more efficient"? Can you show me an
      example or describe a report that is more efficient than the ones we have
      here? What does "better looking" mean—can you give me some idea of
      exactly how you'd like the reports to look?

This enables you and the boss to gain a common understanding of exactly
what is wanted. Expressions like "more efficient" and "better looking" are
so vague, and leave so much room for misinterpretation, that you will save
yourself hours of guesswork if you just ask a few clarifying questions. This
need not sound like interrogation, if you adopt a posture of interest and
curiosity, and also let the person know that your primary concern is to get
the highest-quality results.

8

Refined Listening

Learning how to listen is a continuing process. In the last chapter we looked at some of the complex factors involved: the right psychological attitude, paying attention to the speaker's nonverbal cues, and so on. This chapter examines a number of techniques for fine-tuning your communications skills so that you can become a refined listener—that is, one who hears more than just the words on the surface. The following exercise will help you assess your current listening habits.

Exercise: How Well Do You Listen?*

Rate yourself as a listener by answering the questions below. There are no correct or incorrect answers. Your responses, however, will extend your understanding of yourself as a listener and highlight areas in which improvement might be welcome—to you and to those around you. When you've completed the exercise, read the Profile Analysis to see how your scores compare with those of thousands of others who've taken the same test before you.

1. Circle the term that best describes you as a listener. (Quality of listening includes some of the skills described in Chapter 7: empathy, congruence, lack of defensiveness, not evaluating or judging the other person.)

Superior	Below average
Excellent	Poor
Above average	Terrible
Average	

2. On a scale of 0 to 100 (100 = highest), how would you rate yourself as a listener? _____

*Exercise by Elaina Zuker, reprinted with permission from THE EXECUTIVE FEMALE, a bimonthly magazine published by and distributed exclusively to members of the National Association for Female Executives, 120 East 56th Street, Suite 1440, New York, NY 10022 (212) 371-0740.

3. How do you think the following people would rate you as a listener? (0 to 100)

Your best friend	_____	A subordinate	_____
Your boss	_____	Your spouse	_____
A business colleague	_____		

4. As a listener, how often do you find yourself engaging in these 10 bad listening habits? First, check the appropriate columns. Then tabulate your score using the key below.

Profile Analysis

This is how other people responded to the same questions that you've just answered.

1. Eighty-five percent of all listeners questioned rated themselves as *average* or *less*. Fewer than 5 percent rate themselves as *superior* or *excellent*.
2. On the 0–100 scale, the extreme range is 0–90; the general range is 35–85; and the *average* rating is 55.
3. When comparing the listening self-ratings and projected ratings of others, most respondents believe that their best friend would rate them highest as a listener. And that rating would be higher than the one they gave themselves, where the average was a 55.

   How come? Apparently, best-friend status is such an intimate, special kind of relationship that you couldn't imagine it ever happening unless you *were* a good listener. If you weren't, you and he or she wouldn't be best friends to begin with.

   Going down the list, people who take this test usually think their bosses would rate them higher than they rated themselves. Now part of that is probably wishful thinking. And part of it is true. We *do* tend to listen to our bosses better—whether it's out of respect or fear or whatever doesn't matter.

   The grades for colleague and subordinate work out to be just about the same as the average for all test-takers—that 55 figure again.

   But when we get to spouse—husband or wife—something really dramatic happens. The score here is significantly lower than the 55 average that test-takers gave themselves. And what's interesting is that the figure goes steadily downhill. While newlyweds tend to rate their spouse at the same high level as their best friend, as the marriage goes on, and on, the rating falls. So in a household where the couple has been married 50 years, there could be a lot of talk. But maybe nobody is *really* listening.
4. The average score is 62—7 points higher than the average figure for all test-takers. This suggests that when listening is broken down into specific areas of competence, we rate ourselves better than we do when listening is considered only as a generality. Of course, the best way to discover how well you listen is to ask the people to whom you listen most frequently (your spouse, boss, best friend, and so on). They'll give you an earful.

Frequency

Listening Habit	Almost Always	Usually	Sometimes	Seldom	Almost Never	Score
1. Calling the subject uninteresting						
2. Criticizing the speaker's delivery or mannerisms						
3. Getting overstimulated by something the speaker says						
4. Listening primarily for facts						
5. Trying to outline everything						
6. Faking attention to the speaker						
7. Allowing interfering distractions						
8. Avoiding difficult material						
9. Letting emotion-laden words arouse personal antagonism						
10. Wasting the advantage of thought speed (daydreaming)						

Total Score _____

Key:
For every "Almost Always" checked, give yourself a score of 2.
For every "Usually" checked, give yourself a score of 4.
For every "Sometimes" checked, give yourself a score of 6.
For every "Seldom" checked, give yourself a score of 8.
For every "Almost Never" checked, give yourself a score of 10.

THE ART OF LISTENING

In the work environment, you are called upon to listen countless times a day. A colleague stops into your office, and you interrupt your train of thought for a few minutes to hear her describe a concert she attended the evening before. An employee comes to you with a conflict he is having with a co-worker. A colleague confides in you, over lunch, about a personal problem. At a staff meeting, your boss describes some long-range goals for the department over the next two years and asks you to be part of the team that will help realize those goals. In all these situations, you are being asked to really *be* with the other person. You are being asked to listen.

Most of us worry a lot about giving speeches, making presentations, giving performance evaluations, running meetings—occasions when we'll have to be the speaker. We fret about our notes, the order in which we'll say our piece, how we'll handle questions, and how we'll close. However, when we really think about it—and according to managers in different organizations all over the country—*listening* is the most difficult task in the communications process.

The Japanese symbol for "listen" is made up of the character for "ear" placed within the character for "gate." In effect, we enter into the other person's gate or world. We might have to sacrifice a bit of ourselves to do so. We certainly need a lot of inner security to truly listen to and understand another person.

Barriers to Listening

No one is a naturally good listener—it takes work. As ideas and information travel through the organization, they get distorted by as much as 80 percent. Even information between two people gets distorted and misinterpreted. Part of the problem is that we speak at the rate of 150–160 words per minute, but we think at a rate of 650–700 words per minute. Unless we make a real effort, then, our minds will wander when we are listening to others speak.

Many of our listening problems can be attributed to lack of training. We simply have not been taught how to listen and have developed poor listening habits. For example, we may approach other people with a closed mind or a preconceived idea of what they're going to say. Or we may jump to conclusions, filling in the blanks with our own ideas. Sometimes, too, we make the mistake of listening only for facts, tuning out body language and other subtle forms of communication. Table 5 lists some typical barriers to effective listening and ways in which they can be overcome.

Improving Your Listening Skills

Refined listening involves understanding the meaning of the speaker's total message—the context as well as the content. Principles of good listen-

Table 5. Typical barriers to effective listening.

Barrier	Solution
During a meeting, you take extensive notes. Your motto is, "There's no substitute for documentation." Besides, it gives you something to do during boring meetings and makes you appear interested.	Note taking may be necessary, but it can also be a distraction to the speaker. A written record of a meeting does not necessarily mean you understood what was said. If you are an obsessive note taker, learn to write less and listen more. Faking attentiveness does not work. If that is your motive for scratching out every spoken word, find a more genuine way to look interested.
You finish sentences for the person speaking to you.	Predicting or anticipating is caused by impatience and lack of sensitivity. Under the guise of understanding what the speaker is discussing, you help him or her along. Interrupting, no matter what the intention, has the appearance of rudeness. Focus on listening, not talking.
To save time, you hold an employee meeting while you are waiting for your secretary to put through a phone call.	When the call comes through, it will be a distraction. In this type of environment, neither interaction will be productive. If the speaker wants to talk about anything requiring your full attention, he or she will wait or find another listener. The executive who appears harried, no matter how much she wants to have a positive impact on her staff, will isolate herself if she does not fight distractions.
If a supervisor hands you a resignation two weeks before a production deadline, you scream and beg until you get her commitment to finish the job.	Once you make the atmosphere emotional, listening becomes very difficult. It is impossible to concentrate on delicate issues like employee dissatisfaction when you are expressing outrage. Be particularly aware of certain words that trigger an emotional reaction in you.
At a business presentation, if the subject is uninteresting, you use the time more constructively by secretly doing paperwork.	A good listener assumes the role of staying interested. There is always something to be learned if you are open to it. Your time and the speaker's would be better spent if you concentrated on the program. If you can't, leave.

ing include (1) having an open mind, (2) developing a habit of give and take, (3) listening from the speaker's frame of reference, and (4) staying with the communication at hand—not wandering into the past or daydreaming about the future. To be a refined listener, you must listen to what is being said and how it is being said, paying attention to both the verbal and nonverbal portions of a message. Looking for the sender's cues will give you a better understanding of what is really being communicated.

The Sperry Corporation considers the art of listening so important to its corporate health that it has embarked on a massive advertising and publicity campaign to stress the value of listening. The company has developed a personal listening profile for its employees that stresses ten keys to effective listening. (See Table 6.)

A good first step toward developing refined listening habits is to concentrate when you're in the listening role. Remember to *be curious*. There is always something you can learn by hearing the other person out. Listen until you get the big picture—the entire meaning—so that you can place the message in its appropriate context.

The goal of refined listening is to become attuned to other people so that you can "package" your communications in sophisticated and subtle ways that give others the feeling that you are in harmony with them. Most people offer very rich clues about where they are coming from and where they stand. The more you can learn about the person you are communicating with, the more on target you will be as a communicator. Your assertive messages will then be clear and precise and will give you the highest probability of getting the results you want. The following sections examine several new areas of research into learning and communication that can help you acquire refined listening skills.

MENTAL SETS

Each half of the brain is responsible for a different kind of learning and information processing. All of us use both sides of the brain, but we each have a favored, or dominant, side.

People who favor the left side of the brain approach the world intellectually. They use words to make sense of their experiences, are objective and logical, and think sequentially. Many of them are good administrators, good systems people, and good planners. People who favor the right side of the brain are more intuitive and spontaneous. They think in images, tend to see the larger picture, and are more subjective than objective. Often they are artists or entrepreneurs—people who have a creative, spontaneous approach to life.

Once you tune in to people's mental orientation, you will be able to adjust your communication to suit their world view, their frame of refer-

Table 6. Ten keys to effective listening.

Keys	The Bad Listener	The Good Listener
Find areas of interest.	Tunes out dry subjects.	Seeks opportunities; asks "what's in it for me?"
Judge content, not delivery.	Tunes out if delivery is poor.	Judges content, skips over delivery errors.
Hold your fire.	Tends to enter into argument.	Doesn't judge until comprehension is complete.
Listen for ideas.	Listens for facts.	Listens for central themes.
Be flexible.	Takes intensive notes, using only one system.	Takes fewer notes. Uses four or five different systems, depending on speaker.
Work at listening.	Shows no energy output. Attention is faked.	Works hard; exhibits active body state.
Resist distractions.	Is distracted easily.	Fights or avoids distractions, tolerates bad habits, knows how to concentrate.
Exercise your mind.	Resists difficult expository material; seeks light, recreational material.	Uses heavier material as exercise for the mind.
Keep your mind open.	Reacts to emotional words.	Interprets color words; does not get hung up on them.
Capitalize on fact that *thought* is faster than speech.	Tends to daydream with slow speakers.	Challenges, anticipates, mentally summarizes, weighs the evidence, listens between the lines to tone of voice.

Reprinted from materials developed by Dr. Lyman K. Steil, Department of Rhetoric, University of Minnesota, and Communication Development, Inc., for Sperry Corporation. Copyright 1979. Used by permission of Dr. Steil and Sperry Corporation.

ence. For example, for the intellectual type, you might describe a project in its logical sequence, listing the reasons it would work and focusing on verbal, logical communication. For the creative type, you would be wiser to draw images or pictures, appeal to intuition and emotions, and talk about the exitement that would result from the success of the project. Even though the same project is being described, in each case you are "packaging" your description to suit the other person's frame of reference. This alone gives you an edge.

It is not always easy to figure out a person's mental set. You will have to run a few small experiments to determine which type of communication a person is responsive to. If someone gives you signals of boredom when you describe the logistics of a project, you may be dealing with a creative, intuitive type who won't tune in or become enthusiastic until you literally draw a picture of the project. With practice, you can sharpen this skill into an art.

LEARNING STYLES

When you are trying to communicate your point of view to others, you are really engaging in a teaching process. How can you educate people in your point of view when they have their own way of seeing things? Usually, the problem has little to do with the substance of what you're saying or even with the logic of your arguments. Much more often, it has to do with how an individual approaches the entire learning process. Several learning styles have been identified.

Innovative Learners

Innovative learners learn by speaking, listening, brainstorming, interacting, forming dichotomies, and making up unusual combinations. They go beyond the expected or the usual. They usually ask, "Why?" In communicating with innovative learners, you should present material that involves them, that allows them to interact and to play with possibilities and creative solutions.

Analytic Learners

Analytic learners are observers. They analyze, classify, and draw conclusions. They examine dichotomies and try to figure things out. They usually ask "What?" They want to know the facts. When communicating with this type of person, you can create a good deal of rapport by demonstrating the logic of a certain course of action.

Commonsense Learners

Commonsense learners are similar to analytic learners, but they take a more active experimental stance. They work with abstract concepts, experimenting, building on givens, trying either of two possible alternatives. They usually ask, "How does this work?" With such people, you would do well to present an experimental challenge, since they prefer to explore possibilities rather than to have solutions all wrapped up neatly.

THE BUREAUCRATIC FIRST AID KIT

If you hear "It can't be done" and the person really means . . .	*Do this:*
I don't know how to do it.	Teach the person how.
I don't understand it.	Relate it to something that is already known.
I don't see the value of doing it.	Describe the payoff.
I can't afford to do it (time, money, or risk).	Figure out how to save time, lower cost, or reduce risk.
I'm not allowed to do it.	Find a loophole or offer help in getting approval.
I don't want to do it.	Demonstrate the hidden advantages.

Dynamic Learners

Dynamic learners focus on results—and they follow through. They usually check out the applications of an idea by testing it in reality. They try to resolve dichotomies. They often ask, "What can this become?" "How does this apply?" and "What can I do?" For such people, a smart communicator will present information that answers these questions.

PERSONALITY TYPES

Although everyone is unique, there are basic personality types that can give you clues about how to package your communications. One of the big distinctions is whether a person is task-oriented or people-oriented.

Task-oriented people are quite formal. They control their emotions and focus on the job at hand. In some cases, their concern with technical details, accuracy, and the accomplishment of the task makes it seem as if they are indifferent to the feelings or needs of people around them. *People-oriented* types are more casual and allow their emotions to show. In extreme cases, their concern with finding out how you feel as well as letting you know how they feel makes it seem as if they are interested more in friendly conversation than in business or the task at hand.

There are further refinements within these two groups. Task-oriented people may be concerned with details or concerned with results. People-oriented types may be harmony seekers or excitement seekers.

Details Seekers

Details seekers focus on the details and procedures involved in accomplishing the task. They want to be sure they understand all the fine points before they act. They will usually want to talk through the details and have you assure them that they are correct before they go ahead. They are likely to put off decisions while they gather more information on which to make their choice. The stereotype of the tidy accountant is an extreme example of this type.

In communicating with details seekers, you should establish your concern for accuracy, since this will be one of their prime concerns. If you don't, they may not trust your advice or recommendations. When presenting an idea or a project to details seekers, make sure they feel secure about all the fine points and understand how the parts fit together. Finally, assure them that they have plenty of information, so that they do not try to delay making a decision.

Results Seekers

Results seekers focus on getting the job done so that they can move on to other tasks. They are less concerned with details and procedures than with obstacles that might prevent them from achieving their goals. Typically, they seek just enough information to get the big picture and then quickly decide whether they want to go ahead. Such people think of themselves as organized and efficient in using their time and expect others to be the same way. They don't want to get bogged down in details and are usually willing to take on responsibilities and make quick decisions. The stereotype of the tough corporate executive is based on the extreme characteristics of this type.

It is usually a good idea to be brief with results seekers, since they are rarely interested in details. When they are presented with something different or something that requires taking in a lot of detail, they will often refuse the project outright, because of their disdain for ambiguity and indecision. Often their posture is, "Any decision is better than no decision." In this case, an effective tactic is to demonstrate how the suggested project can contribute to their primary goal.

Harmony Seekers

Harmony seekers focus on interpersonal relationships. They are usually very sensitive to how others feel. Often reluctant to make decisions for fear of offending or upsetting others, they want to "touch bases" with everyone who might be affected by a decision before they go ahead. And they often prefer to maintain the status quo, to keep things as they are rather than take an initiative that might cause social unpleasantness. The stereotype of the shy assistant working behind the scenes is based on the extreme character-istics of this type.

When communicating with harmony seekers, keep in mind their need to maintain pleasant relationships and their fear of rocking the boat. Also, since they often have trouble seeing the forest for the trees, you may have to ask probing questions to find out their goals. You should be patient and thor-ough and show that what you are presenting or recommending is not very different from what is already happening—simply that it is better and/or more of the same.

Excitement Seekers

Excitement seekers focus on the excitement generated by people interact-ing. They are usually quite free to display their own emotions and lend a dramatic backdrop to the situations. Such people may seem self-centered when they tell you of all the exciting and dramatic things they have done or of the famous and successful people they know. But they can also be in-spiring when they get excited about the great things that are about to hap-pen. They are not overly concerned with details or even with task accom-plishment as such; they are usually much more concerned with the personal and social consequences of an action. And if they perceive that an action, an activity, or a project can lead to personal praise or can give their friends pleasure, they are usually quick to act. The stereotype of the gregarious, dramatic politician personifies the excitement seeker.

When you are presenting something to an excitement seeker, emphasize the newness and the exciting personal benefits. Excitement seekers like the idea of being innovators, pioneers, the "first on the block." Don't bog them down in details or intricate logical explanations. They are much more likely to be interested in the groundbreaking aspects of a project than in the spe-cific details.

SENSORY CHANNELS

Another useful system of categorization focuses on the sensory channels people use to process information. Taken from a new field of research called neurolinguistic programming (NLP), it is based on the work of John Grinder, a linguist, and Richard Bandler, a therapist. They began to observe skilled, intuitive communicators who were able to achieve rapport and high-quality communications and attempted to determine *how* this was done. Bandler and Grinder developed a set of formulas, a coding system, of how a person takes in sensory impressions, mentally organizes them in processes like memory and decision making, and then translates the sequence into a response. Bas-ically, they concluded that skilled communicators have a flexible repertoire of communications behaviors, based on the characteristics of the people they are communicating with.

Underlying Bandler and Grinder's theory is the assumption that people rely on one of their sensory channels more of the time than any of the others to interpret their experiences. The five sensory channels are visual (sight), auditory (sound), kinesthetic (touch), olfactory (smell), and gustatory (taste). In our culture, the first three are the most common. That is, some people experience life as a series of pictures (either photographs or movies). Others take in life through sounds, either those they remember or those created by their thought processes. Still others experience life primarily through touching and other bodily sensations.

According to Bandler and Grinder, people send out valuable clues about which system they are using most. Once you know what the system is, you can fine-tune your communication so that it comes to the person directly in the channel in which he or she is most comfortable. One way of detecting these clues is by following a person's eye movements. You can test this out by asking people an open-ended question, such as "What do you recall about the last office you occupied?" Then just watch to see where their eyes go.

If their eyes move *up and to the left*—visual memory—they are probably visually recalling a memory they already have. If the eyes move *up and to the right*—visual construction—they are usually creating a picture of something they have not yet experienced. If the eyes move from *side to side,* people are often going inside and listening to their own internal voices or to the voices of other people. If the eyes move *down and to the right or left,* people are usually sensing how the body feels and are in the kinesthetic mode.

When people just *stare ahead,* they may be recalling something in the visual realm or may simply be processing what they have already heard. Many times when we observe people staring ahead, their eyes not focused on us, we conclude that they are bored or not listening. In fact, often what they are doing is trying to make sense of what they've just heard so they can go on. Instead of barreling ahead, we would be wise to pause, let them process the information, and then continue.

Another way to tell what sensory channel people are using is by the language they use. A visual person will use phrases like "That's the way I see it," "It seems clear to me," "Let's watch this carefully," "I'm getting a vision of how this could work," or "Let's look at this from another perspective." An auditory person will use language like "I hear what you're saying," "That rings a bell," or "It doesn't sound right to me." Someone who is kinesthetic will use physical images: "I'm getting a firm grasp on the situation," "Whenever the new policy takes hold," "We seem to be moving in the right direction," "It just feels right to me," or "Now you're getting a handle on it."

You can go a long way toward achieving rapport with people if you watch and listen for these subtle clues about their sensory orientation. You can never be 100 percent sure, of course, but you can make calculated guesses and then experiment. If you know that someone is visual, for example, you can put your communication in that frame of reference: "Do you see what I mean?" "Is this still hazy, or is it becoming more focused?" You also establish rapport quickly by watching eye movements and then talking to a person in the preferred system.

After you have practiced this a few times, you'll find it becoming quite natural and automatic. You'll be *noticing* much more about people, and you'll find that your communication is more in tune with the other person's.

9

The Assertive Body

You can't judge a book by its cover. Or can you? After all, publishers spend a lot of time and money designing book jackets. Jacket design is a complex art. The front of the jacket must capture the potential reader's attention through graphic design and typography. The spine must convey specific information about author, title, and publisher. The back of the jacket usually sells the book with catchy phrases and testimonials. The flyleaf summarizes the book without saying too much. Covers do give us information.

READING OTHER PEOPLE

People, too, come packaged. A person's cover gives us clues about what is going on inside. Of course, people are dynamic and constantly changing, so the information they give us may be valid for only a short time.

Suppose you are driving along in stop-and-go traffic. The driver in the car next to you is darting forward and jamming on the brakes at every opportunity. Looking over, you see that he is gripping the steering wheel so hard that his knuckles have turned white. His facial muscles are tense and he's yelling and gesturing to no one in particular. Periodically, he frees one hand from the wheel to knead the back of his neck. With these visual clues, would you describe this man as (1) happy-go-lucky, (2) rational and deliberate, or (3) frustrated and angry? Most of us would recognize the signs of an agitated driver and keep our distance.

First Impressions: Image

When you first meet someone, you can tell a lot by his or her appearance, body language, and use of space. Does the person appear neat, clean, and healthy? Are his clothes appropriate to his surroundings? What message is his appearance giving you about how he regards himself?

What about the person's posture? Is her body held erect, or is it slumped over? Do her gestures signal nervousness, anger, or confidence? Does she move with authority? Is she confident in her "territory"? Or does she act suspicious and apprehensive? Does her office tell you what she thinks about her career?

Open the Cover: Style

Every successful author has a style that pleases a particular group of readers. (There are also bad writers who have just not mastered the craft and seem to please no one.) When you get beneath appearances with people, you begin to see their style—their beliefs, values, and approaches to working with others. A co-worker may seem competitive, negative, dependent, or emotional. A friend may be incurably romantic, fearful, domineering, or manipulative. That's part of the person's style.

Reading a person involves learning to look at both image and style. Sometimes the message is quite straightforward. But when the image a person projects is in conflict with his or her essential style, serious misunderstandings can result.

HOW DO WE COMMUNICATE?

In business, as elsewhere, our words are the least of what we say. It has been estimated that we communicate with our body 60 percent of the time; with our voice (tone, timbre, and so on) 30 percent of the time; and with words only 10 percent of the time.* Recent studies have shown that nonverbal messages account for as much as 90 percent of the impact of a total communication. This means that whatever the verbal message, the language of the body—gestures, facial expression, voice, posture, use of space, and eye contact—will have a powerful, and unconscious, effect on the other person.

Think of a time when you were talking to someone and the words or concepts that were conveyed made sense, or seemed to be in your interest, but something just didn't *feel* right. You were probably responding to the person's nonverbal messages. There may have been some incongruence between the words and gestures that the other person was communicating. And because nonverbal signals have such a powerful impact on the total communication, your net impression was that conveyed by the nonverbal messages.

There are many good books on the market that describe what gestures and other forms of body language convey about a person's attitude toward closeness, intimacy, and personal relationships. Here we are concerned with

---

*Ken Cooper, *Nonverbal Communication for Business Success* (New York: AMACOM, 1981).

how body language relates to assertive, aggressive, and nonassertive communication. We will also look at what body language conveys about status, power, dominance, equality, rapport, and harmony.

Nonverbal Messages

We are often completely unaware of our nonverbal behavior and of the effect it has on others. Mike, a young data processing manager, was the leader of a team project. When he saw a videotape of one of the team's meetings, he was shocked to see himself shaking his finger at the group, sitting with his hands folded when other people were talking, and scowling when he wasn't the center of attention. At the close of the session there was almost open rebellion—people didn't want to adopt any of his suggestions. Yet Mike had been certain that he had the group's support as leader. If he had been more self-aware, he might have modified his style, been a better listener, made his contributions slowly, tried to gain consensus as he went along, and ultimately come out with the results he wanted *and* the support of the group. His bold, intrusive, insensitive body language alienated people right from the start. Even though his ideas were excellent, people didn't want them shoved down their throats.

Now let's look at the opposite extreme: nonassertive body language. Julian, a bright engineer and the newcomer in the department, never said a word at departmental meetings. Even when people said things that he knew were inaccurate or infeasible, he was afraid to disagree. As time went on, he did try to open up and speak out, but he was all crouched into his chin, and when he spoke he barely opened his mouth. He never made eye contact with people, looking instead at his notes and papers. And he would preface every statement or opinion with, "I'm not sure about this" and "I don't have all the data in, but I wanted to find out what you people thought." His words and body language communicated very clearly that he was not feeling very confident about what he had to say.

What are some of the nonverbal messages you're sending? What impression do you convey to others? And how can you overcome aggressive or nonassertive patterns so that you will come across more assertively? Effective communication involves (1) learning how to read the messages another person is sending, by deciphering all forms of nonverbal communication that accompany the actual words and responding to the whole message; and (2) being able to send assertive messages in which your verbal and nonverbal cues are in harmony.

Body Language "Language"

Before reading any further you should become familiar with some of the terms used in nonverbal communication. Here are definitions for five frequently used terms.

o *Body language* —the ways in which the physical self communicates, often unconsciously, through gesture, facial expression, body movement.

o *Kinesics* —the study of physical movements and their relationship to communication.

o *Congruence* —when a person's verbal and nonverbal messages say the same thing.

o *Synchrony* —when one person begins to mirror the movements and gestures of another to show agreement or acceptance, or to seek rapport.

o *Territorial space* —the space a person occupies; distance from other people.

Deciphering Nonverbal Communication

It will be helpful in your management career to become familiar with four ways in which people routinely pass on information without using words.

1. *Body language* can tell you a great deal about the person you are negotiating with. If your colleague has his foot on your desk top, if an interviewer has her legs crossed in a figure 4, or if someone you are trying to impress gives you a blank stare, you are being sent important nonverbal messages.

2. There's more information to be found in a person's *voice* —volume, pitch, and resonance—than in the words themselves.

3. Learning how to deal with *territorial space* can help you plan a successful meeting.

4. Take an inventory of a client's *personal effects* —clothing, mementos, office decor—for an idea of the image that person wants to project. Chances are, your client wants to be perceived in that way too.

Before we examine these nonverbal signals, a word of caution is in order. All interpretations of body gestures and movements should be preceded by a qualifier such as "frequently" or "usually." Kinesics is not an exact science, and many uncontrollable variables are involved. A headache may affect posture, for instance. If your client is sitting forward in her chair, you may think she is very interested in what you are saying, when in fact her posture is signaling discomfort and a desire to end the meeting.

No single gesture or movement is the whole message. You are trying to piece together a communications puzzle, so you'll need the main frame in place before you can feel sure of proceeding. Look for clusters of congruent signals. If you get on a bus and the driver speaks very abruptly, you might suspect that he is angry. If his hands are clenched in fists and his breathing is shallow, you can add these two observations to the first and have a cluster of three signals that reinforce the conclusion that he is an angry bus driver.

BODY SIGNALS

The Center

A good place to begin observing the body is a place called the center. It's an imaginary point on the chest at about breastbone level, a vulnerable spot. (If you were wearing a bulletproof vest, it would cover your center.) You lead with your center. It is the most obvious signal of your overall attitude.

Look around you and observe how people are dealing with their centers. Some people not only will expose the center but will aggressively display it like a drill sergeant. A depressed person will slump so that the center is concave. Some people cover the center entirely in a way that indicates, "I am closed off to you." The boss who sits behind his desk with jacket buttoned tightly and arms crossed on his chest while telling you, "I am happy to hear your proposal, Miss Swain," is sending two messages. The second, more powerful message is, "You might as well forget it."

The Head

There are many facets to decoding the messages contained about the head. The individual parts, such as eyebrows and mouth, can convey attitude; the position of the head, whether tilted or rigidly upright, can reflect mood; and the facial expressions can give insight into emotions.

The eyes are particularly expressive. Sometimes, when you think you have successfully masked a feeling—say, the disapproval you felt when a friend told a lie—a twitch of an eyebrow can blow your cover. Think of how many phrases in English make reference to the eyes: shifty-eyed, hawk-eyed, eyeball to eyeball, dead-eyed dick, bedroom eyes. When a camera pans a room and then zooms in on something, it sets the focus of the scene. Making eye contact with another person sets the stage for interaction.

People tend to make eye contact more frequently when they are listening than when they are speaking. There is an etiquette to eye contact, and you would be wise to adhere to it. When you first meet another person, give a quick glance, and then look away. This gives the other person a chance to look you over. To continue to stare would be to invade the person's personal space, and is considered "immoral looking time." That long gaze directed at a romantic interest might be interpreted as a sign of appreciation, but directed at a client it can be taken as a challenge. If your client is uncomfortable and feels invaded, your meeting is off to a bad start. By carefully observing the response your level of eye contact receives, you'll be able to gauge how much eye contact you should use to instill trust and communicate interest.

Movements that bring the hand to the face are worth studying. When people cover their mouth while speaking, they are usually indicating that they are not entirely convinced of what they are saying. Another gesture of uncertainty is touching the nose. One veteran negotiator noticed that his opponent touched his nose whenever he was considering or discussing a proposal, but took his hand away from his face when he was ready to settle.*

Reading body gestures is important for timing. The salesman who can read a client's body language knows when to close the deal. The interviewer who can tell when the prospective employee is feeling favorable knows it is time to make an offer. A common and universally offensive faux pas is interrupting people when they have not finished what they started out to say. A skilled communicator can read the flags another person is holding up to indicate "I wish to speak," "Your turn to speak." When someone wants to speak, he assumes a speaking position. He may actually stand or merely draw up in height. Characteristically, he will lean forward or otherwise dominate the space in front of him. When the speaker has finished a series of thoughts, the pitch of his voice will drop and his body will recede from the dominant speaker's position, relinquishing the floor.

What does your face look like when it is relaxed? You may think it has no expression, but downturned mouth, droopy eyelids, laugh lines around the eyes may give you a sad, disinterested, or elated look whether you intend it or not. A mustache may give the mouth a negative look by pointing the edges of a man's mouth downward.

Look at your head in the mirror. Draw your neck up and throw it back. Do you feel more powerful? Now drop it forward slightly and look down. Do you still feel aggressive? No, now you're in a depressed or defeated posture. Tilt your head to the side and you'll show interest. Rest it heavily in a cupped hand and you'll tell others that you're about to tune out. As you speak, look at the head positions of others for an indication of how your message is being received.

People incline quite literally toward things that attract them and withdraw from things they dislike. The TV commercial for the E. F. Hutton brokerage firm ("When E. F. Hutton talks . . .") make this point graphically. If you are making a proposal and you notice someone leaning back or stepping away from you, be aware that the person is feeling negative about your proposal. Find a way to rekindle your subject's interest.

Posture

Body posture may reveal how someone feels in general. If you know someone who gets headaches frequently, you can visualize the brittle way he holds his head when it hurts. When it is obvious that a person does not

---

*See Gerard I. Nierenberg and Henry H. Calero, *How to Read a Person Like a Book* (St. Louis: Cornerstone, 1972).

feel well, postpone discussions that will lead to decisions. Sometimes timing is more important than content.

Your own body posture is an immediate sign to those around you of how you regard yourself. Standing "tall in the saddle" conveys a leadership image; shifting your weight to one foot and clutching at one arm signals uncertainty.

Hands and Feet

Both hands and feet make open and closed statements. The open palm is offered in friendly greeting; the closed fist is extended aggressively. Two feet on the floor signify readiness to agree; feet crossed in a figure 4 position indicate disagreement.

Synchrony sometimes happens unconsciously when parties find themselves in agreement. At other times, it can be used as a tool for developing empathy with a client. By "putting yourself in someone else's shoes," you begin to feel what that person is feeling. If you lean back in your chair and stretch out your legs, as your boss is doing, you begin to feel relaxed—the conversation is going well. If you are tugging at the back of your neck, just like your administrative assistant, you'll begin to feel the stress that she is feeling.

As you begin to catch on to body language, become more aware of the signals your own body is sending. Try to make the most of signals that enhance your assertive management skills. Train yourself away from gestures that suggest weakness or negative traits. Table 7 lists some typical body signals associated with attitude. Keep in mind, once again, that these are generalizations, and that you should look for clusters of congruent signals in the person you're communicating with before you draw any conclusions.

VOICE CLUES

When someone speaks, you get messages not only from the words but also from the tone of voice, inflection, volume, variety, and timing of the delivery.

Tone

A woman was walking along a crowded street with a young child who was coughing. The mother barked authoritatively, "Cover your mouth." Two passers-by responded to this parental command from childhood and instinctively covered their mouths.

The game "Simon Says" is based on the premise that the brain responds to tone of voice at the same time that (if not sooner than) it responds to meaning. So one must work hard to separate the tone of the game's commands from the actual words being said.

Table 7. Attitude and body signals.

Attitude	Center	Facial Expression	Typical Body Signal Gestures	Posture
Disapproval.	Closed.	Frown.	Finger under nose; eyes narrowed; head shaking; hidden fists; arms crossed on chest.	Tense crossed legs; figure 4 crossed legs; kicking.
Readiness to make a decision.	Open.	Expectant.	Hands stop tugging at clothes; both feet on floor; arms spread; hands on hips.	Sitting erect, on edge of chair.
Desire to terminate conversation.	Partially turned away; feet facing exit.	Mild interest.	Wiping hands together; pat on head; handshake; looking at watch.	Looking away.
Boredom.	Closed.	Blank, droopy eyes.	Drumming on table; foot tapping.	Head in palm of hand.
Lack of understanding.	Turned in.	Quizzical.	Furrowed brow; blank eyes; foot tapping.	Stooped or slumped.
Confidence.	Open, aggressive.	Excitement.	Greater eye contact; feet on desk; steepling fingers; space grabbing; chin thrust out.	Erect, arms behind back, shoulders squared.
Suspicion.	Turned away; feet point to exit.	Scowl.	Nose touching; folded arms; crossed legs; tilted head; eye rubbing; squinting.	Leaning back.
Desire to speak.	Extended to listener.	Nodding.	Tugging at ear; touching arm of other person.	Leaning forward.
Nervousness.	Turned away.	Tense.	Coin jingling; throat clearing; whistling; hand covering mouth; closed hands; neck rubbing; running fingers through hair.	Crossed arms, crossed legs.

Voice can go a long way toward making a presentation effective. A friend recalled a college chaplain who preached too frequently. Students remarked that "he said nothing, but he said it so well." How did he manage that? Well, first, he had wonderful diction. He stood elegantly, lending authority to his words. His gestures kept his delivery varied and visually interesting. His eye contact was superb. His tone ran the gamut of emotion. And his mood ranged from intimate to universal. The fact that, in the end, he had said very little was easy to overlook.

Inflection

Inflection can change the meaning of a single word. Someone walks into a room and says the word "so." Depending on inflection, three different meanings can be conveyed:

> "So?" (defiance—"So what, try and make me!")
> "So—" (transition—"What happens next?")
> "So!" (discovery—"Oh, that's it!")

In the first instance, the "so" sounds aggressive and challenging; in the second, questioning; in the third, surprised and delighted.

Volume

If someone is speaking too loudly, listeners will involuntarily retreat by taking a step backward or tilting the head back. Be aware of how people respond to your voice level. People who are too loud are trying to dominate the conversation or the entire meeting. Rather than make their point, they antagonize other participants.

Variety

Like singers, speakers can be trained in voice. With exercises and feedback you can develop a more interesting speaking manner. By varying pitch, resonance, tempo, and volume, you can make yourself seem confidential, authoritative, entertaining, or persuasive. Develop an ear for speech by analyzing the voice patterns of announcers for TV commercials. Robert Young's "professional" plug for decaffeinated coffee and Crazy Eddie's "huckster" hype for electronic gadgets suggest the range of possibilities.

Timing

Be aware of the tempo and timing of your sentences and phrases. Speaking too quickly will cause you to gobble up words and dilute your meanings. If you drag out your sentences, your listener might become bored or uninterested. It's also important to be sensitive to the timing or pacing of your listener or group, and to pace yourself accordingly. If you speak quickly like a New Yorker, you might have to slow down if you're meeting with someone from Texas or Louisiana. And if you're from the South or Midwest and visiting Boston, you might want to study Yankee speech rhythms if you have to make a presentation. Of course, you can't completely transform your speaking patterns whenever you speak to people from a different part of the country, or another country. However, it is helpful to be aware of the differences, so that you can tune in to others.

TIPS FOR IMPROVING YOUR SPEAKING VOICE

1. Buy a cassette recorder and tape your voice in different situations—under stress, giving directions, arguing, talking on the telephone. Decide what areas need work and use the recorder to practice.

2. Ask a friend for a second opinion. Your friend can also help you overcome bad habits by calling them to your attention when they occur. Sloppy speech habits—such as repeating "you know," stammering or falling over words, rushing your delivery, and clearing your throat—make you seem nervous and weaken your credibility.

3. Enroll in a speech class to gain poise and learn techniques for calming down or projecting your voice. Try to find a speech center that uses videotape playback. This can be invaluable for getting an image of yourself performing. You'll be able to develop good podium habits such as keeping papers quiet, not rocking or swaying, and using body language to punctuate your speech.

4. Make eye contact with the audience during your speech. Move from individual to individual as you make your points so that you can get feedback. If people are looking blank, you may have to change your tack. In the Broadway play *Mass Appeal* the preacher gives the young colleague this advice on addressing the congregation: "If they start coughing you're in trouble, and if they start dropping hymnals, you're finished." It's important to sense when your audience is starting to drift away. You *can* win people back with effective voice techniques.

TERRITORIAL SPACE

People claim air rights. Invisible antennae stretch 18 inches around our bodies and define our "intimate space." When someone invades this bubble of space, alarms go off. We feel threatened and angry and want to bolt. And in a business discussion, that is exactly how you do *not* want others to feel. Some crowding gestures that annoy people are back slapping, talking too loudly or too close to them, and jabbing at them with a finger or a cigar. Police invade intimate space when they question a suspect. All are attempts to dominate. Unless you are in a win/lose situation with someone, this is not a good way to do business.

A wider circle, two to four feet, defines our "personal space." This is comfortable dinner-table distance. "Social space," four to seven feet, is the usual desk-to-visitor distance for office conversations. Be aware of these markings so you can tell if someone is trying to invade your space, or if you might be crowding someone unduly.

Space Is Power

Office conflicts often develop over space. Just sit down at the conference table and spread out your papers. When the person next to you does the same thing, the "overlapping papers" scenario will begin. One infringes on the other's space; the other retaliates. Conflict heightens as space diminishes. If you're trying to bring an issue to a resolution, put the principals in a small room. Negotiation will move along more quickly.

Space Is Visibility

Tall or very large people gain more territorial space and are more noticeable because of their size. Take a cue from this and make yourself more visible. Choose a larger chair. Take a position of importance in the room. Emphasize your strengths so that you become known as the best at something—the best joke teller, the sharpest dresser, the most creative planner. Be careful of confrontations that belittle you, for when you lose size, you lose power. It's easy to lose when you are late, unprepared, apologetic, or intimidated. Keep up! Assertive managers lead. They lead with ideas, initiate conversations, open doors, walk at the head of the pack.

Handling Space at Meetings

Meetings are the key arena where office power is traded or wrested away. The strategies of the boardroom are essential for the assertive manager.

1. The best place to hold a meeting is in your own territory. The next best is neutral territory, such as a restaurant or conference room. The least favorable place is someone else's office. You must take control, and keep control, even in your own office.

2. Know the pattern of dominant/subordinate positions around the conference table. The most important person is at the "head" of the table—the next, at his or her right ("my right-hand man"). The next most important person is at the left of the head. The farther away one is from No. 1, the less power one is perceived to have. Let this guide you in choosing a seat. It will also help you recognize who the players are when you are in a new setting.

3. Learn the dynamics of seating. What configurations are most conducive to cooperation? The person you wish to defuse should be seated with his or her back to the door. It's the position that feels least secure and has the most distractions. If you learn the dynamics, you can maneuver yourself

to the best position for gaining control, opposing something effectively, or simply being noticed.

PERSONAL INVENTORY

Clothes

Whether or not clothes make the man, they certainly unmake the man or woman if they are chosen poorly. Your clothes say a number of things about you. One of the most important is where you are headed. What you wear affects the way people perceive you. So it's not a bad idea to dress for where you're going—that is, as though you already have the promotion you're seeking. You'll take yourself more seriously, and so will others.

No matter what your style, it can suffer from neglect. An expensive French suit will lose its impact if you have a spot on your tie or if a piece of string is trailing from the back of your skirt. Make it a habit to visit the rest room before a meeting or appointment, especially if you have just been outdoors. Do a quick check of hair, teeth, and clothing. Then go into the meeting with confidence.

A good communicator knows that every aspect of a presentation needs to be planned. So if you're interviewing, or speaking before the board, let your clothes help you strike the right tone. Darker colors lend more authority to your appearance. Warm colors are better when you want to come across as creative. Dressing right is part of psyching yourself up for the situation.

Surroundings

Your office makes a statement about your personality (drab, clever, businesslike) and your comprehension of office politics. If you've arranged your space effectively, you're telling others that you are in control.

Approach someone else's office with a mental checklist. What can you learn about this person for small talk? Look around for signs of hobbies. Check artwork, books, photographs, awards. What about special projects? Is there any indication that the competition has been by for a visit? Are there huge backlogs of correspondence, unanswered telephone messages? Is the office attractive, well maintained? All this information will be helpful to you in communicating with the other person.

The assertive person is congruent. Words, body language, voice, appearance, and surroundings all reinforce the same message: This is a competent manager.

10

Criticism, Feedback, Acknowledgments, Bouquets

Most of us think of criticism only in its negative sense—in the sense of blaming, censuring, or reprehending others. Criticism of this type may be intended or unintended. In either case, it is unskilled. It serves only to weaken the criticized person's self-concept and his or her self-esteem.

The Greek root for criticism (*kritikos*) means "able to discern or judge." In ancient Athens, a critic was expected to assess the pluses as well as the minuses of a situation and to judge it accordingly. The goals of the critic were to communicate, to influence, and to motivate. Sound familiar? These are also the goals of any good manager. Criticism, when looked at in this way, is important in the evaluation process. It helps us examine our aims and actions and explore new resources for achieving our goals.

So let us consider an assertive definition of criticism: "information communicated to others in a way that enables them to use it to their advantage; a tool for enhancing personal growth and relationships." This requires a somewhat different stance or philosophy from the blaming approach. Here we are in effect telling others, "I am saying this because it can strengthen our relationship." Let's take a look first at the various ways criticism can be destructive and then examine some techniques for giving—and receiving—criticism assertively.

DESTRUCTIVE CRITICISM

Telling people what's wrong with them is destructive, and seeking to find fault or lay blame does nothing to improve communication or performance. It only hurts people's feelings. Here are some of the forms it takes.

Negative Ways to Give Criticism

1. *Unstated assumptions.* Here the critic assumes that the other person understands the basis for the criticism. For example, "This report doesn't meet our internal requirements." More than likely, these requirements have never been written down and agreed upon by everyone in the organization. They may be clear in the mind of the critic, but unclear in the mind of the receiver.

2. *Unclear alternatives.* Criticizing someone without offering alternatives or positive suggestions for change is not criticism at all. It is simply "sounding off."

3. *Exaggerations, blanket statements.* "You always interrupt people." "You never complete the customer project on time." There is nowhere the recipient can go with such statements. And rarely is it true that someone always or never does something.

4. *Psychoanalyzing.* "Why do you fill out the time sheets this way?" "Why did you show up late at the meeting?" When we attempt to analyze behavior, we succeed only in embarrassing the other person. Most people do not know why they do things in a particular way. Do you?

5. *Poor timing.* Many times, in the heat of our own frustration or needs, we criticize others at the very moment when they are least able to hear what we're trying to convey. It's important to be sensitive to the other person's emotional state before delivering our criticism.

6. *Threats and ultimatums.* Threats may be implied ("If you don't start coming to work on time . . .") or explicit ("You have two weeks to shape up"). Veiled or open, they are the least effective way to deal with criticism. They do nothing more than put the other person on the defensive, so that the person ceases to listen.

Negative Ways to Respond to Criticism

1. *Stonewalling.* A common way of defending ourselves against criticism is to have a rigid answer. This is a passive-aggressive attempt to deny or invalidate the criticism. Some stonewalling answers include "I always do things that way," "I can't help it," "That's not my department."

2. *Making excuses.* Another way we defend ourselves against criticism is to say "Yes, but," and then come out with an explanation. This is a defense of our behavior or our self-image. The "yes" acknowledges the criticism in part; the "but" is an attempt to justify or excuse it.

3. *Retaliating.* Here we play "Can you top this?" and find something the critic does or has done that is worse than the behavior being criticized. Sometimes we will even dredge up items that have nothing to do with the topic being discussed.

4. *Avoidance and withdrawal.* This is a common nonassertive response

to criticism. Typical ways of withdrawing include avoiding eye contact, clamming up, and simply retreating to our desk or office. When we avoid criticism in this manner, we weaken our relationship with the other person. Also, we reinforce the idea of withdrawing as a way to handle criticism instead of learning skills for coping with it positively.

5. *Superficial acceptance.* Here we give lip service to what the critic is saying without really listening or taking it seriously. ("I read you." "I get what you mean.") Sometimes this can be seen as downright hostile.

CONSTRUCTIVE CRITICISM

Constructive criticism begins with an honest evaluation of your motives for expressing criticism to others. If you are convinced that someone's behavior is harmful—to you, to others, or to the organization—then you must begin to explore possibilities for improved behavior. Once you can present your point of view thoughtfully and clearly, and can offer alternatives, you are ready to give constructive criticism. Here are some guidelines:

1. Identify the behavior you want to criticize. Make sure you criticize the *behavior,* not the person.
2. Make your criticism as specific as possible. Tell the person *what* behavior specifically failed to meet your standards or otherwise displeased you. Do not psychoanalyze or evaluate.
3. Make sure that the behavior you are criticizing is something within the person's power to change.
4. Use "I" statements. Let the person know how his or her behavior makes *you* feel. "You" statements lead only to defensiveness, and when that happens the other person will not listen.
5. Make sure the receiver understands what you mean. Check this out by having the person ask you clarifying questions.
6. Don't belabor the point. Lengthy and repeated criticism causes others to tune out. Be brief and concise.
7. Don't allow your own negative feelings or biases to get into your criticism. Avoid putdowns or sarcasm, angry or blaming gestures. Be aware of your body language.
8. Show that you empathize with the person's problems or feelings.
9. Have a good sense of timing. Give the criticism as soon as possible after the incident, but make sure you are cooled off when you approach the other person.
10. Let the person know that even though you may be angry or upset, you want the relationship to continue.
11. Inoculate. Give the other person a small dose for openers before you launch into the full treatment. "I know you're going to be a little uncomfortable when you hear what I have to say." This gives the person a chance to become emotionally prepared.

12. Acknowledge the receiver for being willing to listen to you, and give recognition if the criticism produces a change in attitude or behavior.

RECEIVING CRITICISM ASSERTIVELY

Effective managers receive and deliver criticism clearly, directly, positively, and constructively. When you are able to take in criticism, you demonstrate to others that you are approachable. People will be more likely to give you feedback to your face rather than behind your back. This doesn't mean that you are now the department's punching bag and everyone is free to tell you off. It does mean that others perceive you as an open, assertive person who is willing to change, grow, and work on relationships.

Aggressive people are not approachable. Others stay away from them out of fear that they will respond to criticism with hostility and resentment. Nonassertive people are equally unapproachable. Others avoid them, out of fear that they will be upset and hurt by criticism. Assertive people, on the other hand, are able to listen to the expectations of others without taking every action personally. They value the co-worker or boss who brings mistakes and oversights to their attention. Table 8 summarizes these three different approaches to hearing criticism.

Table 8. Three ways of hearing criticism.

	Nonassertive (*I'm no good*)	Aggressive (*You're no good*)	Assertive (*We're okay*)
Example: Your boss says, "Your performance is not meeting standards lately."			
Thought	I'll never do it right. I'm worthless and incompetent.	That mean SOB is at me again.	I wonder what the boss means? Maybe I can learn from this.
Feeling	Sad, stressed, anxious.	Angry, outraged.	Secure, curious.
Behavior	Isolation, moping, not trying.	Work slowdown, sabotage on the job.	Active attempt to determine how to behave differently.
Outcome	You avoid work and challenges. You put yourself down.	You fall out of favor with the boss, or are fired or demoted.	You and the boss negotiate the problem and come up with a workable solution or compromise. You and your boss feel better about yourselves and each other.

This section explores a number of skills for handling criticism assertively when you are the receiver. These skills will help you:

1. Distinguish between truths that others are telling you about your behavior and the arbitrary rights and wrongs that others choose to find in you.
2. Feel more comfortable when you are told things about your behavior that others do not openly call wrong but only imply are wrong through a critical tone.
3. Learn not to get upset about making mistakes. Errors can be costly and time-consuming, but they are terrific learning experiences. Everyone who has ever tried anything makes mistakes.

As you read through the techniques described below, notice that throughout no attempt is made to call the critic crazy, stupid, or irrational, or to accuse the person of picking on you or finding unnecessary flaws. Of course, you do have a right to defend yourself against criticism if it is untrue or unfair. But whether the criticism is right or wrong, intended or unintended, if you respond with hostility, anger, or resentment, you will reduce the possibilities for productive interaction with your critic in the future. If you can adopt an open, investigative point of view from the outset, you will go a lot further toward coping with criticism.

Empathy—Seeing with Another's Eyes

To receive criticism assertively, you must first try to understand your critic's point of view. Ask questions to find out exactly what your critic means. What you want to know is: *What* did you do, *how* did you do it, and *when* or how often do you do it in a way that displeases the other person?

The more information you can get from the other person about the behavior being criticized, the better you'll be able to understand where he or she is coming from. Your goal in emphathizing is to see the world through the critic's eyes. You want to know, if you were the critic, how you would feel about the behavior. You are not agreeing with the critic or defending yourself. You are simply letting the other person know that you are willing to listen and are trying to understand his or her point of view.

Fogging

If you are being attacked, or perceive that you are being attacked, you have three choices. You can retaliate, you can run, or you can stay where you are and skillfully disarm your opponent. Fogging is a skillful way of taking the wind out of your critic's sails so that rational exploration of the problem can begin. When you give fogging responses, you agree *in principle* with all your critic's comments, without apologizing or explaining. Like a fog bank, you remain impenetrable. You offer no resistance or hard striking surfaces. Here's how it works:

SANDRA: George, your desk always has heaps of paper piled on it.

GEORGE: Yes, you could be right.

SANDRA: Also, you dress in a way that doesn't look very executive. Why, that seersucker suit you had on the other day was very wrinkled.

GEORGE: You're right, Sandra. A wrinkled suit doesn't look very executive.

Get the picture? If your critic is being manipulative or laying blame, he or she will soon find you no fun at all to criticize and will leave you alone.

One of the values of fogging is that it forces you to focus on exactly what the critic is saying, because you are almost parroting what is being said. So it teaches you to be a good listener—to listen to precisely what is being said without trying to read the other person's mind.

You may be thinking that it sounds phony to keep agreeing with someone if you don't really agree. But look at it another way: Almost every critical comment has some grain of truth in it, at least something that is true for the critic, the way he or she sees the reality of the situation. So, if you listen, you might learn something. When people criticize you, they are telling you something about *them,* about their preferences. They are simply letting you know that they'd like you to be a different way. It doesn't mean you have to change, or do anything different. Fogging helps you let the other person know that you have heard the criticism, and are conceding that possibly (not probably, just possibly) there could be a grain of truth in it.

Negative Assertion

A related skill in dealing with criticism is negative assertion. Here you offer a fogging response and then assert yourself, stating your own opinion or telling the other person a bit more about you. So in the case of George and Sandra, George might acknowledge his independence or difference of opinion by saying: "Yes, Sandra, you're right. There are a lot of papers on my desk right now. If they interfered with my current work, I'd probably get rid of them. But they don't seem to bother me." This tells Sandra that George has heard her and is acknowledging her right to criticize, while at the same time he is establishing *his* point of view.

Negative assertion and negative inquiry, discussed next, are called negative because in a sense you are agreeing with the negative statement the other person is making—as a technique to get more information.

Negative Inquiry

Fogging and negative assertion can help you stop manipulative criticism and can make you more assertive in responding to comments from others.

But they still do not prompt your critic to be more assertive. And in the final analysis, your goal as a manager is not only to act assertively but to encourage other people to be open and assertive in their dealings with you.

Negative inquiry is a useful technique for getting your critic to open up and to state clearly what his or her objection is. You simply respond to the criticism with a series of questions to get more detailed information. Suppose that a co-worker approaches you with the comment, ''You're awfully quiet in our departmental meetings.'' You could respond in one of two ways:

''What makes you think that being quiet in meetings is not good?''
''Specifically, what is it about being quiet in meetings that isn't good?''

The first option is likely to make the other person defensive, because you are throwing the emphasis back on the critic (''What makes *you* think . . .''). The second is an assertive, nondefensive way of seeking more information. Your negative inquiry might proceed like this:

FRIEND: You're awfully quiet in our departmental meetings.

YOU: Specifically, what is it about being quiet in meetings that isn't good?

FRIEND: Well, nobody will know that you have good ideas.

YOU: Maybe people won't know. So what?

FRIEND: But they'll ignore you.

YOU: Well, if they do, what's wrong with that?

FRIEND: They'll think our whole group has no ideas.

YOU: Even if they think that, so what?

FRIEND: They'll think we're stupid and shouldn't have the positions we have.

YOU: Well, what if they do?

What you're beginning to discover is that your friend is concerned that your behavior will reflect on her and on the whole department. You are beginning to get her to be assertive about her own fears and insecurities. But you haven't wagged a finger at her, blamed her, or accused her of projecting her own inadequacies onto you. She is probably discovering this on her own.

Negative inquiry is especially useful with people you are close to. It will help you:

1. Become less sensitive to criticism from people you care about so you can listen to what they are telling you.
2. Stop them from giving you repetitive manipulative criticism—from laying all their wrongs and rights on you.
3. Help them to become more assertive about what they want so you can begin to negotiate compromises.

You can even use negative inquiry to try to get a raise or a promotion on the job:

YOU: I've been wondering—I've been here almost a year now, and I think I would like to ask for a raise.

BOSS: So why don't you?

YOU: Okay, I am. Why haven't you given me a raise yet?

BOSS: Quite simple. You don't deserve it.

YOU: I don't understand. Can you be more specific?

BOSS: Well, you're a bit slow getting the reports out on time. And you haven't been delegating much. You continue to do the job yourself, even though you've been promoted. And delegation is what I'm watching you on. That's one of the key skills I look for in managers.

YOU: I didn't know that. I thought you were judging me on how well we turn the work out. I had no idea delegation was the most important thing to you. From now on, I will delegate more. When can we get together to review how I'm doing? And how much delegation would you consider to be "more"? (Here you can press to make sure you have a realistic idea of what your boss means by "delegate more.")

By not becoming defensive, by simply probing and asking more and more questions through negative inquiry, you are eliciting information that can be valuable to you in your future dealings with your boss. You are also getting a clearer picture of what you need to do in order to get a raise.

Negotiation, Feedback, Compromise

Once you have heard your critic out and have acknowledged that there could be some truth to what the other person has said, you are ready to negotiate specific aspects of your behavior that you could or are willing to change in order to meet with your critic's desire.

To take criticism positively, you must look upon it as an opportunity—a chance to learn about your behavior and how you can change it. The important point is to focus on the specifics of the criticism, rather than on your feelings of humiliation, defensiveness, or frustration. If you think that you must be perfect, or that you have to please everyone, you will deny yourself the opportunity to learn, change, and grow.

Everyone gets feedback and criticism from time to time. Take it as the rich opportunity it can be—a chance to find out from other people in your world how they perceive you and how they respond to your behavior and your ways of interacting with them.

THE POWER OF ACKNOWLEDGMENT

Many managers begin assertiveness training because they have a difficult time handling negative feedback and criticism. An equal number, however, have a difficult time with *positive* feedback and acknowledgment.

We are taught early in life to be modest, to discount or not really let on to people that we believe their compliments and flattery. We are equally resistant to acknowledging our good points to ourselves. Yet all of us can probably recount at least one experience when we felt acknowledged and valued. If we received this acknowledgment from a boss or a peer, it is likely that we performed our jobs far more effectively.

Ironically, people who have difficulty listening to criticism also have a difficult time taking in compliments. It is not only modesty that makes it difficult for us to receive compliments; it is also the belief that other people are the final judges of our actions. If we believe that we are the final judge of the appropriateness or intelligence of our actions, we will be able to listen openly to what other people are telling us, positive or negative, and then decide whether it's accurate for us.

As a manager, how often do you take the time and trouble to compliment people, let them know how they're doing and whether their performance meets with your approval? Most of us fail to tell people, during the process, how much we appreciate them—we imagine that they know. And that's the first fallacy: they may or may not know. Even if they do, there certainly isn't any harm in telling them again. In most organizations, people hear about their performance from the boss only when they have goofed up or made a mistake, or when they are being given a formal appraisal.

Positive Strokes for Yourself

We all have a strong need to know how we are doing. Most of us have been judged, criticized, flattered, and complimented throughout our lives. We may think that this is acknowledgment. But in fact true acknowledgment is neither good nor bad. It is simply an affirmation of what is there—a description of the situation, or the behavior, without judgment or evaluation. According to Michael Wyman, a training consultant, "Acknowledgment comes from the heart. It's neither negative nor positive. It is simply a re-cognition, a re-knowing, of the truth."

Of course, the ability to acknowledge others begins with being able to acknowledge yourself. So get into the habit of acknowledging yourself daily. Keep a list of all the things you acknowledge yourself for.

> "I acknowledge myself for completing my paperwork before I went home last night."
> "I acknowledge myself for the negotiation I lost yesterday."

Remember to acknowledge everything about yourself—the highs as well as the lows. And don't beat yourself up for what you didn't accomplish.

Practice this with employees too. Let them know that you are pleased with them or appreciate their work. This need not be for the major projects they complete, or even for anything they complete. You can simply acknowledge people for their efforts, for their enthusiasm, for their loyalty, for their willingness to pitch in and get the job done. If your people are not accustomed to hearing this kind of comment—from you or from anyone else in the organization—you may get some surprised looks at first. But you will be amazed at the difference you can create in people's attitudes by a little acknowledgment.

Affirmations

Another way to acknowledge yourself daily is to write a list of positive statements at the start of the day. Instead of beginning the day with gripes or grumbles, write statements like "Today I am finishing everything that I need to do with ease and concentration, and will even have time for a leisurely lunch." "I am an assertive and competent manager, and my employees and bosses respect me."

It is impossible to really accept and believe acknowledgments from other people if you can't give them to yourself. If you feel that you are competent and worthy, you will be more likely to notice other people's competence and acknowledge them for their skills. If you feel incompetent, you might notice other people's competence, but you will be envious and resentful of them and therefore reluctant to compliment or acknowledge others.

So ask yourself: When was the last time you acknowledged yourself? When was the last time you acknowledged your spouse, your child, a close friend, letting them know how much they and the relationship contribute to your life? And when was the last time you acknowledged any of your peers, subordinates, or bosses (yes, even bosses) for something about them that you have noticed and value?

Bouquets

Once you become skilled and confident at acknowledging others in small ways, try giving the exquisite acknowledgment. Pay people unusual compliments. Say things that you wouldn't ordinarily say, or tell people something about themselves which you know they value highly but which other people have not recognized in them. For example, one of your colleagues might have a reputation for being quite serious and conservative. You think you have noticed a twinkle in her eye and a mischievous look from time to time. Secretly she may be a madcap comedienne, but few people take the trouble to look beyond the surface. By remarking on this subtle quality, you will be paying her an ultimate compliment that makes her feel recognized and valued.

There are infinite variations, of course. The important thing to remember is that acknowledgment starts with you!

11

Meetings

Time spent preparing for and attending meetings can consume up to 50 percent of the average manager's workweek. This amounts to as much as 1,000 hours per manager per year. Considering the salaries of the people involved, meetings can be expensive if they are unproductive. Nonetheless, meetings are a regular part of every manager's life. And as organizations grow and become less hierarchical in structure, there seems to be a trend toward more and more group decisions—hence more meetings.

In organizations plagued with information overload, managers often need to get together with others to make even the simplest decision. These people may be from the same department, from different departments, from other divisions, or from the outside—such as customers, suppliers, consultants, and advertising agencies. Some companies even have meetings with their competitors. Certain industries have created networks of "friendly competitors" in which managers or representatives from the companies get together periodically to exchange information.

The two most common types of meetings are regular staff meetings and meetings with peers. Each can pose special problems for the manager.

STAFF MEETINGS

Like most managers, you probably hold regular meetings with your staff. Here, you're in charge. Your purpose might be to make an announcement, get people to discuss some new development, request their input, or mediate some conflict within the department. What are some of the typical problems that can arise?

One common problem is that certain people never speak up at meetings, even though they may have valuable contributions to make. Sandra J., a young product manager, met with her staff regularly. One member of her staff, Paul, came to every meeting, sat through each one, and listened quietly and attentively, and then went back to his office. Two weeks after one important meeting, Paul wrote Sandra a memo criticizing one of the projects that had been discussed. When Sandra asked Paul why he had not spoken up at the meeting, he said, "I didn't think you wanted to hear a dissenting opinion from me. But from what I know about manufacturing, that thing will rust soon after it's on the shelf. Everybody seemed to think the idea was really feasible and just dandy. I didn't want to put a fly in the ointment. Besides, you never asked me."

Had Sandra simply asked all the members of the meetings what they thought of the suggestions, she would have saved herself some anxiety and uncertainty, saved Paul the two weeks of worrying about whether to write the dissenting memo, and saved everyone's time by discussing the issue at the moment, instead of having to call a special meeting to reopen an issue that she thought was settled.

A variation of this problem is the "silent treatment." Sometimes people keep silent at a meeting, not out of shyness, but as a way of sulking or being the withholding child. These people too may have valuable contributions to make, and their form of hostility is to withhold the information from the group. How can you, as the manager in charge of the meeting, handle such a situation?

One good approach is to take a poll of *all* the members present, especially the quiet ones, to find out what's on their minds. Are they not speaking up because they have nothing to add, because they're afraid of disagreeing, or because they are upset with some person or issue and are responding with the silent treatment? It's best to uncover these problems as early as possible.

You might try saying something like, "Does everyone think what Ann has proposed is a feasible idea? Can anyone think of anything that might go wrong in terms of production, quality control, durability, sales? Has anyone had any experience with something like this that has worked well? Any experience with something not working well?" Your task, as an assertive manager, is to create a climate in which all opinions are valid and valued and no one gets his or her wrists slapped for not going along with the crowd. That way, you'll get what people are thinking out in the open.

At the other extreme is the group member who's outspoken or overtly hostile to other staffers. You may have established a policy of openness and free exchange at meetings, and some people take advantage of the occasion to vent their distrust and disapproval.

When a meeting member is being aggressive and violating other people's rights, you as a manger need to demonstrate control and assertiveness. Often, someone who dominates the meeting or acts in otherwise obnoxious or overbearing ways is suffering from insecurity and a need for attention. The best way to handle such people is not to ignore them or give them negative attention, but to confront the problem directly.

One supervisor in a construction materials company always knew better than everyone else how things should be done, how much budget should be spent, and so on. At staff meetings he habitually shouted at people, even though he was inches away from them. As a veteran supervisor in a noisy factory, he always shouted at people—because on the production floor nobody heard him if he didn't. So shouting became his style. Of course, when he shouted in normal settings, people tuned out rather than in. So he shouted more.

Barney, the leader of the staff meetings, recognized this behavior early on. He began to give the supervisor positive attention, making direct eye contact and indicating in other nonverbal ways that he was really listening. When the supervisor began to feel confident that he was being heard, his shouting diminished.

Another common problem at staff meetings is unclear communication, so that people leave the meeting with different perceptions of agreed-upon actions. For example, you've just ended an all-morning meeting with your staff, during which some decisions were made and different people were to take action and report back to the group. Barbara, the new assistant manager, has volunteered to research the customer market to find out how a new product is selling.

At the next meeting, she reports on three phone calls she has made to old customers in the immediate area. You were expecting a region-by-region breakdown of customers in the three different market categories, along with a report of their sales records over at least one quarter. Also, you prefer to have this material in written form, with support graphs and charts. But at the original meeting, you never specified clearly to Barbara what *form* of research would satisfy your criteria. You never let her know that anecdotal information on three customers was not solid enough for your purposes. You simply assumed her idea of "researching the market" was the same as yours and that she would deliver the information in the way you like to see it.

Neither of you is right or wrong. The point is, if you want the result to be the way you like it, you must be precise and clear when you're giving directions to people or when they volunteer to bring something back to you.

Give assignments in specific terms, and ask people to be more specific whenever they volunteer some service. You must do this assertively, of course, adjusting your voice tone so you do not appear to be a cross-examiner. You simply want to put everyone on the same wavelength. For example, if someone says, "I'll do a report," you can simply ask, "Specifically what will the report include? How long will it be, what will it accomplish, and what form will it be in?" Ask questions until you're satisfied that you have a clear idea of what this report will be like when you see it. Any time a meeting member makes a vague or fuzzy statement, stop the music and ask questions until you're clear on specifically what the speaker means. Encourage other people in the group to do the same. Set a climate of precise, clear, open communication. You will reap high rewards in lessened anxiety and confusion, and greater productivity.

Another way to determine whether people are clear on their duties is to go around the room at the end of the meeting and ask, "What is your understanding of what's expected of you?" Make sure people are specific in terms of dates, procedures, amounts. The more concrete the information, the better. You may feel that it is impolite or unfair to challenge people in this way. On the contrary, you are doing them a service by helping them clarify what they mean and what they're promising to deliver. Fuzzy speaking is often an indicator of fuzzy thinking—and by forcing people to be more specific, you are helping them get their thoughts straight. When people understand exactly what you want, they feel much more comfortable about producing it. They don't waste time or put off a project because they're not sure they are doing it right. An added benefit of this approach is that people on your staff will soon begin to speak with more precision and clarity about everything they do.

Of course, you must practice what you preach. Encourage people to ask questions when you've given directives or suggestions at a meeting. You'll welcome the feedback. Everyone profits from clear communication.

MEETINGS WITH PEERS

Often, you will have to go to a meeting with a group of your peers. Sometimes, the meeting will be led by the natural supervisor or manager of the group. At other times, the meeting will be unsupervised, with the leadership flowing or allowed to surface from within the group. What are some of the potential problems in such a situation?

If the group has a natural leader, power struggles are likely to emerge. These often take the form of "sibling rivalries," not unlike the petty family squabbles in which everyone vies for the parent's attention. People who are normally quite cooperative will snipe at each other's contributions because they want to be seen as the "brightest kid on the block." Many otherwise reasonable and compassionate people become reduced to petty nitpickers at such meetings. The creative flow quickly deteriorates, and soon the group has lost any momentum it was generating. The leader of the meeting has all he or she can do to keep people from more serious conflict. So the group ends up focusing on avoiding conflict rather than on producing a new product or idea.

If you are the acknowledged leader of such a group, there are many steps you can take to manage the meeting assertively. Remember that, as leader, you will have to be a guiding influence rather than a directive force. You must exercise control a lot more subtly than if you were running a meeting with subordinates. If you are too directive with peers, you might be perceived as dominating or pushy. So you will have to keep a low profile.

As the team leader, you would be wise to get some higher-level sanction for the group before the first meeting. This could simply take the form of sending a memo to a department head saying that this task force will be meeting regularly to address a certain problem (even if the department head is *not* the one who appointed the task force). The point is, by the time you are ready to set goals and call the first meeting, members will perceive that you have a mandate to carry out. This will enhance your authority and credibility and make your task easier once the meetings get going.

Before you call the group together, find out the best meeting times for all members. Make sure that the time you finally choose is convenient for the most powerful and influential members of the group, as well as for people who are your acknowledged allies and supporters. This does not mean that you purposely call the meeting at a time when you know some members can't make it (this would be management suicide—such a move could haunt you later on).

To discourage stragglers, establish a policy of starting meetings exactly on time—and stick to the commitment. People will get the message that this is a serious undertaking, not some informal function they can wander into at will. Also, if you hold up the meeting for 10 or 15 minutes waiting for everyone to show, you will be rewarding latecomers and penalizing on-timers.

Agenda

The agenda is one of the most critical parts of planning and running meetings, especially among your peers. Since peers do not work for you, they may feel that coming to meetings is a burden on their time. Therefore, it is important that the time be used as productively as possible.

It's a good idea to establish a working agenda first. Ask members for ideas ahead of time. You can poll them by telephone and ask what items they think should be included in the meeting's agenda. Also ask them to set priorities: Which items do they consider important and which ones peripheral? From this information, you can structure the final agenda, giving highest weight to the items mentioned most frequently. The fact that you asked people for their input will work strongly in your favor later. Members will feel much more involved and committed, and will be much more agreeable to working collaboratively.

Suppose you're calling a meeting with your peers to discuss the new employee incentive program. Production's main agenda item might be tangible rewards for overtime or Saturday work. Finance may be concerned

HOW TO DEAL WITH PROBLEM PEOPLE AT MEETINGS

Latecomer	Start meetings on time—don't wait for stragglers.
Early Leaver	Get a commitment from all members at the beginning of the meeting to stay until the end.
Broken Record	Brings up same point over and over again. Use "group memory" or the minutes of the meeting to remind Broken Record that the point is noted.
Doubting Thomas	As facilitator, get the group to agree not to evaluate any ideas for a period of time, then use this agreement to correct violators.
Headshaker	Disagrees nonverbally. First strategy: ignore. Next: acknowledge behavior, and then deal with negativeness.
Dropout	Nonparticipant. Try asking her opinion during meeting or at break.
Whisperer	As facilitator, walk up close (low-key intervention). Or ask for focus on a single topic.
Loudmouth	Move closer and closer, maintain eye contact. Ask him to be group recorder.
Attacker	Thank the attacker for observation, ask the group what it thinks.
Interpreter	Often says "In other words" or "What she really means." Check this (in public) with original speaker.
Gossip	Ask the group to verify the information.
Know-It-All	Remind the group that all members have expertise; that's the reason for meeting.
Busybody	Before the meeting, ask other members to get Busybody to stop.
Teacher's Pet	Be encouraging, but break eye contact. Get group members to talk to one another. Lessen your omnipotence by reflecting "What do you think?" back to member.

about budget projections from all the plant foremen, and Public Relations may emphasize discussing all the steps of the plan so that the newsletter on the plan can get started. It is up to you to find the common ground and come up with an agenda that takes everyone's needs into consideration.

Before you finalize the agenda, ask yourself some hard questions: "What is the current situation?" "What result is needed?" "What decisions should come out of the meeting?" It is important to set agreed-upon goals *before* the first meeting. Then the agenda simply becomes a document supporting the group's goals. With objectives clearly stated and agreed upon, sidetracking and peripheral discussions will be kept to a minimum, the group will have an easier time staying focused, and you will be better able to control the flow of the discussion and keep things on track.

Proceedings

At the first meeting, make sure all the group memebers know one another by name, rank, and serial number. One helpful technique is to have a quick go-round of introductions, in which members take turns describing their special skills and the unique contributions they can make to the project. This will make people feel that they are part of a team and that their special talents are of value to the group.

Your task as the meeting leader is to get people to cooperate and to use one another as resources. Once the meeting gets going, bounce ideas off different people. For example: "George is making an interesting suggestion here about the Processing Center's time log. Ellen, how does that fit with your experience when they tried that in the Western Region?" In a collaborative environment, everybody plays and everybody wins. Your role is that of facilitator. You must work with the group to generate ideas, pinpoint problems, and identify possible causes. Keep a flip chart, a notebook, or a chalkboard near you to record the information as it is given. So that you won't be distracted from your job as leader, make someone else responsible for the meeting record.

You may find it helpful to focus on desired outcomes rather than problems. Too often, attempts at identifying problems deteriorate into long-winded gripe sessions about unrelated issues. Also, when groups start discussing problems, it is all too easy to attribute cause or blame to other departments, other people, the competition, the weather, and so on. A focus on desired outcomes will put people in a positive frame of mind and get them to think about the ideal situation or goal.

Closure

Once the group has arrived at some tentative workable solutions, your task is to restate what has gone on so far. Ask different people to summarize what, in their view, has transpired at the meeting. If someone is taking minutes, this will help too. Often, the minutes of a meeting come out looking just as vague and fuzzy as the meeting's procedures, because no summary was made of the main points and decisions. You can also seek commitments about action steps. Get people to publicly volunteer to take some action before the next meeting.

TIPS FOR PARTICIPATING ASSERTIVELY IN MEETINGS

Whether you are the leader or a participant in a meeting, there are three important principles to remember for being assertive and persuasive: timing, tone, and tact.

1. *Timing*. Before you decide when to contribute your opinion, consider all the issues that are raised. Decide on your top-priority issues and focus your comments on them. There's no point being assertive just for the sake of being assertive. Unless you have a clear focus on what result you want, and are sensitive to other people's needs and priorities, you may simply be taking up air time and will not gain any advantage.

2. *Tone*. The *way* you present your opinion or contribution is also important. Be clear and assertive. Don't preface your remarks with "This is only my opinion," "I don't really have much data to back this up," or "The rest of you may not agree with this." These discounters will detract from the power of your remarks, and you will lose credibility.

3. *Tact*. Tact is especially important when you are taking a position that is contrary to what the group wants to do. A powerful assertive/persuasive tactic is to acknowledge the value or truth of what another person has said, and then continue with your own view. "Your point about the market share in the West is well taken, Don. We have been slipping in that area. However, I maintain that we shouldn't give up where we already have a considerable foothold." This allows you to get your point across without making the other person lose face.

12

Assertive Writing

Business executives are called upon to use writing skills every day. Each time you write a letter, memo, or report, others are making judgments about you on the basis of what they read on paper. A misspelled word might make readers think that you are careless; a rambling, muddy sentence might lead others to conclude that you are uncertain about what you are saying. Mastering good writing skills can help you get what you want.

ASSERTIVENESS ON PAPER:
HOW TO INFLUENCE YOUR READERS

Assertive writing, like assertive speaking, is clear, open, honest, and to the point. Assertiveness on paper is defined by these characteristics:

It's persuasive. Your business letters are sales letters. You are trying to sell goodwill, yourself, your company, or your product. Once you are clear about the purpose of your letter, how can you get the response you want?

1. Identify who can give you what you want. Address your letter to the person who would make that decision.
2. Figure out how you can make what you want fit into the reader's needs. For instance, if you want an additional staff person, write a memo to your superior showing how adding a staff person would be cost-effective and would make the department more productive.
3. Anticipate all objections, then include the rebuttals in the body of your letter or memo.
4. Determine what would make your reader say yes to your request. Then structure your proposal accordingly. Sometimes the hard sell works best; at other times a soft sell is called for. One client responds to logic, another to emotion.

It's direct. Reading nonassertive writing is like talking to a person who won't meet your eyes. This may take the form of gobbledygook, padded language, or beating around the bush. Be clear, and state exactly what your purpose is and what action you want your reader to take after reading your letter.

It's strong. Assertive writing puts forth your position without apology and without being combative. Make your writing strong by being straightforward. "That's an unacceptable offer" is a much stronger statement than "That's not as tempting an offer as it might be." The active voice is stronger than the passive voice: Instead of saying, "The speech you gave at graduation was a great favorite of mine," say, "I loved your graduation speech."

It's self-enhancing. Assertive writing enhances the writer without violating the rights of others. A good example is the "no" letter. It is a definite art to be able to refuse someone without qualifying your own position, and at the same time making the person feel that you care about his or her feelings. If you can do it well, the person who reads your letter will say, "I can see why my request was turned down."

PREPARING FOR BUSINESS WRITING

Before you can become a good writer, you must come to grips with the hard truth: Writing is not easy. Even people who write for a living have periodic bouts of "writer's block." As Samuel Johnson, the eighteenth-century British critic and man of letters, said, "You learn to write by writing." It's a little like learning to ride a bicycle. No matter how much you read about it, you won't learn how to ride a bicycle until you climb on one and feel what it's like to balance on two wheels. Similarly, you learn to write when you sit down with pad and pencil and convert theory into practice. The good part is that *any* kind of practice helps. Write letters to a friend, keep a journal—just keep writing and it will get easier.

Writing correctly is not necessarily writing well. You can learn to write correctly by studying books about grammar. But the mechanics of usage are not the final test of good writing. That extra flair called style is what makes a piece interesting. To capture someone's attention your writing must be well thought out and easy to follow, and it must strike just the right tone. A course specifically designed for the business writer can help you zero in on the skills you will need. Your company may offer a training course. If not, inquire at schools of continuing education or professional organizations. Several companies offer self-study courses on audiocassettes. Any attempt to work on your writing skills will help.

Some people find it hard to write because they cannot get words down fast enough and then lose their train of thought. If you are one of these people, learning to type may be the answer for you. Or dictate your first draft. Speaking may be easier than writing it out. But remember that dictating is always just a first draft. It may look very different on paper and will need revision.

The first draft—whether dictated, written by hand, or typed—is just that. It's the first of many versions of what you want to say. If you get the idea that it's chiseled in stone the minute you put it on paper, you'll never become a skilled writer. Relax. It's just a draft, so you needn't start at the beginning or worry about any rules. Here are some tips for moving past your fear of writing and getting into the first draft.

1. Get *all* your ideas and thoughts onto paper first, even if they seem jumbled.
2. Don't write in final order. If you've got the fifth paragraph clear in your mind and are hung up on the first, start with the fifth. You can move it later.
3. Use wide spacing between lines and wide margins so you can add copy, make notes to yourself, and reorganize the material. Write or type on only one side of each sheet of paper so that you can cut and paste whole paragraphs if you want to. (Don't feel amateurish about any of this: Professional writers use these tricks.)
4. Don't stop to search for the perfect word. Don't pause to fix grammar. Go back and do it later.

TOOLS FOR GOOD WRITING

The dictionary is the business writer's most important tool. What can it do for you? Defining a word is just the beginning. It will give you the correct grammatical sense so you don't use the word incorrectly. The dictionary will tell you how to make a word plural. It will tell you the correct pronunciation of words should you be called upon to read your writing aloud. Stuck for another word to avoid repeating? Synonyms are given. The dictionary will also tell you when a word is slang, colloquial, or archaic. If so, you may choose to avoid it. How do you break a word if it doesn't fit at the end of the line? Each entry in the dictionary is divided into the proper syllables. The supplements at the beginning or end of the dictionary are full of helpful information: tips for manuscript preparation, proofreader's marks, capitalization rules, a punctuation and grammar guide.

Roget's Thesaurus is another useful guide when you're stuck for a word. You'll soon see how important it is to choose the right word. When you come up with a word that's close, the thesaurus can lead you to the word that's perfect. Say you're writing to a customer to appease a complaint. You want to say that the shipment did not arrive on time because of a mistake on the part of the shipping supervisor. But "mistake" is a little too strong;

it places too much blame. A better word, you discover from the thesaurus, is "oversight." The thesaurus lists words that are similar, but not necessarily substitutes. That's why you need a dictionary right beside it to determine the exact meaning of each word you use.

Quoted material can add interest to your writing if it's chosen appropriately. Use it to inject some humor or to personalize what you are saying. *Bartlett's Familiar Quotations* and *Stevenson's Home Book of Quotations* are two well-known collections. *Peter's Quotations for Our Times* has modern, timely anecdotes and sayings.

A book of usage is another valuable addition to your desktop library. Then when you are in a quandary about whether to say "This situation will *effect* your company" or "This situation will *affect* your company," you can be sure. If you wish to consult some fine books on usage, here are a few suggestions.

> *The Practical Stylist*, 4th ed., by Sheridan Baker (New York: Harper & Row, 1980)
>
> *The Careful Writer: A Modern Guide to English Usage*, by Theodore Bernstein (New York: Atheneum, 1965)
>
> *Writing Without Teachers*, by Peter Elbow (New York: Oxford, 1975)
>
> *The Elements of Style*, 3rd ed., by William Strunk, Jr., and E. B. White (New York: Macmillan, 1978)
>
> *On Writing Well: An Informal Guide to Writing Nonfiction*, by William Zinzer (New York: Harper & Row, 1976)
>
> *The Communication of Ideas*, put out by the Royal Bank of Canada (available at no cost, by request, from: Royal Bank of Canada, Box 6001, Montreal, Quebec, Canada H3C 3A9)

Become thoroughly familiar with one or two of these sources so you can find the information you need.

Another important tool of business writing is your own ability to exercise quality control. And it's for extremely selfish reasons. Everything that comes out of your department reflects on your reputation. Suppose a memo leaves your office that reads, "New methods are *necessary* to overcome *insufficient* trading *nad* neglect." You let it go, thinking your secretary sure has lots to learn. But someone upstairs is thinking, "Boy, D.R. sure has lots to learn about management." Make it clear to your secretary that you expect perfection. Anyone can use a dictionary; anyone can correct mistakes.

Another thing you can do is circulate examples of good writing. Explain why it's good. If a news item explains a problem succinctly, if a letter is concise but arresting, if a report summarizes a complex subject in an orderly readable fashion—point this out to your staff. Conversely, circulate "disasters" that come into your office. Examples of bad writing are just as constructive as well-written pieces.

Remember to praise good results and to demonstrate the value of editing by always going over your work and making changes. Hire outside editors for major projects.

TIPS FOR WRITING EFFICIENTLY

Your writing tasks will seem less formidable if you adopt a formula for tackling your projects. Here are some tips for directing your writing energy.

1. *Do your research first.* There are three reasons to gather your information *before* you begin writing. First, your actual writing time will be shorter and the task will seem less awesome. Second, when you have all the facts and statistics laid out before you, the whole picture will be clearer. Your sentences and paragraphs will organize themselves around the information. Finally, the writing itself will proceed more smoothly. If you keep taking time out to search for a fact, you will lose your train of thought.

2. *Outline your piece of writing.* Begin with what you want the reader to know or do after reading it. Then list three or four supportive points. Try to imagine the *person* who will be sitting down to read your work. Draw up the reader's objections, the specific facts he or she will need, and figure out what you can say that will make your reader pay attention to you.

3. *Keep it simple.* Spend less time trying to be clever or unusual and more time making your writing as clear and straightforward as possible.

4. *Check your work.* The more you practice the art of careful writing and reviewing, the more automatic good writing will become. Here is a checklist to help you perform this task quickly. Whether you are writing a letter, memo, report, proposal, or press release, ask yourself these questions about your work:

○ Is it complete? Have you supplied all the information? Will your reader have to read your mind to understand your message? Have you answered all possible questions?

○ Is it concise? Have you eliminated all unnecessary words, phrases, and information?

○ Is it clear? Is the information presented in an orderly way? Have you used simple but precise language? Have you said enough, but not too much? Are your paragraphs logical and organized?

○ Is it correct? Have you checked all information for accuracy? Have you cleared your facts with all necessary authorities in your organization, including the legal department? Did you go over spelling, punctuation, and grammar?

○ Is it appropriate? Is the tone right—pleasant, firm, but not antagonistic? Will your writing bring the desired action? Is the language human, free of pomposity and gobbledygook?

PITFALLS TO EFFECTIVE WRITING

Writing gets to be gobbledygook when it says too much or says the same thing twice. You may think that saying more about a subject will make it clearer. On the contrary. It's the simple statement that's easiest to interpret.

Redundant phrases say the same thing twice. The italicized part of each expression below is redundant.

separate *out*
attach *together*
consensus of *opinion*
close *off*
large *in size*
octagonal *in shape*
contains *within*
stand *up*
continue *on*
true facts

Superfluous phrases say more than is needed. Be clear and concise.

afford an opportunity   (allow)
at your earliest convenience   (soon)
in the amount of   (for)
at such time as   (when)
attached you will find   (attached is)
owing to the fact that   (because)
for the purpose of   (for)
in the majority of instances   (usually)

Pompous words are much too showy. Use simple, colloquial words.

terminate   (fire)
excessive amount   (too much)
accordingly   (so)
optimum   (best)
facilitate   (ease)
subsequent to   (after)
become cognizant of   (know)

Clichés make writing trite. Clichés are expressions used so many times that they have lost their meaning. See if you can think of better, fresher ways to rewrite the phrases in italics below:

How's the weather down there? It's *raining cats and dogs* here.
The chairman of the board was *conspicuous by his absence.*
Be careful of Jim Smith—he's *sly as a fox.*
Boyd seems disorganized but there's *method in his madness.*
You would think *in this day and age* that Ken would know better.
It *goes without saying* that Jones is the person to please.

When we meet Tuesday, let's get right *down to brass tacks.*
Here's that report I promised you—*better late than never.*
Production keeps growing by *leaps and bounds.*

THE SENTENCE

Turn to a paragraph in a popular magazine. Count the number of words in each sentence, then divide by the number of sentences to get the average sentence length. Chances are it is fewer than 15 words. It was once fashionable to write sentences that were 100 words long. But just as hemlines change with the times, so sentence length goes through phases. In the Victorian era, the average sentence was 29 words; today, it is fewer than 15. Of course, within any given paragraph some will be short, some long.

To make your writing more interesting, vary your sentence structure. The same material can be presented in several ways. For example:

- *Two simple sentences:* The sales manager consulted his parts book. He placed an order for 40 bolts.
- *Compound sentence with conjunction:* The sales manager consulted his parts book, and he placed an order for 40 bolts.
- *Compound sentence without conjunction:* The sales manager consulted his parts book; he then placed an order for 40 bolts.
- *Complex sentence:* After consulting his parts book, the sales manager placed an order for 40 bolts.
- *Compound-complex sentence:* The manager, who was in charge of sales, consulted his parts book; he placed an order for 40 bolts.

Let your sentences work for you. The Dale Carnegie course teaches three ways to remember things: by association, by repetition, and by impression. When you construct sentences use these methods. Choose memorable examples, make comparisons, and use quotations or anecdotes to reinforce a point. The proverb "One picture is worth a thousand words" can be applied to your writing. Use words to "paint" a picture for your reader. If you are trying to sell vacation condominiums, "picture" your reader stretched out by the pool. Use colorful, descriptive adjectives to portray the setting.

Structure your sentences so that the most important thought comes at the end. What is read last stays longest: "All absences will be recorded, *without exception.*"

THE PARAGRAPH

Every paragraph has a topic sentence—usually, but not always, the opening sentence—that outlines its main point or purpose. A paragraph may instruct, review, evaluate, or persuade. Make the purpose clear in the topic sentence. Next, introduce supportive material to make the main point clearer. Present your weakest argument first and lead up to the strongest. Each paragraph that follows should link up in some way to the one that precedes it. You might build on the closing thought of the last paragraph or use a transitional word like "therefore," "nevertheless," or "however."

The effectiveness of your writing depends on your ability to organize your material so that it is presented in a clear, orderly way. The paragraph is a building block. Plan your material so that ideas are brought out one after another, each supporting and adding to what went before.

THE BUSINESS LETTER

The Assertive "In" Basket

Nothing makes a business letter less assertive than beginning with an excuse for being so late to reply. The person at the other end begins to wonder if you care at all. There will never be a better time than now. Here are some tips for handling your mail assertively.

1. Handle mail only once. Develop a system for categorizing letters as you read them, dealing with what is urgent and dispersing what is not.
2. A quick answer may do. If you can reply with a yes or no, or single piece of information, write your response on the letter itself.
3. Devise standard types of responses (*not* form letters) for situations that arise frequently.
4. Delegate answering duties. Reroute a letter that could be answered by someone else. Request copies.
5. Let your secretary handle routine mail. It need not come across your desk at all.
6. Create a mail time. Set aside a portion of your day to handle mail.

Writing to Your Reader

Business letters are written to people. If you remember that a real person will be sitting down to read your letter, you will produce a more personable, compelling letter. Develop a sensitivity to the reader, as if you were having a conversation. Use the person's name if you know it, and be sure to spell it correctly. If you start your letter with "Dear Sir" or "Dear Madam"—with the implication that anyone can read the letter—your writing will probably be just as impersonal. But if you direct your letter to Bill Schmidt, vice president of marketing, you can begin to form an impression of Bill even if you don't know him personally. The more you can learn about his reputation, the size of his staff, and his company's productivity and marketing strategy, the better you'll be able to tailor the letter to his interests.

If you are answering a prior letter from Bill, you will have many clues to help you personalize your response. Check the signature, stationery, and typewriter. Is the letter neat, correct, interesting? Are there traces of humor? Where does the writer live—in a big city or a small town? Has he written with sympathy, sarcasm, aggression, warmth?

Assertive Openers

You can never get what you want if you can't get the other person to read your letter. Here are a few suggestions that will get you influence right from the start.

1. Begin with a question. "How would you like to be in Bermuda right now?"
2. Begin with an assertion. "I've got an idea that could save you $100 a day!"
3. Begin with something the reader wants to know. "We've got the answer to your heating problems!"
4. Begin with humor. "I saw this timely piece of graffiti on the subway, 'E.T.—phone home already.' Well, Ted, you and I have been working on this phone company deal for several months now. I think we're finally ready to bring it to a close!" Humor can be effective in defusing someone's anger, but it can backfire if it makes fun of the reader. Beware of off-color, religious, ethnic, or political humor. Used well, humor can set people at ease and make your reply memorable.

The Art of Persuasion

To write persuasively, you must know what it is you want and must organize your letter around that goal. You'll be using sales techniques; subtle manipulation will help. Think through what would make the reader do, believe, or buy what you want.

Have you ever stopped a busy person on the street? Picture yourself on a sidewalk. Approaching you is an acquaintance you've been trying to reach. He's walking very quickly and he's deep in thought. What do you do? You can stop him. Impede his progress. Then ask a few questions. Or you can say hello and reverse your direction. Walk along beside him, talking as you go. Now ask a few questions. Which course of action is likely to get results?

The "I know how you feel" approach works. When you travel in the same direction as your readers, they will get the feeling that you see things their way and that you want to help.

Use the 4-P formula: *picture, promise, prove,* and then *push.* You are probably familiar with the first three. Describe what you are offering, explain how it will help, and give data and statistics to support your claims. Then what? Say something friendly and sign your name? No. The fourth P is a key element in getting what you want. Push. Tell the reader exactly what to do: "Call this toll-free number immediately to receive your trial issue of *Hearth and Home*. Or tell the reader exactly what will happen: "I will be telephoning you Wednesday, June 9, to see if you approve of this contract. And I hope we can close the deal that same day over lunch." The closing part of your letter, since it is the last thing read, is the first remembered. An influential closing can go far toward getting the results you want.

When Your Letter Says Yes

It's fun to be able to say yes to someone. A "yes" letter is easier to write and more pleasant to receive than a refusal. Keep these points in mind to help your "yes" letters enhance your reader's impression of you.

1. Say yes quickly. If you know you're going to say yes, don't leave the letter sitting in the file for a week. You'll keep the recipient in the dark for that week. A brief note is better than a delayed masterpiece.

2. A "yes" letter that costs something may be a good investment. A customer has been to the store with a defective appliance, and then to a parts/repair shop, and finally to the manufacturer. Your response to his agitated letter begins, "I'd be upset too. That's why we're sending you a replacement mixer with our apologies for your inconvenience. Just return the defective model to us. . . ."

3. Give something extra. A young consumer wrote to General Mills seeking information for a school project.

Dear General Mills:

I love Cheerios. I eat them every morning. For a Christmas present my parents gave me a case of Cheerios. My teacher wants me to find out if it is good for me to eat so many Cheerios. Can you help me with this science project?

Sincerely,

Melissa

She received this reply:

Dear Melissa,

Most children would be healthier if they ate a breakfast like yours. Of course, a good diet is balanced throughout the day with other things—protein, fruits, and vegetables. You need all your vitamins and minerals to stay healthy.

I'm sending you three things: a booklet called "Start Your Day the Cheerios Way on the Road to Good Nutrition," to help you with your science project; some coupons for future purchases of Cheerios; and a sticker for your school notebook that says "You Made Cheerios Number One."

Your friend,

A. J. Smith

Product Information Officer

When Your Letter Says No

If you must say no, soften the blow by saying something positive first.

We love to hear from writers like you who have perceived our needs so well. Unfortunately, your idea was so on target that it has already been assigned to another writer for the October issue. Don't be discouraged. Send us another idea. We depend on creative people like you to keep our magazine current.

When you are answering a complaint, be sure the reader knows you have taken him seriously.

I appreciate your taking the time to write to us about your disappointment with the Electronic blender. Thoughtful consumers are our most reliable source of product information.

I reviewed the packaging and accompanying literature for the blender with the product designer. I assure you we do not want to deceive customers just to attract a sale. Our review showed the following claims for the blender:

○ Ten speeds.
○ Easy to clean.
○ Will pulse at any speed.
○ Suitable for making crushed ice drinks.

Elsewhere on the box the optional accessories were pictured, including the ice crusher. It was not our intention to promote the blender as an ice crusher, and I call your attention to the note on page 5 of the booklet: "Be sure to crush ice cubes to medium consistency before adding to liquid in the blender (we recommend using Attachment 4405, Ice Crusher.)"

I am sure you understand that we cannot refund purchase price simply because a customer wants another model. We can, however, guarantee you perfect frozen daiquiris every time if you purchase the ice crusher attachment. An order form is enclosed for your convenience.

The Unexpected Letters

There are times when sending an unexpected letter or memo can have enormous impact. For example, you were asked to present long-range goals for your department. Joe did the research and it paid off in a terrific presentation. Send him a personal note that is a pat on the back. The note reminds him that you are (1) a nice guy and (2) in a position to praise him.

Acknowledge an employee in writing for public service outside the office, particularly if he or she has received an award. Send a letter to the clients who rejected your sales campaign—thank them for their time and their helpful criticism. Pass information and clippings to colleagues. Recognize a public servant or a good customer with a short note. When you write unnecessary correspondence you will appear assertive to others, because you are taking the initiative and showing your appreciation and concern.

EDITING YOUR WRITING—OR BEING ASSERTIVE WITH YOURSELF

No piece of paper should leave your desk without a careful inspection—in fact, two inspections: the first to revise your written material and the second to follow the copy into print. A word processor or dictating machine is not an excuse to avoid revising your work. But it can save you time and help you make your work letter-perfect.

Cutting

The bulk of your task is to eliminate all of your writing that is distracting, repetitive, or unnecessary. Deletion involves pruning away excess material to strengthen your piece, much as a gardener cuts away deadwood to make a tree look better and grow stronger. In your writing the main thought may be lost in unnecessary words, phrases, and sentences. Go through your draft and eliminate all the words you can without changing the meaning. Strive for simplicity, but don't lose sight of your style. A 10 percent cut in wordage is a good but modest goal.

Rewriting

The next step in the process of revision is to improve the quality of your writing by tightening your logic, making your phrasing more precise, and getting your sentences to flow in interesting ways. Often a sentence can be improved by repositioning a single word or phrase. The meaning becomes clearer or the sentence reads better. FDR's famous statement "The only thing we have to fear is fear itself" exemplifies a principle of repositioning—that is, the end of the sentence carries the greatest emphasis. Would it have been as dramatic if FDR had said, "Fear itself is the only thing we have to fear"?

Notice how repositioning the word *only* in the following sentence changes the meaning and the flow. The reader should not have to question meaning.

Only I want to go to the dance with him.   (*no one else wants to*)
I want *only* to go to the dance with him.   (*I want nothing else*)
I want to go *only* to the dance with him.   (*nowhere else with him*)
I want to go to the dance *only* with him.   (*no one else will do*)

Editing

To be a successful editor, you need some objectivity. Put yourself in the shoes of your reader and then be very critical. Be aware of using certain words repeatedly. Go over your text and circle words you intend to change. If your copy is handwritten, get it typed. It will seem more impersonal.

Use a dictionary to check spelling and use of words. Spelling is especially critical. Mistakes in spelling make writing look sloppy—and you can't afford that if you want to be taken seriously. There are some basic rules you can memorize, but, above all, remember that for every rule there are exceptions. So, whenever you are in doubt, look the word up in your dictionary. You will find a few words that trip you up again and again. Make a list of them in a notebook. Keep track of your own pitfalls and watch for them when you write.

Finally, look for typos and messy pages. Your signature on a sloppy page will create the impression that you don't care. Written communications represent you. You wouldn't visit someone with your hem hanging down, your shirttail out, your shoes dusty, and your hair unkempt. Make your communiques as smart and stylish as you are.

Exercise: Test Your Editing Skills

The following paragraph contains no capitals and no punctuation. Test your editing skills by making corrections.

the new medium could start carrying pay tv and advertiser supported programming over a planned 30 or so channels as early as 1986 it is likely to make its most immediate appeal to rural areas where ordinary tv reception is so poor and program choices are few and to city dwellers in areas not wired for cable our primary market will be the nonserved and the underserved predicts a spokesman for satellite television corporation one of nine companies that have lined up to start the new service hoping for fcc construction permits within 90 days admits william bresnan chairman of group w cable a subsidiary of westinghouse electric they are needed in rural areas we can't reach unaffected by the new fcc rules are the large 12 ft backyard dishes that can already listen in on a whole variety of satellite signals including the prime time offerings of the cable outfits most of the new broadcasts will probably be scrambled to prevent unauthorized tapping

Exercise: Test Your Spelling

Circle the correct spelling of each word. If you miss even one, make the dictionary an indispensable part of your desktop library—and use it whenever you write.

attendance	attendence
goverment	government
excede	exceed
seperate	separate
commitment	committment
cemetery	cemetary
publicly	publically
supersede	supercede
accomodate	accommodate
inadvertant	inadvertent
dissension	dissention
quandry	quandary
fourty	forty
perscription	prescription
arguement	argument

mispell	misspell
symbollic	symbolic
milage	mileage
cancelation	cancellation
descendant	decendant
equipt	equipped
alotted	allotted
perogative	prerogative
achieve	acheive
pronunciation	pronounciation
proceed	procede
disasterous	disastrous
concensus	consensus

13

Managing Stress

Today's workplace is a much safer environment physically than it was even a decade ago. Construction workers wear hardhats; factory workers have blood tests on jobs where the environment may harbor dangerous substances; unions keep a diligent watch over conditions on the job. Even so, occupational hazards remain with us. Miners still get black lung disease; urban teachers still get mugged in the classroom. Many other jobs involve physical risk day after day. Stress, however, is the most pervasive occupational hazard in today's workplace.

Stress can endanger your health. It is associated with heart attacks, migraine headaches, peptic ulcers, renal disease, hypertension, asthma, and other physical ailments. Some doctors link stress to depression, anxiety, alcoholism, drug addiction, and the breakdown of interpersonal relationships.

In the workplace, stress is a double-edged sword. It may endanger your job as well as your health. Stress results in low productivity and high absenteeism. *The New York Times* reported that American industry lost between $10 billion and $20 billion annually for executives alone through lost workdays, hospitalization, and early death caused by stress. Other sources put this figure as high as $25 billion annually and expect it to double in the coming years.

Understanding stress and learning how to control it are essential to your success as a manager. You need to perform well and keep yourself physically and mentally fit. At the same time, you need to keep your department functioning cohesively and efficiently. Both tasks are undermined by stress.

WHAT IS STRESS?

When things are running along smoothly, your body functions in a state of *homeostasis*. You sleep, wake, go to work, eat, and move about, maintaining a normal range of body temperature, blood pressure, pulse, and respiration rate. Your physiological and mental states are in equilibrium. But then something happens and all these functions go haywire.

You're threatened. Your body prepares to respond to that distress. A car comes careening around the corner, tires squealing; it wavers and then veers out of control toward the playground. Your son is ten yards away. Without hesitating you leap over the seesaw, shove the child out of the car's path, and hurl yourself after him. What happened inside your body to enable you to do that?

When the body perceives danger, your pulse quickens. Your eyes dilate. Your lungs take in extra oxygen and send it straight to your muscles to prepare them for strenuous activity. Your digestion slows down while your blood-clotting capability increases. Your hearing improves. The endocrine system secretes epinephrine (adrenaline), which stimulates the nervous system.

The purpose of this flow of extra juices through your body is to help you respond better. Aroused, you are able to handle extraordinary situations. This is known as the "fright-flight-fight" response. You are prepared to run from danger or to fight back.

Where does "fright" come in? Imagine this scene. You receive a telephone call from the vice president of personnel. Could he see you at 3:15? You have an hour to stew. Your mind begins working. You've heard they are cutting some staff. There have been rumors about transferring a department or two out of the state. And shouldn't your performance evaluation be completed by now—is this meeting to tell you that your head's on the chopping block? By 3:00 your body is in full "fright." Your adrenaline is pumping. You're on pins and needles with every nerve ending alert, while you pace the floor, chew your nails, and try to drink enough water to moisten your dry mouth. Then it's 3:15. You walk through the vice president's door and he extends his hand and says, "Jim, I have some good news for you."

What happens to "flight or fight"? Of course, flight and fight are not necessary. But the body has already interpreted the situation as dangerous to life and limb and has built up its defenses. In office situations, particularly the kind where the work is mental rather than physical, people react to psychological distress just as if it were physiological stress. So the body goes through all those changes, creating a surge of energy, concentration, and power to perform in the expected crisis—yet nothing happens. The body must use even more energy to recuperate, and you end up feeling drained.

What if you do fight? What happens next is nature's way of adding a safety valve. The pancreas has been sending sugar into the parts of the body that will have the most work to do. Now the nervous system releases noradrenaline, a chemical that stabilizes blood pressure and keeps the heart functioning. When you actually use your distress readiness for a physical task—

say, you are experiencing stress in the locker room and then you begin to play football—your body produces more noradrenaline than adrenaline. This neutralizes the effects of the adrenaline and keeps your body from going into "overdrive." But if you are sitting at your desk and not getting exercise, no noradrenaline is produced, and the adrenaline remains in your system. This can have harmful effects.

Is stress always harmful? If you are watching a horror movie and have three or four false-alarm frights, will that quickening pulse, boost of adrenaline, and rapid heartbeat hurt you? No. In fact it is good for your body to have stress episodes, particularly if they are isolated, short-lived, and followed by recuperation time.

But what if your job itself is a horror movie and your boss stars as Mr. Hyde? He's moody and comes in every morning after a fight with his wife, looking for a scapegoat. He's predictable only in that nothing pleases him. And you're the one who always gets in the path of his anger. Then you're working in a situation of chronic stress, and that is harmful. You experience stress repeatedly, with no time for real recuperation. Your body is producing adrenaline but little noradrenaline, and it's in a constant state of alert. According to Dr. Paul J. Rosch, president of the American Institute of Stress, chronic stress lowers resistance to disease by interfering with the body's immune system. Chronic stress has a second side effect: the buildup of cholesterol and the increased likelihood of heart disease.

What are the symptoms? When stress goes beyond temporary preparation for emergency, it may lead to such symptoms as restlessness, excessive smoking, low-grade infections, irritability, anxiety, tension, stuttering and stammering, an inability to concentrate, and fatigue. When you feel any of these, you need a rest.

If you do not rest, you may advance to some of these symptoms: migraines, stomachaches, dizziness, sweating, random behavior, lethargy, hypertension, indigestion, accident-proneness, chest pain, insomnia, depression, backache, eating irregularities, frigidity, impotence, fatigue, absenteeism, and reduced quantity and quality of work. If you reach this stage of stress reaction, take heed: You are not coping well. The sad outcome of untreated chronic stress may be heart attack, ulcer, stroke, alcoholism, drug addiction, psychosis, suicide, or cancer. But stress can be deflected and turned into beneficial energy if you learn some effective coping skills. So take time to stop and rethink some of your behavior.

What are the causes? Stress is the original "good news/bad news" joke. You can get stress from either happy life experiences or tragic ones. Every major event in life means adaptation, and that produces anxiety.

Stress can be measured in various ways. For example, Drs. Thomas H. Holmes and Richard Rahe, professors at the University of Washington, developed a scale that used points to rate the stress caused by major life experiences.

Work-related problems are only one cause of stress, but they are a major cause. Researchers who presented a study called "Lifestyles/Personal Health Care in Different Occupations" to the American Academy of Family Physicians in 1979 drew this conclusion: "Although a major source of stress, work was not the sole culprit in producing such conditions as allergies, migraine headaches, backaches, and anxiety. But more problems tend to have their roots in the workplace than in the home."

EVALUATING STRESS AT WORK

Tension and anxiety can hit you in the workplace in many ways. Stress in the workplace can be divided into two categories: stress caused by changes (or events), and stress caused by ongoing conditions.* Stress from the first source is traumatic and requires immediate adaptation. Stress arising in the second instance is more subtle and often goes unrecognized. For instance, you may not realize that it is stressful for you to be unable to use your journalism skills when your job is to type, not edit, the company newsletter. This type of stress keeps eating at you because you cannot easily make a change or adapt to it. Here are some of the factors that can be stressful in the workplace:

Changes or Events

Changing jobs
Major changes in instructions, policies, or procedures
Requirement to work more hours per week than normal
Sudden significant increase in the activity level, or pace, of work
Major reorganization
Demotion
Losing a job

Ongoing Conditions

Feedback only when performance is unsatisfactory
Conflict between your unit and others
Underutilization of skills
Unclear standards
Conflicting demands
Being left out of decision making
Perceived lack of career progress
Inequity in reward systems
Lack of control over work
Restricted social interaction
Repetitive work
Piecework reward system
Management responsibility

*John D. Adams, *Understanding and Managing Stress: A Book of Readings* (San Diego: University Associates, 1980).

Inadequate support of supervisor
Long hours
Travel
Deadlines
Highly competitive atmosphere
Unclear job responsibilities

Today's managers face an added burden. Once it was possible to learn how to handle specific problems on the job by looking to the past. If your predecessor kept good records, you could follow those guidelines and make efficient adaptations of your own. But the modern work environment is in constant flux. Problems arise that no one has encountered before. Changes caused by rapid company growth, new technology, competing products, expansion of the manager's role—these unprogrammed events have variables that cannot be controlled or predicted. There is no body of research to tell what approach worked before. Anxiety about finding the right solution when there is no "right solution" cripples office leadership. It's even difficult to identify the problem when so many aspects of the business seem to be changing.

JOB BURN-OUT

What happens to someone on the job—whether that job is manager, factory worker, or housewife—who has not been able to manage stress? The person ends up burning out—exhausting his or her physical and mental resources.

Job burn-out is a psychological condition that affects your whole life—not just your work, but your interpersonal relationships outside of work, your enjoyment of your hobbies, and your outlook on life. It may leave you listless, depressed, and feeling cheated. It may also leave you seriously ill. A vicious cycle begins. You are less able to perform; you care less about performing. Then others begin to notice your lack of interest and become critical of your attitude. First you feel like a failure, then you're perceived as a failure. You isolate yourself because you feel both contagious and shunned. As one worker observed, "In this company it's an unwritten policy that you work together, but burn out alone."* Three variables affect burn-out:

1. *The type of person you are.* Not everyone who suffers from stress will succumb to job burn-out. One person can enjoy the job even while his or her blood pressure climbs. Another person, usually one whose energy and

*Quoted in Robert Veninga and James Spradley, *Job Burn-Out*.

expectations are heavily invested in work success, cannot handle the stress. This highly motivated person is a prime candidate for job burn-out. An unmotivated person might suffer from "rust-out," or terminal on-the-job boredom. But the person with idealized goals, whose standards are high, and who is intensely driven to compete and win is a prime candidate. As one manager put it, "To burn out you must first have been on fire."

2. *Your perspective.* If you perceive yourself as the hub around which all else revolves, you're the indispensable man or woman. A large corporation lost five top executives in the crash of a small jet airplane. The corporate stock dipped for a day or two, but the company was not devastated. Competent people emerged from the wings and filled in. Work went on. Yet each of those executives might have worked overtime, brought work home, and cut vacations short thinking that without their extra effort the company would collapse. Indispensable people mask the threatening thought that the world could go on without them.

A report of the Institute of Life Insurance several years ago noted that top managers who could easily afford long, uninterrupted vacations were not taking them. Instead they took a week here and there, long weekends, "working vacations"—but they never really gave themselves enough time to restore their energy supply. A recent study of executive vacation patterns added an alarming note: Today's executives are likely to suffer *more* stress on vacation. They worry about things going wrong back at the office, others taking over their jobs and getting ahead. The healthy approach is to be committed enough to want to do a good job but detached enough to know when you've done it.

3. *Your values and motives.* The values you bring to the workplace govern your response to what happens there. For example, you may have a very strong commitment to the work ethic, and may unconsciously see work as a "should." Some American women are joining the workforce for economic or philosophical reasons. Others hear the question "What do you do?" and feel subtle echoes of the work ethic; they get anxious that "housewife" is not enough of an answer. Such women are candidates for job burn-out.

"Workaholism" also puts managers at risk for burn-out. An effective manager exercises power to get things done and to achieve goals. Sure, being on the line every day takes its toll. But there is also the thrill of being where the action is, feeling important, and making things happen. The adrenaline "fix" can become as real as the alcoholic's need for a drink.

Workaholics are compulsive managers. They build fires just to put them out. They thrive on conflict, crisis, and control. One "reformed" workaholic described victims of the syndrome as: "Tense, depressed, aggressive or at least quietly stubborn, oppressed with feelings of inferiority and at the same time acting quite superior, perfectionistic and rigid, overpowered with a sense of loneliness, basically self-centered, defiant in a world apart from others."* Not only is the compulsive manager a candidate for job burn-out; he or she is creating an atmosphere for department burn-out.

COPING WITH STRESS AND BURN-OUT

Change, technology, broken dreams, tense interpersonal relationships, fears about world developments—all can lead to anxiety, stress, and a life that seems out of control. Stress can sideline you, throw your engine into "park" when you really need to be in "drive." When you develop coping skills despite these stresses, you learn to view life realistically. You regain your power and self-esteem and get back in control.

You have to learn how stress affects you. Two people may experience the same event with entirely different reactions. Consider an event from childhood—say, an outing at the beach with your parents. Your brother remembers only the trip home in the family car. He recalls that your father was tired and hit a dog and did not stop to help it. The day was spoiled for him and that's all he remembers. Your memory, on the other hand, is of playing in the surf with your father lifting you up over the waves. You recall a wonderful time. In adult life you may look forward to beach outings, while your brother finds them stressful. Similarly, in the workplace, what is stressful to one person may be challenging to another. You have to learn your own "stress points," your particular Achilles' heel.

Your goal is to take charge of your job (and your life) so that you can control what happens before it controls you. There are many aspects of your job that could produce stress. Some you can change, but others you cannot. As you slip into stress and start to burn out, you will have no idea what's causing the problem unless you learn how to read the signs.

When your refrigerator breaks down, you get out the owner's guide and read, "Avoid unnecessary, costly service calls. Five easy items to check yourself—before calling for service." Your owner's guide for your emotional well-being would list the following five trouble spots for checking at times of breakdown. If you can pinpoint the problem, you stand a better chance of relieving the stress.

1. *Your individual perception of stress.* Have you ever stood in a long bank line at lunchtime and watched people's behavior? Some are lost in thought, while others fume and complain aloud about the terrible service. One man is very concerned about his place in line; another reads a book and puts the time to good use. Do you find minor inconveniences like waiting in traffic extremely stressful? The more stress you experience in a routine situation, the greater your risk of burn-out. The perception of stress is some-

---

*Warren Oates, *Confessions of a Workaholic: The Facts About Work Addiction* (New York: Abingdon Press, 1972).

thing you can change. Try approaching stressful situations with the thought "So what if _____. I can always do _____."

2. *The demands of your environment.* Remember mood rings? Something in your body chemistry caused the ring to indicate your mood by changing color. You may change moods with the weather. Some people are soothed by a rainy day; others get depressed. Red tide strikes the ocean in the middle of your vacation and the children cannot go in the water. Your stress is much greater than that of vacationers with no children. A family moves to a large city. Some members love the change; others react with anxiety and tension. To change a stressful environment, you may need to make "flight" an option. Sometimes, quitting a dead-end job is the only way to separate yourself from its stress.

3. *Family pressures.* Since you spend part of each day at home and part of it at the office, work stress and family troubles interact daily. Stress at home carries over to the job—and vice versa. The argument you have with your spouse before you leave for work is not forgotten at the train station. The stressful aftereffects travel with you to your office and to your relationships there. At different times during your career, family pressures will mount. The death of a parent, child, or spouse; a rebellious adolescent; divorce or separation—all these things hamper your ability to cope.

4. *Problems at work.* Two years ago it seemed like such a great job. Now it's unfulfilling. Few adults are stress-free on the job. But many, even under stress, will say they are happy. Your expectations about your job make a difference. A man who measures success in terms of salary will feel less stress when he gets frequent raises. A woman with hidden talents who works at a routine office job builds up intense anger that she has not been discovered. Someone who needs to be loved rather than respected reacts to office conflict very badly. You have two choices: Change the job, or change your expectations.

5. *Stress safety valves that aren't working.* It really helps to be able to do something to relieve the pressure. Exercise is reliable. So are having a good friend to talk to, pursuing a hobby, and getting some rest. But some people choose alcohol or tranquilizers and create other problems. Workaholics think that by spending more time at work, they can get things under control. Instead, they become less and less efficient and the stress builds. When you pursue something that "should" bring relief but doesn't, stop and look for another solution.

Each of these five "trouble spots" could be a cause of job burn-out. All five can go wrong at once. But rarely is stress linked to just one cause, because our lives are not that fragmented. So when you begin to feel the first symptoms of stress—the headaches, the tension at the back of your neck, digestive problems, fatigue, it's time to consult your checklist. Evaluate what could be causing you problems. You, too, may be able to avoid a costly service call (or a costly life experience) if you identify the trouble and take action to alleviate it.

Before you gird up to combat stress, one reminder is in order. Not all stress is bad. Think about stage fright. Every actor knows that it's real. Good actors are keyed up by the time they go on stage. Some vomit before most performances. But this stress serves a useful purpose. The actor learns to take charge of the energy and transfer it to the task at hand. The same nervous energy that caused sweating palms and rapid, shallow breathing backstage is used for expressive gestures and an eloquently projected voice once the curtain rises. Many performers feel that their nervousness adds an extra electricity and excitement that was not there during rehearsals.

We need stress to be able to respond to emergencies and to challenges. Without it life would be flat and emotionless. Learning how to perceive stress, and understanding how to take charge of it and make it work for you, is what keeps it from being destructive. That's why assertiveness skills are an important part of managing stress, both at home and on the job.

Another hopeful note: People who are able to progress from manager, to executive, to the room at the top find that life at the top is much less stressful. Whether there actually is less stress or whether those who negotiate the tough climb successfully are better able to handle stress is uncertain. Still, according to a report of the Metropolitan Life Insurance Company, men at the top have a mortality rate 37 percent lower than those with similar backgrounds who did not reach the top; women have a mortality rate 29 percent lower.

SOME PROGRAMS CORPORATIONS HAVE FOUND HELPFUL

Diet and Exercise

Employees can be encouraged, even taught, to practice good nutrition. The company cafeteria can participate by serving a diet plate and having salad choices. When managers are required to take cardiovascular stress tests each year, corrective measures can be pursued to control weight, alcoholism, and coffee or tea addiction. Some companies have gymnasiums or offer exercise classes during the workday to encourage stress reduction and body fitness. You should pick some form of exercise that fits into your daily routine—jogging, swimming, bicycling, aerobic dancing, or walking to work.

Time Management

Most people do not think they have enough time to accomplish what needs to be done. And falling behind can make you feel overwhelmed and depressed. Do you feel that the quality of your work is slipping because

ASSERTIVE STRESS FIGHTERS

○ When you know you have to refuse someone, say no right away. Apply this to tasks and invitations.

○ Allow extra time for everything. Arrive early.

○ Write angry letters and rip them up.

○ Don't rely on memory for addresses or telephone numbers of your appointments.

○ Say "so what" more often than "what if."

○ Always carry "waiting work"—or a good book to read—so lines or travel do not frustrate you.

○ Double-check meeting places, times, and dates.

○ Look for some humorous aspect to any disaster.

○ Keep extra supplies of pens, stamps, pads, and other frequently used items.

you're always under pressure? You *can* get your time under control. Many organizations, community colleges, and business schools sponsor time management seminars. This may be a wonderful investment. You can learn to organize your day to include space for work and relaxation. Many jobs can be done automatically; other jobs need full concentration. Use your prime time (when your efficiency is at its peak) to tackle your most important tasks. Practicing assertiveness and saying no to people's demands will often save you lots of time.

Procrastination is a human disease. With twelve hours to do something, it takes twelve; with two hours, it gets done in two. The head of a prestigious New York design firm was the last to leave the building each day. She locked the doors precisely at 5:30 and opened them (weekdays only) at 8:30. Her staff members knew they were expected to perform at peak efficiency during those work hours and were not allowed to stay late or come in on weekends. And they did. You can spend less time doing more if you work at time management. Some pointers:

1. Set goals. This gives you perspective and direction.
2. Establish objectives. Have a time frame for reaching your goals. What do you want to accomplish today, by next week, by next year, and so on?
3. Set priorities. Head for the most important things first.
4. Analyze your use of time. Are you spinning your wheels, wasting too much time? Or not taking enough time to relax?
5. Plan. Schedule your time to reach your objectives.
6. Relax. Plan time for leisure. It's essential.

Programmed Relaxation

Many people have found transcendental meditation (TM) to be a valuable tool for detaching themselves from the events around them and relaxing. Those who practice TM feel that it helps them cope with daily pressure. At Equitable Life Assurance, employees can go to a laboratory to obtain biofeedback on their anxious, tense feelings. The feedback makes them aware of tension and of the effectiveness of their relaxation programs.

A relaxation/meditation technique developed by Dr. Herbert Benson of Harvard University* is used in many companies and takes only a few minutes to learn. The essentials are:

1. Get comfortable. Sit or lie down, and loosen clothing.
2. Relax each part of your body, "thinking" or "willing" it into relaxation (name each part).
3. Inhale. Be aware of the air as it fills your lungs.
4. Exhale, repeating a neutral word. Choose one that does not have thought associations.
5. Try not to be distracted.
6. Practice the breathing exercises for up to 20 minutes. Then sit quietly with eyes closed. Get up slowly.

Those who practice relaxation techniques are benefiting in two ways. First, they actually do rest. In addition, they see things differently. The brain has two hemispheres: The left hemisphere controls our analytical, rational, and verbal impulses; the right hemisphere is our subjective, intuitive, creative side. Most stress comes from rational and verbal stimuli. In other words, when we are undergoing stress, the left side of our brain is working most of the time. We get locked into physical responses dictated by that part of the nervous system. If we can tune into the other side of our brain—by using relaxation techniques, going to a concert, painting a picture, and so on—we can increase the possibilities for new solutions or give ourselves a much needed rest.

ATTITUDES THAT CAN HELP

Desensitizing

Desensitizing is like wading into a cold lake instead of diving in. Before you get to a threatening event or confrontation, you relax, imagine yourself there, and get used to the discomfort you will feel. You also rehearse "stroke" messages that will give you encouragement and protect your self-image (such as "you're calm, you can handle this").

The Relaxation Response (Boston: G. K. Hall, 1976).

Worried about that important meeting tomorrow? Relax and imagine the first steps toward the scene. For instance, you might see yourself asleep in bed, then getting dressed, eating, driving to work, entering the office, getting coffee, and finally going to the meeting. At each stage you try to hold on to your relaxed state so that it becomes part of the scenario. Gradually you work your way through it. The acid test is carrying this anxiety-free memory with you to the real encounter. It works!

Flexibility

"There's more than one way to approach this." That's the attitude of the flexible person. Rigid structures (and people) are unable to weather severe storms. Architects know they must build an allowance for sway into plans for skyscrapers. People who are unable to bend can get knocked down by stress. Task-oriented managers often have trouble being flexible. Goals become so important in life and at work that tunnel vision sets in. When you focus on one path to a destination, you lose sight of many other ways you might get there.

To be flexible is to say, "That's not working—time to try another approach." Some managers have the mistaken notion that if they give up on something—a style of leadership, an operations system—they are weak. In fact, it takes a strong leader to reevaluate goals, assess progress, and change direction when necessary.

Reality Testing

Reality testing is important in mastering stress. Reality testing puts reason up against emotion. Is what you're feeling (anxiety, fear, anger, intimidation) appropriate to what is happening? Let's see how the process works.

It's time for your annual physical at Executive Health Services. Each year for the past five years, these checkups have been very routine. But this year, your fortieth, you grow more anxious as the date approaches. The night before the exam, tossing in bed, you do some reality testing. Do I have any physical symptoms to cause me worry? No. Have my previous checkups revealed any problems? No. Does my family history give me reason for concern? Well, my father had his first heart attack at 40. But he was 30 pounds overweight and I'm in good shape. Your cause of worry is revealed and with it a rational piece of information that can relieve your concern.

Objectivity

Decision making can be very stressful. Here are some tips for making objective, stress-free decisions.

1. Get some distance. When you stand back from the issue you can see it objectively. You need to identify the issues involved and the feelings they are producing in you.

2. Play "what if." Treat your decision like a game of chess. What would happen if you moved your knight? Would moving your pawn be better? If you did, what would your opponent's next move be? In other words, what are the repercussions? What are your rights in this situation? What will this move mean to your career? If you win the battle, will you lose the war?

3. Separate your "wants" from your "shoulds." Knowing what you really want to do may free you to do what you know you should. (You're allowed to feel righteous.)

Once you've considered all the options, looked at the probable results of your actions, and accepted the feelings involved, your decision will be based on logic, not rationalization.

Role Reversal

Role reversal can help you get enough distance from a stressful situation to see it objectively. Think of a situation in which someone else is causing you stress. Pretend you are that "problem person." Now bring yourself into the scene. As the problem person, try to relate to yourself. Take a good look at your strengths and weaknesses. What complaints would the problem person have? What would make your relationship work better? Now get back to reality and make some of these changes. Take steps to resolve the conflict yourself.

TIPS FOR MANAGING STRESSFUL JOBS

1. *Learn to manage and cope with stress.* In order to do your job, you have to be free to do it, free from crippling effects of stress. There are few stress-free jobs. Pretending that stress isn't real doesn't help. Finding solutions does. And the first step to finding solutions is isolating the cause of your stress. You may feel discontent with your whole job and not realize that something specific is causing the problem. Make yourself more aware of the stress factors. Make a list of everything that irks you, every complaint. Keep it going for several days. Then arrange your complaints in order of severity. Decide which ones you can do something about.

2. *Alter your perspective.* Ever tell a story months after an event and say, "Well, I can laugh about it now, but at the time it certainly wasn't funny." When stress builds, things can blow up out of proportion. Stepping back from what's happening and treating it like a piece of theater is a wonderful way to see things differently. A headache, an empty stomach, family problems can make a small slight seem like a huge insult.

3. *Check behind the scenes.* Sometimes managers don't realize that there is more going on in the workplace than meets the eye (or ear). Again, treat what goes on at the office like a piece of theater. Your job description is the

script of the play; but what you actually need to do to get recognition may be hidden behind the scenes. You may think your major duties are to write 12 pieces of advertising copy a week. The real test of whether you succeed may be whether you can supply your boss with ten new jokes each week. Break the unwritten rules and you may run into stress head on.

4. *Learn how to read stress signs.* You can treat the symptoms. That headache behind your left eye, the ramrod neck, the quivering hands—those are the signals that stress is setting in. Recognize your own weakness. Stop and do something. Take a rest, exercise, go for a walk. Or work on reducing the source of the stress. That may mean lowering your expectations. If your goals are realistic and attainable, you will experience the pleasure of accomplishment and the boost that it gives your ego. One completed task may make you feel better than five ambitious but half-finished projects. At a meeting of a women's group, a bestselling author was asked how she managed to write her book and keep up with her house and child at the same time. "Easy," she replied. "I gave up housework." The audience breathed a sigh of relief. Knowing your limitations is necessary for coping with stress.

5. *Change what you can.* Make a list of all the functions you perform on the job, even small, trivial things. Make a second list of all the people you interact with each day—in person, by telephone, or through the mail (include the coffee cart attendant, the security guard). Then make a list of all the conditions surrounding your job (include commuting, the copier that always breaks down, the slow-moving elevator, the lighting, the temperature). Then circle each person, function, or condition that adds to your work stress. What can you do to make changes? Can you improve communications, suggest alternative job structures, recommend safety improvements, be more receptive to staff suggestions? If as a manager you are able to make the workplace more human, you will benefit from the improved atmosphere and the improved motivation of your staff.

STYLES OF MANAGEMENT—ARE YOU A STRESS CARRIER?

Sometimes when one employee burns out, she causes a whole department to burn out around her. The disease is catching. Employees sometimes sense this and try to avoid a department member who is beginning to burn out, and this breeds more malcontent.

Another way for a whole department to burn out is to have a stress carrier for a boss, even if the boss himself is not burning out. If you are a burn-out boss, chances are that management skills such as problem solving, motivational strategy, and management by objectives are less important to you than corporate games. So confrontations are win/lose situations. Subordinates are after your job. And most communication is nonverbal. As a result, your staff members are not committed to the corporation. In fact, they feel gypped of job satisfaction. (Table 9 lists some common burn-out styles and ways of dealing with them.)

You as a manager should continually assess your impact as a boss. Read the body language of those who work for you. Look for signs of burn-out and determine whether you are the cause. Consider yourself a burn-out monitor. Learn all you can about stress so that you can help employees who have burn-out problems and combat the spread of burn-out in your department. Find out what is being done and what can be done at the corporate level to prevent or treat burn-out—for example, training programs on management techniques, stress management, time management, health care. Keep the satisfaction level high in your department. Review performance and give specific instructions for improvement. Provide lateral moves for the dissatisfied. Encourage continuing education so that employees keep growing and improving their skills. Finally, it's important to show your employees that you appreciate them as human beings, not just as workers. Cultivate and express interest in their families, hobbies, and outside interests.

Remember, too, that you are a subordinate as well as a manager. You must learn how to respond to your boss's style while keeping your own style intact. Change is more likely if you approach your boss in the following ways:

1. Use every communications method open to you—written notes and phone calls as well as planned conferences. Be specific, clear, and concise.

2. Don't attack. Try to find a way of saying what you want that will make the change seem like a benefit to your boss.

3. Give your boss positive feedback. Everyone responds to positive reinforcement. When the boss does something that helps rather than hinders your work, say so.

4. Handle critical suggestions with kid gloves. Start your statements with "I feel," "I need," "I think" rather than making accusatory "you did" statements. Go easy. One well-thought-out suggestion that leads to change could have a beneficial ripple effect throughout the company.

Finally, as a manager, don't be intimidated by change. Every change—even a sought-after promotion—involves loss. There are good-byes, loss of support, and tearing away from the familiar. If you dwell on a loss, your anxiety will increase. Instead, view it as something exciting and expect the best. Why? Because past experiences have been successful. Your worries about starting over can be lessened by planning, rehearsing solutions for problems you anticipate, and testing reality.

To cope with stress effectively, remember that you need information. You can't make decisions until you know all the possible options for action. If you know where you are headed, your choices will be grounded in reality. Remember, too, that you must act freely. A decision not your own, or one based on guilt, leads to anger. Finally, anticipate crises before they overtake you. Being ready eliminates anxiety.

Table 9. "Burn-out" styles of managing.

Management Style	If It's Your Boss . . .	If You're the Boss . . .
HYPERCRITICAL. Tone is angry or testy. Unable to compliment. Employees have high turnover rate. Poor communicator.	Assert yourself against unfair criticism. Find something to compliment your boss about.	Learn how to give positive feedback. Learn how to motivate workers in a positive way.
PLAYED-OUT. Waiting for retirement. Doesn't want to cause problems or try new things. Survival is important. Defeated by the system. Doesn't heed subordinates' suggestions. Staff is low in productivity. Bitter.	Demand approval of work, but do not expect rewards. Do not waste energy trying to change things; risk is too threatening to such a boss. Find ways to view your lack of supervision positively; think of it as freedom.	You are blocking productivity, causing absenteeism. If you are unable to get a new job, look into early retirement.
NO CONFLICT. Values love over achievement. Sees the best in everyone, excuses mistakes. Never fires anyone. Loyalty is most important. Likes self-starters.	Stop looking to the boss for structure. Direct your energies into jobs that others will notice. Don't be fooled by the boss's manipulative acts of kindness.	Learn how to be a mentor. The relationship can be caring and productive. You need help with self-esteem and conflict management. Observe the devotion good leaders get from subordinates.
SILENT. Noncommunicator. Gives no feedback to employees—no criticism or praise—and no direction. Will not discuss problems. Creates crises by not involving others in planning. Workers have role conflict, no job satisfaction.	Your anxiety is caused by role conflict and not knowing what is expected of you. Inquire about corporate programs for breaking through communications barriers. Use confrontation to demand feedback.	Your silence is giving you a sense of power. Your employees cannot do as well when you withhold information. Get training in communications skills.
SLAVE DRIVER. Authoritarian. Never pleased with others' performance. Can always do it better. Personal success is most important. Gives no positive reinforcement. Everything is win/lose. Sets arbitrarily high standards, then punishes for lack of achievement.	Use reality testing to assure yourself that you've done a good job. Organize a group of employees to confront the boss. Use company's boss-performance review if you can, or have a conference with the boss's superior. Restructure authority so workers have some.	Learn how to give praise. Ask subordinates for their opinion of what's wrong. Be thick-skinned when they tell you. Autocratic behavior is inappropriate in the workplace.

Exercise: Stress and Burn-Out Inventory*

This exercise is designed to help you step back from your routine and take a look at yourself, an honest look. Do your current attitudes, behavior, circumstances make you a burn-out candidate? Check as many personality traits as apply to you:

_____ dynamic	_____ principled
_____ charismatic	_____ responsible
_____ goal-oriented	_____ impatient
_____ idealistic	_____ demanding
_____ dedicated	_____ intense
_____ high achiever	_____ thorough
_____ committed	_____ independent
_____ competent	

If over half of these categories describe you, read on.

Warning Signals

Check the column which best describes your behavior currently and in the recent past. Add up your total scores for each category and record them in the spaces provided.

	not at all	rarely	occasionally	usually	very often
Physical	0	1	2	3	4
1. I have headaches, colds, flu.					
2. I suffer from backaches.					
3. I am in a hurry, rushing.					
4. I have digestive problems (upset stomach, diarrhea).					
5. My blood pressure is high.					
6. I feel tired.					

Total _____

---

*This exercise was designed by Joan Alevras Stampfel, Executive Director of Resource Center Inc., a management development corporation located at 273 Hillside Ave., Nutley, NJ 07110 (201) 661-2195. Exercise reprinted with permission from THE EXECUTIVE FEMALE, a bimonthly magazine published and distributed exclusively to members of the National Association for Female Executives, 120 East 56th Street, Suite 1440, New York, NY 10022 (212) 371-0740.

	not at all	rarely	occasionally	usually	very often
	0	1	2	3	4

Behavioral
7. I am impatient with others.
8. I am irritable in a wide variety of settings.
9. I am critical of others.
10. I have trouble accepting criticism.
11. I complain to others but do not take action to improve a situation.
12. I am demanding of myself and others.

Total _____

Emotional
13. I have to push myself to keep going on a project.
14. I use anger or sarcasm when making a point.
15. I tell myself, "I am really not doing as well as I could."
16. I doubt that I can get the job done.
17. I do not believe that others really like me.
18. I fly off the handle more than I have in the past.

Total _____

Intellectual
19. I have been forgetting important dates/assignments.
20. I find it hard to concentrate.
21. I find myself daydreaming.
22. I find it difficult to make decisions.
23. I have been putting off important tasks.
24. I have too many things on my mind at once.

Total _____

	not at all	rarely	occasionally	usually	very often
	0	1	2	3	4

Organizational

25. My relationships at work are not satisfying.

26. I am not getting support for my decisions.

27. I do not believe others can do the job as well as I can.

28. I feel tense at work.

29. I feel confused about what I am really supposed to be doing on the job.

30. The time pressures at work do not allow me to complete tasks properly.

Total —————————

Subtotals:

Physical

Behavioral

Emotional

Intellectual

Organizational

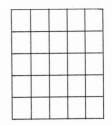

Total —————————

Now check your burn-out range:

0–29 = Safe

You seem to be reacting to life events in a way which does not deplete your resources or your ability to take care of yourself.

30–59 = Average

You could be taking better care of yourself. Your standards for yourself and others are unusually high, and this causes you to have frequent run-ins with reality.

60–89 = Warning

You are very close to burning out. You are probably encountering many difficulties and disappointments and having a hard time adjusting to events. Your resources are being depleted faster than you can replace them.

90–120 = Danger

You are experiencing burn-out; reality is in conflict with your hard-driving ways and high ideals. Since you have probably exhausted your ability to adjust, you need a vacation, a rest, and a support system that can sustain you.

Also check your most vulnerable areas—your two highest scores. Pay particular attention to these areas of your life, and begin today to take positive steps to develop your healthy coping skills.

Coping Behaviors

Each of us has developed measures for taking care of ourselves. As you go through the following items, check the responses which best describe your habits. How often do you use these measures to relax?

	not at all	rarely	occasionally	usually	very often
	0	1	2	3	4
1. I get enough sleep.					
2. I take enough time to eat.					
3. I take a drink to relax.					
4. I drink coffee, tea, or soda and eat snacks.					
5. I seek out people to talk to.					
6. I smoke.					
7. I use tranquilizers/stimulants to get through the day.					
8. I use humor to get my point across.					
9. I leave my work area for a temporary break.					
10. I eat lunch away from work.					
11. I use sick days as I need them.					
12. I use aspirin, medications, drugs.					
13. I use relaxation techniques (meditation, yoga).					
14. I use informal relaxation techniques (deliberate "daydreaming," deep breathing).					
15. I plan for quiet, unscheduled time.					
16. I keep an up-to-date "life goals" plan.					
17. I participate in physical exercise.					
18. I watch television, go to movies or shows.					
19. I am active in noncompetitive physical activities.					

	not at all	rarely	occasionally	usually	very often
	0	1	2	3	4
20. I schedule leisure reading time.					
21. I break up my routine.					
22. I chew my fingernails, gum, mints, candy.					
23. I pay attention to good grooming habits (hair cuts, clothes that fit, are appropriate, cleaned and pressed).					
24. I acknowledge others for the good job they are doing.					
25. I say "no" to unrealistic demands or requests.					
26. I schedule times for my hobbies, interests.					
Other: _____					

Now look at how you have answered the above questions. Pay particular attention to your responses to numbers 3, 4, 6, 7, 12, 18, and 22. If you are predominantly using these measures to the exclusion of others, you probably are not renewing your own resources adequately. Plan to increase your use of these other methods by scheduling them into your life on a regular basis. One good way to assure your involvement is to make a commitment with a friend to do some of these activities together. Join a gym. Plan a program. Commit to a course. Make an appointment to talk with your supervisor about your concerns and changing needs; if a supervisor is not readily available, talk with a co-worker about the changes and adjustments you can make in your workplace. Find and practice ways to keep renewing yourself. You'll start to see the results in every aspect of your life.

14

Building Support Systems

Have you encountered any of the following situations in the past six months on the job?

- o A co-worker is promoted to a position that you would have liked, but you didn't even know the opening was available.
- o A proposal of yours that you thought was a sure winner is killed without explanation. You haven't any idea how to find out what happened to it.
- o You overhear two colleagues ridiculing your choice of clothing for the regional sales meeting.
- o You want to change jobs, but you have no information about pay scales in similar companies, what benefits you should look for, and, most important, where to look for a job.
- o You notice that R. S. always comes to meetings equipped with statistics, figures, and support material. You have no idea where she gets that information.

If you've identified with even one of these situations, you need a support system. Or maybe you just need to recognize that you have a support system but are not using it.

HOW SUPPORT SYSTEMS HELP

A closer look at the situations described above suggests that there are five different types of support systems that can help you become a more effective manager.

Lateral Networking

Your co-worker heard about that job opening from an old friend. Four managers who worked together when they first joined the company continue to meet for breakfast once a week even though they now are located in different departments. When one of them mentioned that there would be a job opening in her department soon, the co-worker was not hesitant to suggest himself, and to ask a favor. He said, "Gee, that would be a great job for me. I've been taking some night courses in statistics to help me land a job in market research. I'd be very interested in talking to someone about that job. Do you think you could put in a word for me?"

If you are losing out on opportunities because you aren't in touch with company gossip, take a cue from this co-worker. Maintain contacts with old friends. It's to your advantage to have broad-based recognition in the company, along with a tie-in to the office grapevine. Keep your contacts up to date about your training and accomplishments, and don't be afraid to ask for a favor when you need it. You will be learning the art of lateral networking.

Vertical Networking

Your proposal arrived at the meeting without groundwork. It was presented cold. No one was prepared to defend it. One element in the proposal—using a direct-mail campaign to increase sales—hit on a pet peeve of the ranking vice president. Even though it was not an essential part of the proposal, it soured the vice president on the idea. The oversights should be obvious.

You would have done much better with your proposal if you had developed a contact with someone above you on the company ladder. Such a contact could have helped you hone the proposal so that it had a better chance of gaining approval. Your contact could have carried your proposal into the meeting and become spokesman for it. Of course, ahead of time you would have discussed critical points with the contact and supplied supportive material. In return, you would "owe him one." That's how vertical networking works.

Mentoring

That regional sales meeting your division was invited to was held at a resort in the Poconos. Some employees managed to find out ahead of time that the chief executive officer liked to conduct business sessions in office attire, then allow everyone to change to leisurewear for recreational activities. You arrived with a suitcase packed with business clothes, ill-prepared for the four days of meetings.

Every company has unwritten rules, or protocol, that govern behavior. These are learned best from a mentor—someone who has played the game longer than you have. A relationship with a mentor would have saved the situation described above. The mentor would have previewed the new experience for you—your first regional sales meeting—and given you vital information about what to wear, where to sit, and what activities were "in." This would have kept you from making mistakes and landing flat on your face. At the same time, you would have had the advantage of arriving at the meeting confident, with game plan in hand. Your success in turn would gain your mentor the reputation of being a good groomer. Such is the mentoring process.

Citywide Networking

Let's say your section has six management-level people. Two of the six always seem to have inside knowledge about job openings, who's making what salary, what companies are losing money, policies on hiring women and laying people off, and so on. What do they do with this information? They are a step ahead of the other four in spotting trends, so their ideas seem new and creative. If they get a job offer, or want to pursue an opening, they have ways to get the information they need—salaries, benefits, people to contact. How do they do it? They join associations or professional groups that draw people from across the profession together. A banker might join a group of regional finance officers to gain valuable contacts outside his own bank network. By contributing to that organization, he builds a reputation as a team player, someone who gets around, an idea man. It's called citywide networking.

National Networking

True, R. S. always comes to meetings with an arsenal of information, but she doesn't just pull it out of the air. She belongs to national networks that attract people from her whole profession. If she's an architect she might belong to the American Institute of Architects and the Alumni Association of Parsons School of Design. To expand contacts to groups that might affect her occupation, she also belongs to the Guild for Religious Architects and the National Commission on Architectural Barriers to the Handicapped. She supports the Architectural Heritage Foundation and, through this organization, has contacts with famous designers, builders, politicians, and preservationists. But she also receives mailings that keep her informed about legislation which might affect her trade. Newsletters, copies of speeches, and conventions are very fertile by-products of belonging to these organizations. By associating yourself with national groups you will be able to see the big picture. These are the benefits of national networking.

WHAT IT TAKES TO GET AHEAD

"No man is an island," John Donne observed, and nowhere is this truer than in the working world. Each person's job performance interfaces with another's to enhance or detract from productivity. An employee's technical

talents and abilities are measured along with the ability to work coopera-
tively with others. In a management job, the ability to lead and motivate
others may be just as important as individual job performance.

Moves up the organizational ladder hardly ever happen in a straight line.
Rather, moving up is like an unpredictable trip around the track of a pinball
machine—bumping off the corners, richocheting off the flippers, ringing a
bell here or there—with each event changing the course of the game and the
probability of achieving the goal.

Your support system is the people in your life who can help you keep on
course toward your goal. More than likely, it is a varied group. It may
include the friend who would commiserate with you over a drink if you lost
an account; the company vice president who is married to your mother's
best friend; and the "insider" in your profession who knows everything
that's happening. There may even be a college professor you've kept in
touch with who serves as a role model.

If you are an assertive manager, or trying to be, getting ahead is one of
your goals. Your support system can provide you with the information,
emotional support, contacts, role models, and confidence you need. It's a
crucial part of your success. Charles Luckman, a manufacturing executive
and architect, defined success succinctly back in 1955 in *The New York
Mirror:* "Success is that old ABC—ability, breaks, and courage." Understanding these three components of success can help you work out your own
support systems.

Ability

Any networker will tell you that ability is the first prerequisite for seeking
support. No one else can or will prop you up on your job if you can't
function on your own. Once someone gives you a contact or a recommen-
dation, his reputation as well as yours is on the line. Being competent at
what you do is absolutely necessary, but it's just a starting point.

Breaks

Some people spend their whole career waiting for "luck" to give them
that big break. If up to now you've thought success had anything to do with
being in the right place at the right time, or were sitting behind your desk
waiting to be noticed for doing such a good job, begin to take charge of
developing your own career.

Have you ever returned from a vacation with a group of friends or cou-
ples and discovered that one of you managed to get a gorgeous tan while
the rest of you either fried or were pale by comparison? Looking back, what
happened? Did Pete "get all the breaks"? Sure, he may have started out
with a complexion that tanned more easily than some. But he probably
worked hard at getting that tan. He was the one who covered himself with

creams and lotions, who kept shifting his body to get the right angle of the sun's rays, and who got on the beach for the best tanning times. That's what building support systems is all about—positioning yourself so you take advantage of the breaks that are out there.

Courage

In the management sphere, courage means a willingness to take risks. The payoff, when taking a risk works, is that you benefit by growing and developing into an effective manager. Taking a risk might mean trying a very different approach to solving a problem. Do be sure you've assessed the options, weighed the risk factor, and thought about the outcomes that each possible option could produce. If you've done all that, you are ready to take an "educated risk."

Here's one type of risk: Offer your talents to an organization that's influential in your field. The risk is rejection. You can minimize the risk by working very hard, trying to get along with others at all levels in the organization, making sure your efforts get recognition, and not expecting immediate results. You may need to work at low-level duties for a while. Other risks include leaving your job when it's secure but not challenging; making a lateral move just to get a different angle on an upward climb; and presenting yourself as a candidate for a higher-level job. Taking calculated risks is the only way you can move yourself toward success.

BUILDING A NETWORK

Developing a support system is an activity, not a happening. It's as old as the "old boy network" and as familiar as "you scratch my back, I'll scratch yours." Your active role is critical. In developing a network, you are structuring around yourself the kinds of people and support you will need to get you where you want go.

How Networks Work

Networking is a means of making contacts, of linking up with people and ideas, of getting and giving information. Every connection you make is a two-way circuit—sometimes conducting and at other times receiving information, contacts, and support. But always the circuit leads from you or to you.

In a larger sense, networking is like a complex solar system. You are the sun of your own universe, and your network orbits around you. It exists for you and continues through your effort. Without your involvement, there is no system or structure. The people listed in your address book are simply people you know; they do not become resources until you call upon them.

At the same time, each component of your networking universe is the center of his or her own universe, with its own planetary system. (Because we are not really dealing with astronomy, you can be a sun in your solar system and simultaneously be a planet in your friend's.) This may sound like chaos, but it works in surprising and creative ways for those who catch on to the networking process. That's not all. Every person who is the hub of his or her own network, and a component of your network, may also be part of someone else's network. One of your emotional supporters may be someone else's resource for contacts. Linkages are a constant surprise.

Networks can be formal or informal. Generally they are informal, with no bureaucracy or hierarchy, because they are always in flux and are based on cooperation rather than competition. They have leadership but are not dependent on leaders. In a network, the purpose of leadership is to enable and facilitate rather than to control or exercise power. There is a tacit understanding that every member is a self-reliant part that joins with others to form a whole. So no one member is indispensable; nor is anyone's identity completely wrapped up in the network.

Some networks do have official titles, such as the Women's Forum and the Boston Health Collective. But the process itself is invisible. Networks are the intangible links, communications, friendships, trusts, and values that spring up in relationships. These change—start up, stop, redefine themselves—without formal announcement. Networkers form clusters of interaction and channels of communication as needs and issues emerge.

If you are ready to begin networking, you have several immediate tasks. You must determine what your abilities are and how you can contribute to others. You will have to evaluate your own needs so you know what you want. Then you can begin to catalog the people who can fill key roles in your network. Finally, you will have to support your supporters.

Your Resources and Goals

Networking is a reciprocal arrangement. You'll be giving your own talents and resources to others in exchange for their support. What you have to offer may be as simple as making some telephone calls, proofreading a report, or attending a meeting in someone's place. Or it may mean teaching a skill like public speaking or tennis, passing on information about a prospective client, or leading someone to a valuable contact. There is probably something you do very well. Whatever that something is, follow the adage for effective bridge playing and "lead with your strength." Do that something in grand style.

You will also need to establish your goals. You may not be able to sit down and write out a list of your long-term goals, but you probably do know some short-term ones. This is the place to begin while you are trying to nail down what you eventually want to head toward. Perhaps you foresee that knowing how to utilize computer systems will be an important skill in your industry. Getting computer knowledge is then a short-term goal. As you continue in networking, your goals will be changing. And since you will still be growing, you'll continue to set new ones.

Whom Do You Know?

You don't need to set up an office or hang out a shingle to build a network, but a few basics will come in handy. First, you'll need an address book (or Rolodex or file cards) for keeping track of all your contacts—the ones you know now, and the ones you will be meeting. You'll also need a datebook. A large part of developing a network involves going places where you can meet people and keeping in contact with your best supporters. Good networkers make frequent lunch dates. Finally, a telephone or writing pad is useful for keeping in touch with those you cannot see with any frequency. A note or call once a year keeps your contacts alive.

Begin assembling a file box of the people you already know. Get them in some kind of order. You'll quickly find that your supporters fall into several categories: those who give you information; those you turn to for emotional support; and those who are resources for social or professional contacts.

The people who give you information may do so in several settings. Successful men and women learn to work while they play. As a result, many deals are worked out on the golf course between people who also meet in business clothes on other occasions. To identify your information network and to cultivate new contacts, try to determine the places where your contacts are productive as well as fun—for example, country clubs, college clubs, organizations you belong to, lunch tables, tennis courts.

Your emotional supporters are easily spotted. Just imagine something bad happening. You run for the telephone. Whom do you call? Who in your life gives you encouragement, an ego boost, a pep talk when you need it? If you find that your emotional needs are not being met by your present network, it's time to develop new relationships. Think about joining a club, religious organization, or self-help group, or rekindling an old friendship.

People who are contact resources come from every field, so do not make the mistake of limiting yourself to your own profession. Civic clubs, such as Rotary and Junior League, are wonderful arenas to meet people who are well positioned in all occupations in your city and who can help you find the kind of help you are seeking.

A middle-management supervisor at an insurance company met the editor of the local paper at a Kiwanis Club luncheon. With the editor's help, the manager was able to get some publicity for a sweat-equity housing rehabilitation program in the inner city. Not only did the manager donate his time; he also arranged to have the insurance company set up a small revolving loan fund to assist participating city dwellers. The end result of the link-up at the Kiwanis Club? Publicity for a worthwhile project, a public relations boost for the company, and some visibility for the manager. And, since good networking always ends up being reciprocal, a good story for the editor. Once you devise a system for remembering linkages and contacts, you'll get better at networking in social situations. You'll find some parties, groups, and organizations to be much better than others as sources for meeting resource people.

Nurturing Your Network

Friends and contacts will keep giving you leads only for so long. If you do not take charge and follow through—and get back to your contacts to let them know what happened—you will soon find that your sources have dried up.

Networking is based on trust: trust in the reciprocal arrangement of the system and faith in the performance commitment of those who ask for help. It's give and take. That's what keeps the system balanced. You needn't give tit for tat, but you do need to put into the process as much as you get out of it. Just let someone down by taking advantage or goofing off, and you'll soon see that you have lost that person as a contact (and probably most of your "overlapping" network, since word gets around).

Remember that your network is made up of relationships with people. Networking turns exploitive if you do not nurture the relationships behind the expectations. How can you keep these relationships personal? Keep in touch with old friends and colleagues, either by telephone or with an occasional note. See new friends for lunch or drinks, invite them to social events, or share something—say, theater tickets you cannot use. Also, continue to see them in the context in which you met—the Junior Chamber of Commerce, your town's improvement council, and so on.

Rules of the Road

In your workplace there are unspoken rules. You need to ferret them out and learn them (that's where having a mentor is helpful). Networking has its own set of unwritten rules, which you should master before you make some costly mistakes. Patricia Wagner and Leif Smith of the Denver-based Open Network developed a handbook called *The Networking Game*. They suggest an etiquette of networking based on five simple rules that can help you as you explore your own support systems.

Rule 1: "Be useful." As a networker your role is like that of a computer terminal operator. You don't have to remember every little detail. If someone asks you whether you know a place to get training in public speaking, you need only remember that a friend took a course at one of the colleges in your city. You don't necessarily have to remember who taught it, what it cost, when it was held, and so forth. If you try to remember everything, you'll become overwhelmed by the details and demands. So keep it simple. Remember *where* to get the information you need rather than the information itself.

Rule 2: "Don't be boring." Protect your valuable resources. If you waste other people's time, they'll soon be avoiding you. An associate might ask to be introduced to your-friend-the-television-producer because he wants to learn about "the production end of things." If you realize that all he really wants to do is promote the same bad idea for a pilot that he's been pushing all over town, don't waste your resource. After all, you can't send everyone you know to the same friend. You've got to learn how to make quick judgments about what a person needs and who could really help.

Rule 3: "Listen." Hearing is a function; listening is an art. Careful listening will make you a more effective networker. You'll "hear" the underlying currents, and you'll be able to read body language, tone of voice, and choice of words. Sometimes being a good listener means knowing what the person *isn't* saying he wants. Let your listening test out your hunches about people. Then listen to your own internal response to this person. In networking you are always asking yourself, "Can I work with this person?"

Rule 4: "Ask questions." The questions you ask show how well you understand other people's messages. A good question can help someone clarify a statement, opinion, or position. It can even take the place of advice! One caution: Do not interrupt the other person with your questions. Wait until he or she is through. Questions will lead you to valuable information about people and how you can link with them.

Rule 5: "Don't make assumptions." First impressions carry very little weight in networking. That lunch-club speaker whose delivery turns you off may turn out to have family ties to the foundation you've applied to for a grant. That guy in tele-electronics, a field worlds apart from your banking domain, will turn out to be from the very town in Utah where your company is making an investment. He can tell you about the economic problems and potential of that area in a way that no written material can. Networkers do not have to like each other or to share personal interests in order to form an alliance. They join together over a reciprocal issue. It can work in surprising ways.

Exercise: Identifying Your Supporters

Below are some definitions of the people who should be included in your network.* Your supporters fall into two broad categories: maintainers (people who help you get your job done competently and effectively) and propellers (people who push you into new areas to promote your advancement). Identify the people in your life who function for you in these roles now. Then identify the people you would like to

*From Lee Gardenschwartz and Anita Rowe, *Beyond Sanity and Survival* (Training and Consulting Associates, 4550 Via Marina, Suite 106, Marina del Rey, CA 90291).

play these roles in the future. Try to establish a time frame for developing your supporters.

Maintainers

Keystones. People who form the core of your network and are fundamental to getting your job done. (for example, your secretary or administrative assistant).

_____

_____

Experts. People in your field whom you respect and value as professional contacts and would recommend to others; people on whose professional competence you would stake your reputation.

_____

_____

Tangential helpers. People in related fields who help you get your job done (for example, a writer needs an editor, a graphic designer, and a publisher).

_____

_____

Propellers

Mentors. People who guide your career, provide you with opportunity and access, and teach you the ropes.

_____

_____

Role Models. People whose professional behavior stimulates ideas for your future—those who have achieved what you aspire to and who serve as examples to be emulated.

_____

_____

Hubs. People who refer you to additional sources of information and suggest helpful connections.

_____

_____

Challengers. People who force you to look at the direction you are taking and to face some important questions in your life.

_____

_____

Promoters/recommenders. People who advise you of opportunities and encourage your visibility.

Remember that your supporters are not necessarily people you like or people you are in contact with every day. They are the people who can help you acquire the skills and information you need to attain your goals.

THE PROTÉGÉ/MENTOR RELATIONSHIP

The concept of mutualism in the biological world best reflects the process of mentoring. An example of mutualism is the relationship between the hermit crab and the hydroid colony. A hermit crab is a transient occupant of abandoned mollusk shells. Usually a colony of hydroids is already growing on the shell when the hermit crab takes it as its home. The crab lives in the shell and protrudes its head and claws to get food and move about. The hydroids live on the shell's surface, eat the crab's leftover food, and have a means of transportation (the crab travels around with the shell on its back). In return, the hydroids' stinging cells protect the hermit crab from invasion. Neither creature invites the relationship, yet it is beneficial to both and harmful to neither. It is not parasitic.

In mentoring, a younger person, a protégé, and an older, more experienced person, a mentor, form a relationship that is beneficial to each. This aspect of the arrangement keeps it from being exploitive or manipulative. In the typical protégé/mentor relationship, the age difference is 8 to 15 years. Usually by the time people are 40 they are beyond being protégés. Either they have achieved the necessary development by that age or they have missed it.

How to Find a Mentor

If you work for a business organization, get yourself to places where you can mix with a variety of corporate executives. Your workday is filled with opportunities: carpools, commuter trains, the cafeteria, special committees (the 75th Anniversary Dinner), company-supported projects with high visibility (such as the United Way or Junior Achievement), the company baseball team, company outings, cocktail parties, dances (be sure to mix widely), the company newsletter, meetings, elevator rides, training programs, and conferences.

Small businessmen or private professionals, such as dentists and designers, do not move up through a company, but they do have to establish themselves within their profession. One answer is to find role models within the profession who have proven achievement records. If you are an independent businessman, try joining a professional organization. The proven achievers, or those with access to them, can usually be found in these associations. To meet them, you must make yourself visible and useful to the association by donating your time and talent. You should also keep in touch with faculty members whose work and style you admire. Renowned academics, who are the "trainers" for the professions, are wonderful resources both for information and for contacts.

For both the company executive and the independent businessman, mentors can be earned, sought, or arranged.

Mentors can be earned. Janet had a successful career as a publicist with a public relations firm. Her keen interest in politics motivated her to put extra effort into a promotion for her firm's client, Congressman L. H. W. She liked his record and respected him personally. So the next time he ran for office, Janet volunteered as a campaign worker. Her diligent work, both as a professional and as a volunteer, did not go unnoticed. The congressman began to compliment her efforts and seek her opinions. Janet became brave enough to mention her own political ambitions to him: She wanted to run for mayor. He encouraged her toward a more realistic short-term goal: a seat on the city council. He endorsed her candidacy and guided her career by helping her choose effective committees to work on. Janet won the council seat and continues to be loyal to him and to support his campaigns. He continues to prod her toward larger goals.

Mentors can be sought. Bert had a natural love for science. Since his father owned a pharmacy, becoming a pharmacist seemed a natural choice. In the eight years following school, Bert took over more and more of the store's responsibility. But he was discontent. Eventually it dawned on Bert that he was in the right sphere, but the wrong field. Medicine was right— but he wanted to be the prescribing doctor, not the pharmacist. Bert sought out three prominent doctors who did business with the pharmacy and discussed his ambitions with them. All three offered advice and contacts, but one offered something more. He took a personal interest and delight in Bert's plans. They became partners in getting Bert through medical school. Bert's mentor was available for emotional support and medical information, and eventually offered Bert a partnership after he finished his training.

Mentors can be arranged. The Jewel Companies, Inc., a U.S. food conglomerate, assigns every MBA trainee to an official mentor. In turn, every trainee who becomes a manager must serve as a mentor. The relationship is taken seriously at Jewel and has been quite successful. Through mentoring, Jewel is able to identify new employees with high potential and move them along rapidly to positions of greater responsibility.

If your company, like many others, is wary of formal assignments of mentors, you can orchestrate your own arrangement. When Dan joined a large aluminum company as an economic forecaster, he knew no one who was well placed in the company. But he discovered he had two good outside contacts. Dan's economics professor had been a college roommate of the vice president of national sales. Dan's father belonged to the same tennis club as the company's personnel director. Dan asked both men to arrange introductions, which they did. And when Dan's father asked the personnel director to "keep an eye out for my son," he added that his son also played a good game of tennis. Several weeks later, Dan's father arranged a doubles match with his partner, Dan, and the personnel director. After a few matches, and some powerful first serves, Dan had himself a mentor.

Tasks of the Protégé

A mentor is not a fairy godmother who grants you three upwardly mobile wishes. The relationship is symbiotic—that is, mutually enhancing. So something is expected of the protégé. Here is how to be the sort of protégé who contributes to a mentor relationship.

Keep performance level high. There are many capable, talented people courting success. If a mentor is going to risk getting involved with you and put his or her reputation on the line, the least you can do in return is to perform at your best. You should give the mentor's suggestions a chance to work. Remember, too, that when you ask someone advice and act on it, you are paying that person a supreme compliment.

Be assertive. Seek out other positive relationships. Find ways to contribute to the organization, learn new skills, try new experiences. Being a protégé involves following through on the suggestions of the mentor, even if this involves taking risks, meeting new people, and growing.

Welcome criticism. Since your purpose in having a mentor is to develop, criticism will be inevitable. It helps you change direction, set new goals, focus on what's important. Welcome constructive criticism from your mentor and view it as a means of improving your professional skills. Don't take it personally.

Be loyal. Loyalty is an essential part of the protégé/mentor bargain, whether that bargain is implicit or explicit. You are responsible for staying in touch, reporting back, and keeping information confidential when it was meant for you only. The mentor, by supporting younger staff members, is trying to build a power base. He or she will count on you for support and expect you to stay "on the team." When you've outgrown your mentor, try to find a constructive way to build a different type of relationship.

Tasks of the Mentor

The protégé/mentor relationship is a close one. The mentor's guidance resembles a parent's caring and concern, encouraging the development of the child and then letting go. The mentor may serve as a teacher, sponsor, host and guide, exemplar, or counselor. In these roles, the mentor has several tasks.

Share your skills, knowledge, experience, and contacts. As a mentor, you must pass along an insider's trade secrets so that your protégé can function more effectively in the organization. Show your protégé how business gets done and how to formulate strategies for achieving goals. Prod the protégé to seek recognition assertively, rather than waiting to be recognized.

Believe in the protégé's ability to make a valuable contribution. If you are a believer, you will bring out the positive and increase your protégé's self-esteem. Seeing the protégé's assets from your vantage point, you can judge where his or her talents will best fit in.

Make a commitment to help the protégé develop. This may mean time and effort and some emotional stake in your protégé's success. If you have a flock of protégés, you will not have much time for mentoring. Make sure you are not using the relationship to flatter your ego.

Be willing to let go. The average protégé/mentor relationship may last two or three years, sometimes longer if there is a need. The pretext for the relationship is the development of the protégé, so when that happens, the protégé must become independent. Occasionally, the partnership continues in another form. Ending a mentor relationship is sometimes quite difficult because of ego or dependency needs. It is important to recognize when your protégé is getting anxious to be flying alone. Two particularly difficult situations are the mentor who is threatened at the prospect of a student surpassing his or her own achievements, and the protégé/mentor relationship that becomes sexually entangled.

THE PEER/MENTOR PARTNERSHIP

A peer/mentor partnership evolves when two people of similar professional levels but different talents link up in a way that matches the strength of one to the weakness of the other. In a sense, two opposites join together to become interlocking parts of a balanced whole. This idea is embodied in the Chinese yin/yang symbol and is reflected in many parts of nature. Examples are light and darkness, male and female.

The peer/mentor "contract" involves setting goals, building egos, offering encouragement, evaluating progress, and sharing skills. For example, one person may enjoy public speaking and be able to get up and give a terrific presentation with prepared material. The other may be very creative, great with ideas, able to get things orderly on paper, but freezes in front of a group. These two people could help each other directly by teaming up so that one operates behind the scenes and the other goes public. Or they could share their skills by coaching each other in weak areas.

Before setting goals, the peer/mentors assess their strengths and weaknesses to make clear what they need from each other, and what they can offer. Goals may be immediate or long term, professional or personal. The peer/mentors assist each other in evaluating the goals and the commitment level required to meet them.

Once a goal is established, the peer/mentors work together to build a strategy—that is, a specific set of "how-tos" for moving from point A to point B. The goal of being selected to give a presentation at the spring sales meeting might have this three-point strategy: (1) enroll in a public speaking course, (2) research and prepare a report for presentation at the monthly staff meeting, and (3) schedule a meeting with the department head to present the sales meeting proposal.

The peer/mentors should meet regularly to assess their progress and to re-examine their goals and methods if necessary. If a goal is no longer on target or if it is not attainable under the present strategy, alternatives must be explored and a new plan developed.

Praise and encouragement are important throughout the process. Each partner prods the other to keep developing, working, and taking the necessary risks. Because both people have something invested in the effort, the success is mutually rewarding. Peer/mentors celebrate together.

Epilogue

Now that you've read this book, I hope you have some new insight into what assertiveness is—and what it is not. It is *not* pushiness or giving peremptory orders or demanding your way all the time. It *is* being aware of what you want and knowing a wide variety of techniques for relating to other people, techniques that will give you positive influence with them.

As you work on developing your repertoire of assertiveness skills, remember that the truly assertive person is an expert in communicating with others. This means stating your ideas and feelings clearly, both with words and with body language. But it also means tuning in to the many kinds of signals that other people are sending you. By being genuinely attentive to those who work with you and being flexible in your ways of relating to them, you will achieve much better results than you ever could by always being preoccupied with how to express your own needs. This, then, is the paradoxical gift that distinguishes an assertive person: to be heard you must first know how to listen.

Think of the skills of assertiveness as experiments in effective communication, with you as the scientist. If a technique doesn't work well for you the first time, modify it and try again. Or try another approach.

Remember, it's your lab, and there are many variables and formulas for achieving effective results.

Happy Discoveries!

"How Assertive Are You?" Exercise Scorecard

	Positive — SELF — Negative	Positive — SELF AND PEERS — Negative	Positive — SELF AND BOSS — Negative	Positive — SELF AND SUBORDINATES — Negative	Positive — TOTALS — Negative
BELIEFS	3. ___ 4. ___ 7. ___ 8. ___ 11. ___ 12. ___ 15. ___ 16. ___	19. ___ 20. ___ 23. ___ 24. ___ 27. ___ 28. ___ 31. ___ 32. ___	35. ___ 36. ___ 39. ___ 40. ___ 43. ___ 44. ___ 47. ___ 48. ___	51. ___ 52. ___ 55. ___ 56. ___ 59. ___ 60. ___ 63. ___ 64. ___	**TOTAL BELIEFS** Positive ___ Negative ___
ACTIONS	1. ___ 2. ___ 5. ___ 6. ___ 9. ___ 10. ___ 13. ___ 14. ___	17. ___ 18. ___ 21. ___ 22. ___ 25. ___ 26. ___ 29. ___ 30. ___	33. ___ 34. ___ 37. ___ 38. ___ 41. ___ 42. ___ 45. ___ 46. ___	49. ___ 50. ___ 53. ___ 54. ___ 57. ___ 58. ___ 61. ___ 62. ___	**TOTAL ACTIONS** Positive ___ Negative ___
BELIEFS AND ACTIONS	Positive Negative SELF	Positive Negative SELF AND PEERS	Positive Negative SELF AND BOSS	Positive Negative SELF AND SUBORDINATES	Positive Negative TOTALS

Copyrignt Success Strategies, Inc. 1985

See exercise on pages 35–39.

Index

ability, need for, in networking, 186
acceptance, as element in communication process, 94-95
acceptance, superficial, as negative response to criticism, 132
acknowledgment
  affirmations as, 139
  bouquets as, 139
  difficulty with, 137-138
  of self, 138-139
actions, as indicator of intentions, 58
advice, and defensiveness, 103
affirmations, as self-acknowledgment, 139
agenda, for meetings, 144-146
aggressive behavior, 13-14
aggressive coach/counselor, 89
aggressive delegator, 79
aggressive performance appraiser, 91
all-or-nothing thinking
  as cause of guilt feelings, 51
  as cognitive distortion, 42
Alpha leadership style, 6
analytic learning style, 112
anger
  blaming for, 47
  causes of, 45
  constructive, 46-48
  and cool thoughts, 48-49
  expressing, steps in, 48
  healthy response to, 45
  and hot thoughts, 48-49
  ownership of, 47

  unhealthy responses to, 44-45
anxiousness, originating with parents, 41
arguing, and counseling, 88
assertive behavior, 14
Assertive Bill of Rights, 16, 17
  and guilt, 51
  and identifying personal rights, 53
assertive coach/counselor, 89
assertive delegator, 78-79
assertive feelings, 73
assertiveness
  definition of, 12
  effect of others' thoughts on, 27
  in-born nature of, 41
  and self-image, 18-20
  skills and techniques, 52
assertive performance appraiser, 90
assertive philosophy, 15-17
assertive/responsive scores, 74
assumptions, unstated, and destructive criticism, 131
auditory (sound) sensory channel, 116
authentic communication, 93
authority, challenge to, 3
avoidance, as negative response to criticism, 131-132
avoidance of feelings, as barrier to communication, 99-100

Bandler, Richard, and NLP, 115-117
Bartlett's Familiar Quotations, use of, in writing, 151

behavior, changing, to become more assertive, 17-18
belief(s)
  -changers, 32-34
  choice of, 28
  new, 28-33
Benson, Herbert, and relaxa-
  tion/meditation technique, 172
Beta leadership style, 6
birth rate, effect of, on workforce, 2
blue collar jobs, shift away from, 2
body language
  as communication device, 121
  definition of, 121
  see also communication, nonverbal
body signals
  and the body center, 122
  and hands and feet, 124
  and the head, 122-123
  and posture, 123-124
body's immune system, and effect of
  stress, 164
books, for reference use in writing,
  150-152
Boston Health Collective, as example of
  network, 188
bouquets, as form of acknowledgment,
  139
brain, use of left and right sides of,
  110-112
breaks, need for, in networking, 186-
  187
Burns, David, on cognitive distortions,
  41-44
business, decline of confidence in, 3
business letter(s)
  "no," 158
  openers for, 156
  persuasive, 156-157
  reader of, writing to, 155-156
  unexpected, value of, 158
  "yes," 157
business organizations, changes in, 5-6

The Careful Writer, use of, in writing,
  151
catastrophizing, 43

center, of the body, and body signals,
  122
cholesterol, and stress, 164
church, decline of confidence in, 3
citywide networking, 185
civic clubs, and networking, 189-190
clarification, request for, in communication, 104
clichés, as pitfall of writing, 153-154
closure, of meetings, 146
clothes, as communication device, 129
coaching and counseling
  assertive, 87-88
  definitions of, 84
  guidelines for, 88-89
  pitfalls of, 85-86
  principles of, 86-87
cognitive distortion, 41-44
  definition of, 41
  exercise on, 44
commonsense learning style, 112
communication
  barriers to, 98-101
  and the brain, 110-112
  checklist, 102-103
  defensive, 100-101
  definition of, 93
  elements of, 96-97
  importance of, 92-93
  laws of, 96-97
  voice qualities in, 124-127
  win/win, 97-98
communication, nonverbal
  awareness of, 120
  body signals in, 122-124, 125
  importance of, 119-120
  terms of, 120-121
  ways of, 121
The Communication of Ideas, use of, in
  writing, 151
competition, increase of, in workforce,
  3
compliments, handling, 42
compromise, in responding to criticism,
  137
confidence in others, lack of, and
  coaching, 85

congruence
  as element in communications process, 93
  between verbal and nonverbal communication, 121
consequences step, of DESC process, 65-66
cool thoughts, 48-49
counseling
  and apparent conflict with disciplining, 87-88
  see also coaching and counseling
courage, need for, in networking, 187
criticism
  constructive, 132-133
  definition of, 130
  and defensiveness, 103
  destructive, 130-132
  in mentoring relationship, 195
  negative, giving, 131
  negative, responding to, 131-132
  receiving, assertively, 133-137
cutting, of writing, 159

decision making, workers demand for participation in, 4
defensive communication
  avoiding, 101-103
  listeners in, 100-101
  responding to, 103-104
  speakers in, 100
delegation
  assertive, 80-82
  checklist, 81
  definition of, 77
  exercise for, 82-84
  guidelines for, 79-80
  reasons for, 77-78
  style, 78-79
depression
  as flight response, 40
  as result of inward anger, 44
DESC process, of scripting, 64-66
  exercise for, 66-68
describe step, of DESC process, 64-65
desensitizing, for relief of stress, 172-173

desires step toward self-awareness, 57-58
detail seekers, as task-oriented personality type, 114
dichotomous thinking, 42
dictionary, use of, in writing, 150
diet, for relief of stress, 170
disqualifying the positive, as cognitive distortion, 42
dress, and effect on self-image, 121
dynamic learning style, 113

editing, of writing, 159-160
emotional reasoning, as cognitive distortion, 43
emotional responses to problems, inefficiency of, 40-41
empathy
  as element in communication process, 93-94
  in responding to criticism, 134
Equitable Life Assurance, and use of biofeedback for relaxation, 172
exaggerations, as negative communication method, 131
excitement seekers, as people-oriented personality type, 115
excuses, as negative response to criticism, 131
exercise, for relief of stress, 170
exercises:
  Building New Beliefs, 32-33
  Changing a Bargain, 34-35
  Choosing a Model, 21
  Clearing Up Distortions, 44
  Dealing with Anger, 45-46
  Examining Your Work Goals and Values, 8-11
  Feeling Good About Yourself, 20-21
  How Assertive a Manager Are You, 74-77
  How Assertive Are You? Assessing Your Business Relationships, 35-39, 199
  How Well Do You Listen?, 105-107
  Identifying Your Supporters, 191-193
  Keeping an Anger Record, 49-50

exercises (*continued*)
Making Sound Delegation Decisions, 82-84
Self-Image/Career Inventory, 22-26
Speaking for Yourself, 63-64
Stress and Burn-Out Inventory, 178-182
Test Your Editing Skills, 160
Test Your Spelling, 160-161
Writing a DESC Script, 66-68
express step, of DESC process, 65

fear
as barrier to communication, 99
as cause of nonassertive behavior, 13
originating with parents, 41
feedback
on behavior change, 18
in responding to criticism, 137
feelings step toward self-awareness, 57
feeling statements, 60-61
fight-or-flight survival instinct, 40
and stress, 163-164
first impressions, 118-119
first-level managers, and assertive/responsive scores, 74
flexibility, as relief for stress, 173
and stress, 163-164
fogging, to disarm critic, 134-135
fortune telling, in jumping to conclusions, 42
fright, and stress, 163

Gellermann, Bill, on win/win communication, 98
goals
and avoiding defensive communication, 101
for behavior change, 17, 19
and delegation, 79
in networking, 188-189
as relief for stress, 171
Gordon, Thomas, and I-language assertion, 63
government
decline of confidence in, 3

and increase in share of labor force, 2
Grinder, John, and NLP, 115-117
guilt
as basis of problems with assertiveness, 49
and cognitive distortions, 51
originating with parents, 41
as result of inward anger, 44
gustatory (taste) sensory channel, 116

hands and feet, and body signals, 124
harmony seekers, as people-oriented personality type, 114-115
head, and body signals, 122-123
hierarchical business organization, decrease in, 5, 6-7
higher-level managers, and assertive/responsive scores, 74
Holmes, Thomas H., on stress measurement, 164
hot thoughts, 48-49

industrial centers, shift in labor force away from, 2
inflection, of voice, and communication, 126
innovative learning style, 112
institutions, decline of confidence in, 3
intention statements, 61-62
intentions step toward self-awareness, 58
interpretation step toward self-awareness, 56-57
interpretive statements, 60
intimate space, 127
see also territorial space
"I" statements
and assertion, 62-63
definition of, 58-59
feeling statements as, 60-61
intention statements as, 61-62
interpretive statements as, 60
"I want" statements as, 61
sense statements as, 59-60
"I want" statements, 61

Japanese management, influence of, on
    U.S. business, 5-6
job burn-out
    definition of, 166
    exercise for, 178-182
    signs of, 168-170
    variables affecting, 166-168
Johnson, Samuel, on writing, 149
jumping to conclusions, as cognitive
    distortion, 42

kinesics, 121
kinesthetic (touch) sensory channel, 116

labeling
    as cause of anger, 45
    as cognitive distortion, 43
language, positive, and effect on self-
    image, 22
lateral networking, 183-184
leadership styles, 6-7
learning styles, 112-113
Lee, Irving, on communication, 96
leisure society, move toward, 4
"Lifestyles/Personal Health Care in
    Different Occupations," on stress,
    165
listening
    barriers to, 108, 109
    and coaching, 86, 88
    difficulty in, 108
    exercise for, 105-107
    improving skills of, 108-110
    Japanese symbol for, 108
    keys to, 111
    refined, 108
lose/lose communication, 97
Luckman, Charles, on success, 186

magnification and minimization
    as cause of anger, 45
    as cognitive distortion, 43
    as cause of guilt feelings, 57
mail, handling of, 155
managerial style
    Alpha, 6

Beta, 6
changes in, 1-11
coaching and counseling in, 84-89
delegation in, 77-84
emotional resources for, 73
and performance appraisal, 89
manager(s)
    and assertive/responsive scores, 74
    future, 7-8
    goals of, 1
    Michael's competent, 6
meetings
    agenda for, 144-146
    assertive participation in, 146-147
    closure of, 146
    importance of territorial space in,
        128-129
    with peers, 143-146
    problem people at, 145
    proceedings of, 146
    staff, 140-143
    time spent in, 140
mental filter, as cognitive distortion, 42
mentoring relationship
    beginning a, 193-195
    between peer/mentors, 196-197
    reciprocity in, 193
    as support system, 184-185
    tasks of mentor in, 195-196
    tasks of protégé in, 195
Michael, Donald, on the competent
    manager, 6
midcareer bulge, 2
mind reading
    as cause of anger, 45
    in jumping to conclusions, 42
money, savings of, through delegation,
    78

national networking, 185
negative assertion, in responding to crit-
    icism, 135
negative inquiry, in responding to criti-
    cism, 135-137
negotiation, in responding to criticism,
    137

network(s)
  beginning, 189
  citywide, 185
  civic clubs and, 189-190
  definition of, 187-188
  exercise for, 191-193
  lateral, 183-184
  national, 185
  nurturing, 190
  reciprocity in, 188-189
  rules of, 190-191
  vertical, 184
neurolinguistic programming (NLP),
  115-117
nonassertive behavior, 12-13
nonassertive coach/counselor, 89
nonassertive delegator, 79
nonassertive performance appraiser, 90-
  91
nonverbal expression of feelings, 60
"nothing personal" belief changer, 32
  and saying no, 71

objectivity, as relief for stress, 173-174
office, appearance of, as communication
  device, 129
olfactory (smell) sensory channel, 116
On Writing Well, use of, in writing,
  151
overgeneralization, as cognitive distortion, 42
ownership, of anger, 47

paragraph, structure of, 154-155
paraphrasing, use of, in communication,
  104
parents, and instilling negative self-feel-
  ings, 41
passive aggression, 40
peer/mentor partnership, 196-197
peers, meetings with
  agenda for, 144-146
  closure of, 146
  leader of, 143-144
  proceedings of, 146
people-oriented personality types, 113,
  114-115

perceptions, checking, in communication, 104
perfectionist attitude, 42
performance appraisal, 89-91
performance standards, and delegation,
  79
personal effects
  clothing as, 129
  as communication device, 121
  office as, 129
personality types, 113-115
personalizing, as cognitive distortion,
  43
personal space, 128
  see also territorial space
Peter's Quotations for Our Times, use
  of, in writing, 151
physical diseases, as result of inward
  anger, 44
physical signs of feelings, 57
pompous words, as pitfall of writing,
  153
positive emotional anchors, 54-55
positive strokes, as self-acknowledgment, 138-139
posture, and body signals, 123-124
power, expressed in space, 128
The Practical Stylist, use of, in writing,
  151
prizing, feeling toward other person,
  94-95
procrastination, and stress, 171
protégé/mentor relationship, *see* mentoring

Rahe, Richard, on stress measurement,
  164
reality testing, as relief for stress, 173
redundant phrases, as pitfall of writing,
  153
relaxation techniques, for relief of
  stress, 172
"renegotiating a bargain" belief-changer, 34
responsive emotions, 73
results seekers, as task-oriented personality type, 114

retaliation, as negative response to criticism, 131
rewriting, 159
"rewriting the rules" belief-changer, 32
rights
  others', importance of, 28
  personal, identifying, 53
Rogers, Carl
  on congruence in communication, 93
  on unconditional positive regard, 94-95
Roget's Thesaurus, use of, in writing, 150-151
role model
  exercise for choosing, 21
  value of, in behavior change, 18
role reversal, as relief for stress, 174
Rosch, Paul J., on stress, 164

saying no, 70-72
  skills for, 71-72
  steps toward, 70-71
  value of, 70-71
Schwartz, Peter, and Alpha/Beta leadership styles, 6
scripting
  definition of, 64
  DESC process of, 64-66
  exercise for, 66-68
secretary, delegation to, 81
self-awareness, steps toward better, 56-58
self-disclosure, 55-56
self-esteem, and self-disclosure, 55
self-image
  basis of, 18-19
  building, 20, 21-22
  exercise for, 22-26
self-messages, as basis of feelings, 53-54
sense statements, 59-60
senses step toward self-awareness, 56
sensory channels, for information processing, 115-117
sentence, structure of, 154
setting limits
  definition of, 68

  pitfalls in, 69-70
  rules for, 68-69
Shaw, Malcolm, and assertive/responsive test instrument, 74
shoulds
  as cause of anger, 45
  as cognitive distortion, 43
shyness, and coaching, 85
skills, lack of, and coaching, 85-86
Smith, Leif, *The Networking Game,* 190
Social Security
  effect of, on older male workers, 2
  future changes in, 3
social space, 128
  see also territorial space
space, *see* territorial space
specify step, of DESC process, 65
Sperry Corporation, and listening skills, 110
staff meetings, 140-143
Stevenson's Home Book of Quotations, use of, in writing, 151
stonewalling, as negative response to criticism, 131
stress
  carrier, 175-176
  causes of, 164-165
  definition of, 162-163
  desensitizing as relief for, 172-173
  diet and exercise as relief for, 170
  exercise for, 178-182
  flexibility as relief for, 173
  -ful jobs, managing, 174-175
  harmfulness of, 164
  and job burn-out, 166-168
  as the new work-place hazard, 162
  objectivity as relief for, 173-174
  reality testing as relief for, 173
  relaxation techniques as relief for, 172
  responses to, 163-164
  role reversal as relief for, 174
  signs of, 168-170
  symptoms of, 164
  time management as relief for, 170-171

stress (*continued*)
  transcendental meditation (TM) as re-
    lief for, 172
  value of, 170
  at work, 165-166
subordinates
  development of, through coaching
    and counseling, 84
  growth of, through delegation, 78
Sunbelt, shifts in labor force to, 2
superfluous phrases, as pitfall of writing, 153
support system(s)
  citywide networking as, 185
  importance of, 185-186
  lateral networking as, 183-184
  mentoring as, 184-185
  national networking as, 185
  vertical networking as, 184
survival instincts, 40
synchrony
  and body signals, 124
  in nonverbal communication, 121

tact, in meetings, 147
task-oriented personality types, 113-114
territorial space
  as communication device, 121
  invasion of, 127-128
  at meetings, 128-129
  and nonverbal communication, 121
  as power, 128
  as visibility, 128
threats, and destructive criticism, 131
time
  effective use of, and delegation, 77
  lack of, and coaching, 85
  management, for relief of stress, 170-
    171
timing
  in communication, 97
  and criticism, 131
  in meetings, 147
  and reading body signals, 123
  and voice communication, 127
tone, in meetings, 147

tone, of voice, and communication,
  124-126
training, and delegation, 80
transcendental meditation (TM), for relief of stress, 172
trust, and self-disclosure, 55

unconditional positive regard, 94-95
unions, shift away from, 2
U.S. Department of Labor, studies of
  workers by, 3

variety, in voice, and communication,
  126
vertical networking, 184
visibility, as a result of space, 128
visual (sight) sensory channel, 116
voice
  as communication device, 121
  improving, 127
  inflection of, 126
  timing of, 126-127
  tone of, 124-126
  variety in, 126
  volume of, 126

Wagner, Patricia, *The Networking
  Game*, 190
white collar jobs, shift toward, 2
win/lose communication, 97
win/win communication, 97-98
women, in labor force, 2-3
Women's Forum, as example of network, 188
workaholics, and tendency toward burn-
  out, 167
workers, changing nature of, 3-5
work ethic, decline of, 4
workforce, changing nature of, 2-3
writing, assertive
  and business letters, 155-158
  characteristics of, 148-149
  cutting of, 159
  dictating, 150
  difficulty of, 149-150

editing and rewriting in, 159-160
exercises for, 160-161
paragraph structure for, 154-155
pitfalls of, 153-154
tips for, 152
tools for, 150-152

Writing Without Teachers, use of, in
  writing, 151
Wycott, Edgar B., on laws of communication, 96-97
Wyman, Michael, on acknowledgment,
  138